The Complete
Small Business
Internet Guide

Tom and Lori Heatherington

201 W. 103rd St.   Indianapolis, IN 46290

Overview

1	**Reinventing Business**	1
2	**Internet: Hype or Hyperlink?**	9
3	**Using the Net to Help Manage Your Business**	23
4	**Internet Marketing**	55
5	**Choose Your Weapons**	67
6	**Mastering Your Domain**	83
7	**The Net as a Communication Tool**	93
8	**Creating Your Web Site**	107
9	**Microsoft FrontPage 98**	119
10	**Graphics and FrontPage 98**	155
11	**Open for Business**	167
12	**The Key to Success**	187
13	**Web Site Toolbox**	203
14	**What's Next?**	199
15	**Glossary of Geek Speak**	215
	Appendix	243
	Index	251

Contents

1 Reinventing Business   1

Introduction 1
How this all began 1
Welcome to *The Complete Small Business Internet Guide* 3
The purpose of this book 3
Who needs this book? 5
What is unique about this book? 5
What this book is not 5
Will this book teach me everything there is to know
about the Internet? 5
What about attending an Internet seminar or class? 6
Why is this a Windows 98 (and Windows 95) "only" book? 6
Why does this book feature only Microsoft software products? 6
How to use this book with the bonus CD and the Internet 7
Bonus CD 8

2 Internet: Hype or Hyperlink?   9

How big is the Internet? 9
Is the Internet a serious tool for business? 10
Should my business be on the Internet? 11
What are the benefits of having a business Web site? 11
Do I have to be a computer programmer to create a Web site? 13
How do I determine if my business is right for the Web? 13
Internet security 15
What is a firewall and do I need one? 15
Should I be afraid of hackers? 16
Can I prevent visitors from viewing my Web site HTML code? 16
What do I need to know about computer viruses? 16
Does this mean that there is no threat from viruses? 17
What you should know about e-mail security 17
What are secure messages? 18
How do digital IDs work? 18
Where do I get a digital ID? 18
How do I obtain a digital ID and add it to my e-mail account? 19
Are credit card numbers floating around in cyberspace? 19
What about dishonest Internet merchants
and stolen credit cards? 20

Is fraud a big problem on the Net? 20
What about investment scams on the Internet? 20
What is a secure versus a non-secure transaction? 21
How do I know if I am conducting a transaction on a *secure* site? 21

3   Using the Net to Help Manage Your Business   23

Electronic online commerce (e-commerce) 23
What is the difference between e-commerce and
real commerce? 23
Electronic commerce considerations 24
Is e-commerce for real and is it right for small business? 25
Growing your business 25
The Web offers a better, less expensive solution 26
So, how easy is easy? 27
What is e-commerce (electronic commerce)? 28
Is e-commerce right for my business? 28
Can anyone host my online store? 29
Information intoxication 30
Search engines and search services 30
What is the difference between browsing and searching
on the Web? 31
Using search engines 32
How do I locate someone's e-mail address on the Net? 38
The dark side of the Net 39
Is it true that pornography is rampant on the Net? 39
Is there any way to minimize this exposure? 39
Push versus pull 40
What is "Push" technology? 40
Should I consider using Push technology to reach
my customers? 41
What are channels and what can I do with them? 41
Where do I find a list of available channels? 42
How much do subscriptions cost? 42
How do I subscribe to a Web site? 42
How do I browse offline? 43
Business productivity links 43

4   Internet Marketing   55

Marketing definition 55
How is Internet marketing different from
conventional marketing? 56
Online advertising and public relations overview 57

Online marketing tactics 60
    Conventional press releases 60
    Nonconventional press releases 60
    What if I just don't have time to distribute a press release? 61
    How do I deliver my advertising message on the Web? 61
    Reciprocal link free for all 61
    Will I be able to charge others to advertise on my site? 62
    Should I list or advertise with a city-specific service? 62
    What about positioning my Web site in an online
    shopping mall? 62
    How do I use the Web for sales promotion? 63
Newsgroup marketing 63
    Using newsgroups to promote your Web site 63
    How do I create a newsgroup? 63
    What do I do if someone attacks my company in a newsgroup? 64
Effective e-mail marketing 64
    Suggestions 64
    What is automated mail (autoresponder or autobot)? 65
    Produce an e-newsletter 65
    Direct e-marketing (electronic direct mail) 66
    What are automated mailing lists (listserv)? 66

5 Choose Your Weapons   **67**

What you will need to start today 67
    Why you should buy or upgrade to Microsoft Office 97 68
    How can I justify the cost of Office 97? 69
    What about exchanging documents between Office 97
    and earlier versions? 70
    Microsoft Internet Explorer 4.0 70
    Why do I need FrontPage 98? 72
Are you connected? 75
    Defining your connected office 76
    What hardware should I buy, what do I really need? 76
    Computer sources 76
    What software will I need? 77
    How do I connect to the Internet? 77
Getting wired—connectivity options 77
    Modems 77
    What is a modem? 78
    What are the differences between modem speeds? 78
    Is it true that a modem can be difficult to use? 81
    Modem summary 82

6   Mastering Your Domain   **83**

Establishing your domain 83

What is a domain? 83

What is a domain name? 83

What is an IP address? 84

What is a domain classification? 84

What is the advantage of owning my domain? 85

How do I obtain a domain name? 86

Are there any rules about domain names? 86

What if someone has already taken my domain name? 86

What does it cost to register my unique domain name? 87

What will it cost to activate my domain name? 87

Virtual domains versus dedicated domains 87

What should I consider when choosing where
to host my domain? 88

Why should I choose Netcom to host my domain? 88

What if I already use a different Internet Service Provider? 90

Registering your domain 91

7   The Net as a Communication Tool   **93**

The Net as a communication tool (e-mail) 93

E-mail, *"Killer App"* of the Internet 93

What is e-mail netiquette? 94

What is "SPAM?" 96

What is the best e-mail program to use? 96

Microsoft Outlook Express (Domain e-mail setup) 97

Using filters to block SPAM or unsolicited e-mail 100

How do I attach or send a document, spreadsheet,
or graphics file with an e-mail message? 101

How to add/delete e-mail accounts (users) to your new domain 103

E-mail configuration using the Netcom Business Center 103

Audio and video Web site communication 105

What are the benefits of Internet broadcasting? 105

What are some applications for Internet broadcasting? 105

How does it work? 106

8   Creating Your Web Site   **107**

Plan your work 107

Define your Web site goal(s) 108

Develop a Web site strategy 108

How do I determine what content I should include
in my Web site? 109

Planning your Web site layout 111

How big is a "page?" 112

Why are graphics so important to a well-designed Web site? 112

Should I include links to other sites? 113

Web site maintenance considerations 113

Web site design considerations 114

Web site design recommendations 114

Things you should *not* do when building your site 115

Web site—ready, set, go! 116

Copying text and graphics from other resources 116

After you have completed building your Web site 118

9   Microsoft FrontPage 98   119

FrontPage 98 introduction 119

FrontPage Explorer 120

Viewing and working with the FrontPage Explorer 120

The All Files view 121

The Navigation view 121

The Hyperlink view(s) 122

The Themes view 122

Applying a FrontPage theme to your Web site 122

The Tasks view 123

Creating new pages 123

Spell checking 124

The FrontPage Editor 125

How to use FrontPage 98 126

Opening existing pages in the FrontPage Editor 126

Building a new page—entering content 127

Add a bulleted list 128

Create a hyperlink 128

Importing an image 130

Setting the page properties (and other page elements) 131

Setting the properties of other page elements 131

Saving the current page 132

Previewing your new page 132

Shared borders and navigation bars 133

Navigation bars 134

What are tables? (Pay attention to your table manners) 135

HTML META tags 137

What are META tags and why must I use them? 137

The <Keywords> tag 139

The <Description> tag 140

The <TITLE> tag 141

Optimize your page titles wherever possible 142
Miscellaneous <other> META tags 142
Configuring the Refresh option using FrontPage 98 143
HTML—tips, tricks, and help 144
HTML reference sites online 145
Advanced features of FrontPage 98 146
Active Page Elements 146
Interactive Web page forms 147
Adding a feedback form 148
Publishing your Web site on the Internet 149
FrontPage Server Extensions 152
FrontPage database integration 152

10   Graphics and FrontPage 98   155

Working with graphics 155
Speed thrills—think fast! (as in download) 157
Size is important—think small! 158
Get the jump on the next page 160
Fine-tuning graphics 160
What are transparent graphics? 160
How to make an image (color) transparent 161
Creating image maps 162
How to create image hotspots 162
Placing text over images 164
Where can I find royalty-free graphics? 164
How can I transfer my company logo and brochures
to my Web site? 165
Graphics resources online 165

11   Open for Business   167

Before you flip the switch 167
Intellectual property and Internet law 167
Building your Web site development team 168
Copyright infringement 170
Trademarks on the Net 171
Jurisdiction over online activities 172
Conducting sweepstakes and contests online 173
Framing, linking, and META lines 174
Related online reference sites 176

Creating your online store 176
    What is a shopping basket? 177
    What do I need to know about taking credit card
    payments online? 178
    How do I obtain a merchant account? 179
    What if I already have an existing bank relationship? 180
    What should I expect from a merchant bank provider? 180
    What is a transaction? 181
    What should I expect from a credit card processing
    service provider? 181
    Are there other online payment options that I should consider? 181
    Online checking account drafts 182
    What is a PIN-based online credit card clearing? 183
    Summary for taking credit cards over the Internet 184
    One final thought 185

12   The Key to Success   187

Positioning your domain on the Web 187
    How will customers find my Web site? 187
    Registering your domain with search engines and directories 189
    Strategic search engine positioning 189
    How can I improve the standing of my Web site
    with all search engines? 190
    How long before my site begins to show up in search engines? 190
    Will I be notified when my site has been listed
    with a search engine? 190
    What assurances do I have that my site will be
    accepted by major search engines? Can they refuse
    to list my site? 191
    What is a META (search) engine? 191
    Hide your text to get discovered! 191
    Hide your hyperlinks and get discovered! 192
    What are phantom Web pages? 192
    Ready, set, submit! 192
    Things *not* to do when submitting your site to a search engine 193
    Listing your site with the major search engines 194
    Verify your listing regularly 198

13   Web Site Toolbox   199

Netcom Business Center—client resources 199
    Toolbox 200
    Support 201
    Internet Explorer quick tips and tricks 202

Windows 98 tips 203
Should I upgrade to Windows 98? 203
Use that "new" button 204
Update Windows 98 painlessly in the future 204
Make your programs open and run faster 205
Squeeze more space from your hard drive 205

14   What's Next?   207

Your business must continue to grow, or it may eventually go away 207
What is the migration path of products and services
for my business? 208
Where do I go from here? 208
Intranets—interlinking the virtual office 208
Who can use an Intranet? 208
What are the benefits of using an Intranet? 209
When will my business need dedicated Internet access? 210
Which dedicated access service is right for my business? 210
Small business networking—the next step 211
Y2K —the year 2000 controversy 212
How did all this happen? 212
What can I do to prepare? 213
Y2K resources on the Web 213
Lessons learned 214
Embrace the chaos! 214

15   Glossary of Geek Speak   215

If you didn't find it here 241

Appendix   Software Installation   243

System requirements 243
System requirements for Netcomplete with Internet Explorer 4.0 244
Installation instructions 244
Contacting Netcom 244
Hosting offer.. 245
FrontPage 98 installation 245
Internet Explorer 4.0 installation 247
Image Composer installation 247
Image Composer overview 248
Image Composer online resources 249

Index   251

About the Authors

Tom and Lori Heatherington (<u>www.webunet.com</u>)

At the grass roots level, few people have been more involved in helping to shape the business component of the Internet than Tom and Lori Heatherington.

Before "Internet," Tom spent 13 years with NEC America's Paging/Wireless division. In 1994, after five years as Vice President of Sales, Tom resigned his position to help launch PICnet as one of the first ISPs in the nation. Lori managed the sales and marketing departments and was the market research-analyst for their newly established ISP. During its short, but innovative history, PICnet was responsible for many noteworthy industry firsts. Among them:

- PICnet was the first ISP partner of <u>broadcast.com</u> (formerly AudioNet) and aired the first live sporting event in the world over the Internet. <u>http://www.broadcast.com/</u>
- It was the first ISP to offer "Wireless E-mail" (Internet e-mail sent to an alphanumeric pager).
- It produced two successful videos that instructed new users on how to use the Internet and its complex software.

At the time it was acquired by Netcom On-Line Communications, Inc., PICnet's customer list read like a Who's Who in Dallas Fort Worth. Companies such as Frito-Lay, the Texas Rangers Baseball Club, the Dallas Symphony, the Dallas Morning News and many of the major TV and radio stations in the area relied on PICnet both for service and Internet consultation.

As President of Netcom Interactive (formerly PICnet), Tom's subsidiary created the Netcom Business Center. This was the first fully automatic IP provisioning engine in the world. As a result, Netcom subsequently became one of the largest domain hosting companies on the planet. Netcom hosting also became the first "Premiere Partner" of the InterNIC.

Over the years, Tom and Lori have written articles about Internet technology and its marketing related elements. They have been interviewed and quoted on TV, radio, and newspapers. They have conducted seminars and been asked to host or speak at numerous industry gatherings.

In June of 1998, Tom joined Lori as a full-time partner with her consulting company, the Webunet Group. Their first order of business was to complete this book on which they had been collaborating for the past year. As a team, Tom and Lori's most compelling quality is in their ability to take complex technology and present in such a way that any neophyte will find it interesting and easy to understand. As partners and in separate roles, they have already helped thousands of people learn how to "Web-u-tize" their businesses.

Tom studied Business and History at Albemarle College in North Carolina after serving four years in the Navy, which included a tour in Vietnam. Lori holds a degree in marketing from Dallas Baptist University. Tom and Lori live in Plano, Texas, and are proud parents to three beautiful teenage daughters.

Contributing Authors

John Weekley (www.weekley.com)

John Weekley is President of Weekley/Group/McKinney, a successful Dallas-based public relations, advertising, and public affairs consulting firm established in 1979. A third-generation public relations professional, he is also associated with nationally recognized public relations expert Joe McNamara in StratCom (www.stratcompr.com), a Texas strategic communications and crisis management company.

Having previously been an officer and director of several publicly held corporations as well as area civic groups, John's extensive background in business and communications is responsible for his also being a part of several LLPs, advising companies on everything from venture capital structuring to management consulting and organizational behavior.

One of the many early clients and friends of PICnet, John was quick to realize the enormous potential for communication's opportunities via the Internet. John spent considerable time as a disciple of this new medium introducing his clients, business associates, and some local civic organizations to the Net.

A frequent speaker before university, business, and public interest groups on planning, public relations, and political and public affairs topics, John has authored several manuals on applying sound business and communications principles to the Internet Web hosting business.

Weekley/Group/McKinney was among the first public relations firm to establish a presence on the World Wide Web. John Weekley is also the Political Analyst for Dallas-Ft. Worth's NBC affiliate KXAS-TV, and worked with news executive John Sparks to make it the first commercial television station in the world to establish a Web page. (www.kxas.com)

> "Who you are and what you do always speaks louder and longer than who you say you are and what you say you do." - Joseph McNamara

Bret Madole and **Larry Jones** are attorneys with the law offices of David, Goodman, and Madole in Dallas, Texas. The firm has significant experience in trademark, copyright, trade secret, intellectual property licensing (including trademark, software and product licensing), and trademark and trade secret enforcement and litigation. The firm has unique experience in the handling of Internet/Online licensing, trade secret, trademark, copyright, contract, indemnification and other matters peculiar to the Internet. (www.david-goodman.com/)

Bret A. Madole, born Oklahoma City, Oklahoma, December 3, 1960; admitted to bar, 1987, Texas. Education: Birmingham-Southern College (B.S. cum laude, 1983); University of Virginia (J.D., 1986). Author: "Instruments and Transfers-Proposed Amendments to Articles 3 and 4 and the New Article 4A," Texas Association of Bank Counsel, 1989. Co-Author, "Protecting and Realizing Upon The Issuer's Right to Reimbursement," Letter of Credit, A Practitioners Workshop, New York, 1990. Co-Author, "Drafting Letters of Credit," Real Estate Documents, Workouts and Closings, University of Houston Law Center, March, 1991. Speaker, "Practical and Legal Aspects of Doing Business on the Internet," Institute of Real Estate Manages Legal Seminar, 1997. Member: Texas Association of Bank Counsel; Dallas Association of Young Lawyers; Intellectual Property Section Dallas Bar Association, State Bar of Texas; Chairman, Sports Law Committee, Dallas Bar Association, 1991, Board of Directors 1997. Board of Directors, Dallas All Sports Association. Council, Sports and Entertainment Section, Dallas Bar Association, 1996-97.

Larry E. Jones, born Fort Smith, Arkansas, October 31, 1956; admitted to bar, 1992, Texas. Education: University of Arkansas (B.A. Journalism 1978); University of Arkansas School of Law (J.D. with high honors, 1992). Editor-In-Chief, Arkansas Law Review, 1991-92; Intra-School Moot Court Champion, 1991; Outstanding Graduate Award, 1992; School Publications Award, 1992. Instructor: "Legal Aspects of Doing Business on the Internet," Institute of Real Estate Managers' Legal Issues Seminar, 1997. Member: Texas Bar Association; Dallas Bar Association; American Bar Association. Admitted to practice: United States District Court for the Northern District of Texas, United States Fifth Circuit Court of Appeals.

Dedication

This book is dedicated to the women in our lives—our wonderful mothers, Rita and Lenore, who bear the ultimate responsibility for this work, and our beautiful daughters Erin , Lexie and Trish. We love you!

Acknowledgements

To our family, friends, and business associates we offer our most sincere appreciation and gratitude for helping to bring this project to life and encouraging us throughout the process. We would like to extend a very special thank you to those people who have helped shape our Internet destiny.

First, we are proud to recognize Boyd Christensen and thank him for including us in his Internet dream and sharing his entrepreneurial adventure with us.

We would like to extend a very special thank you to Michael Bledsoe for his wisdom and advice, and his brother Mac who trusted our guidance and allowed us to feature the Drew Bledsoe Foundation.

We also thank the original crew at PICnet, Bill Wadley, James McGill, Brock Rowe, and Bruce Christensen for helping us begin our Internet journey.

Special thanks also go to the contributing authors of this book, John Weekley, Bret Madole and Larry Jones for sharing their expertise.

Also, a special thank you to Eric Spivey and his Netcom team for believing in this project.

To the MCP staff, we thank you all sincerely for your guidance, especially John Pierce and Debbie Parisi.

Finally, last but certainly not least, we owe an extraordinary debt of gratitude to Catherine Weekley, who single-handedly chanpioned this project, wrestled corporate executives, and overcame countless obstacles to bring this book to completion. We thank you for your dedication and commitment.

Foreword

One of the biggest challenges facing growing businesses today is how to easily set up an Internet Web presence and leverage it to provide information, generate revenues, and/or reduce costs of business operations. Microsoft has made significant investments in products to help make this an easier process for emerging businesses. *The Complete Small Business Internet Guide* reviews how these Microsoft products, along with Netcom's hosting services, can quickly and easily provide any business with the platforms, applications, and services to market and transact its business on the Web.

- Cameron Myhrvold
  Vice President, Internet Customer Unit
  Microsoft Corporation

Reinventing Business

The Internet is reinventing how business does business.

Introduction

How this all began

In 1992 (about 40 Web-*years* before the Internet was opened to the public), I bought my first Harley-Davidson motorcycle. I had been riding bikes for almost 20 years and had owned three, but buying a Harley was something I had fantasized about for a long time. Back then, Harley-Davidson dealers had a waiting list of eager buyers and new bikes of any model were scarce. By way of a friend, I learned of a dealer in Kansas City who, through some miraculous circumstance, had some inventory. I flew to KC, saw the bike of my dreams, bought it, and rode my new 1992 Lowrider 600 miles back home to Dallas, Texas.

At that time, few of my friends or associates were aware that I was also a "closet geek." I had been a computer devotee and an avid online user for many years. When I finally decided to park my new Harley and give the paint a chance to finish curing, I fired up my modem, connected to CompuServe and joined the Harley-Davidson forum. Soon afterward, I responded to a posting from a Michael Bledsoe who was planning to attend the Black Hills Rally in Sturgis, South Dakota, in August. We got to know each other online and over time, we talked about Harleys, the Sturgis rally, computers, world events, and a host of other topics, but mostly we talked about Harley-Davidson motorcycles.

Michael had an interesting background. He founded one of the first telecommunications consulting firms in the 1970s, he had taken a company public, produced car racing videos for television and was currently the owner of an online "store" on the CompuServe network when we first met each other. Michael and I became very good friends and he took on the role as mentor for me through the building phase and eventual acquisition of PICnet[1] by Netcom.

That summer, Lori and I met Michael and some of his friends in Sturgis for the 54th annual Black Hills Rally. We rode together all week and got to know and respect each other. The following year his brother Mac Bledsoe, a high-school teacher and football coach who had been riding Harleys for more than 20 years, joined him. We developed a deep friendship and over the years have visited each other's homes and vacationed together.

Brother Mac was not a computer user back then. Aside from checking grades or attendance records at his school, Mac knew very little about computers or the cyber-world that his brother and I inhabited. Around this time, his oldest son Drew had just been drafted by the NFL's New England Patriots as the starting quarterback, and like most pro athletes today he was offered a huge salary and signing bonus for a multi-year contract. However, unlike many of the "star athletes" we read about today, Drew felt compelled to give something back.

For the past 25 years, his father had been travelling the Northwest delivering lectures and seminars on effective parenting techniques. Mac was uniquely qualified to speak with considerable authority on this subject. In addition to having taught school and coached young people for almost a quarter of a century, he and his beautiful wife Barbara were almost done raising two outstanding sons, Drew and Adam. Drew decided to fund a foundation whose charter would be to disseminate his father's parenting message to parents and organizations that needed it the most.

The Drew Bledsoe Foundation was launched with father Mac as president. Mac was still not a computer user yet, but as an educator he was very much aware of what was being talked about concerning the Internet and the Internet being made available for commercial purposes. He and I spoke frequently about the possibilities that the Internet offered his foundation's purpose in taking its message to the world. He bought his first computer for the foundation and began his learning process. He had serious work to do, and he had a *lot* of questions.

Mac called me sometime in late 1996 and said that he was ready to begin establishing the Drew Bledsoe Foundation online. He had been "playing around" on his new Windows 95 computer and was beginning to feel more comfortable. Mac asked the question I have heard thousands of times before: *"Now what should I do?"*

The Drew Bledsoe Foundation was a typical representation of what most small businesses in America look like today. It had three employees, a limited budget, a pressing need to generate awareness for its products and services, and a need to develop a revenue stream so that it could grow and become self-sufficient. The foundation had a mission and it knew its vocation, but it did not have the knowledge or technical expertise necessary to launch a Web site.

I advised Mac to buy Microsoft Office 97 so that he could import all of his seminar notes and workbook information into Word and be able to save it as HTML files. I also recommended that he buy Microsoft FrontPage 97. I told him that although it was one of the easiest HTML editors to use, FrontPage was also one of the most powerful programs and would automate many of the processes that would typically require a programmer on staff.

In short, I gave Mac the advice that has been incorporated into this book.

Consequently, I decided to use the Drew Bledsoe Foundation Web site as a real-world example throughout this book when I need to illustrate a procedure or technique. Mac is like the millions of other small business people who are faced with this quandary about the Internet and how it relates to their business. Most find themselves asking nearly all of the questions included in this book.

Welcome to *The Complete Small Business Internet Guide*

The purpose of this book

The Complete Small Business Internet Guide offers real-world practical advice, experience, and results. The contributors to this book are individuals who are professionally involved or employed in the Internet industry.

The mission of this book is to address basic Internet questions for small businesses and offer cost-effective, reliable, easy-to-understand solutions and recommendations. Furthermore, this book is a first of its kind. The electronic version (CD included) integrates the interactive capabilities of office suite technology.

For you to receive the maximum benefit from this book, we are assuming that you have a fundamental understanding of:

- How to send and receive e-mail
- How to use the basic features of a web browser (Microsoft Explorer, Netscape, and so on)
- Rudimentary word processing skills

However, if this is your introduction to the Internet and the concepts discussed in this book, you may want to consider purchasing a basic primer such as *Sams Teach Yourself the Internet in 24 Hours* by Sams Publishing.

Also, as a new user there are some outstanding resources online that you may find helpful, visit:

- Learn the Net, a Web site dedicated to helping you save time and money when roaming through cyberspace. `http://www.learnthenet.com/english/index.html`
- The English Server is a progressive student-run cooperative publishing online since 1990. It distributes over eighteen thousand works representing a wide range of topics. `http://english-www.hss.cmu.edu/internet/aboutbasics.html`

This book was written for you, the quintessential "common individual." It aims to shorten the learning curve for the average working man or woman who wants to establish a Web site but has limited time to devote to the process.

This book was created for people who do not have the time or capital to invest exploring every new business abstraction that gains a mention on the evening news. Our purpose is to sift through all the noise and offer realistic advice as to what is *really* important and meaningful with the Internet, and offer advice as to what degree you should involve yourself. Simply stated, we believe that if you are in business, you must be involved with the Internet, you need to *Webutize* your company.

This book is tailored specifically for small business owners who need practical answers to everyday Internet questions. In our business we speak with people from all walks of life who express the same frustration with this *Internet thing*.

- "There is just *too much information to absorb* to make an intelligent, educated decision about building a Web site."
- "The technology changes too fast."
- "I'm *confused* by the technology and I *don't have the time* to invest to learn it."
- "Can you recommend a book that will *get me started*?"
- "Just tell me what I need to know to put my business on the Internet and be successful?"

We have built million dollar businesses around Internet technology and have helped scores of other businesses position and market themselves successfully on the Internet. We know what is practical, what is hype, and what works. *We've been there, done that, but didn't have time to collect the T-shirts.* We have literally grown up with the business of the Internet and have a solid understanding of what's important and what's frivolity.

Who needs this book?

You need this book if you're investigating the possibilities of the Internet and:

- You want to learn why the Internet is considered a powerful business tool and why your business should be online.
- You want to learn how to use the Internet to enhance business communication with customers and vendors.
- You want to learn how to display your existing marketing/sales information (brochures and catalogues) online.
- You want to learn how to create a Web site for your business.
- You want easy-to-understand small business Internet marketing advice.

 • Your VCR displays 12:00 more than twice per day because learning how to withdraw cash from an ATM machine is all the programming you care to ever learn.

What is unique about this book?

A number of very significant things are unique about this book. Most importantly, this book is a comprehensive guide based on experiential learning. The target market for this book is the small business owner. The goal of this book is to help small business owners understand that the Internet is a business tool and that Internet marketing involves more than just having a Web site and that Web site ownership doesn't stop at creation (it's a fairly long term investment).

What this book is not

 This book is *not* another Internet 101 history of the Internet, hype-driven, diatribes about the demise of the paper transaction and the emergence of the digital planet. Nor is it a technical How To software manual. This book is *not* targeted to super-geeks, the early adopters of new bleeding-edge technology. This book was not designed to introduce or dissect every new software plug-in and helper application or HTML version update. Also, this book will not make predictions about which Web browser will become the de-facto standard for the universe.

Will this book teach me everything there is to know about the Internet?

Why bother?

No single book, company, course, seminar, or Web site can teach you *everything* there is to know about the Internet. Fortunately, you do not need to understand everything about the Internet to maximize its potential anymore than you need to understand the mechanics of a combustion engine to drive your car. What you will receive from this book is a methodical overview to help you make an informed decision about how you should invest your resources in the online world to maximize your business' online return on investment.

What about attending an Internet seminar or class?

We encourage you to increase your understanding of the Internet at every possible relevant opportunity. The only drawback to Internet seminars or classes is that you are forced to follow the entire presentation at the author or presenter's pace. As an example, I recently attended a conference that was advertised as a "Doing Business on the Internet" seminar. As with most types of these programs, the presenter felt compelled to provide the audience with a one-hour history of the Internet and a l-o-n-g-e-r presentation about software application tools, such as, Telnet, FTP, Gopher, IRC, and so on.

Although the background information was educational, as an experienced Internet user, I would have preferred to fast-forward or hyperlink out of that portion of the presentation. After all, I was there to learn how to do business on the Internet. Therefore, ask for an agenda or syllabus before you invest your time and money in an Internet seminar or class.

Why is this a Windows 98 (and Windows 95) "only" book?

Windows (95 and Windows 98) was chosen as our operating platform of preference because Windows is easy to use, reliable, cost-effective, readily available, and well-supported. Also, a small business owner does not require a full-time programmer to maintain a Windows operating system. Furthermore, we chose Windows 95/98 based on the growing market share in the consumer desktop computer market and its majority share in the business environment. For other compelling reasons why Windows 98 gets our vote, refer to "Windows 98 Tips" in Chapter 13.

Why does this book feature only Microsoft software products?

We standardized on Microsoft software because of the complete integration of the operating system (Windows 95/98/NT) with the desktop (Office 97), the browser (Internet Explorer 4.x) and because of the Web publishing capability of FrontPage 98. The holistic view of Microsoft's product offerings allows us to spend less time on the technology and more time on the essence of creating a Web presence that will ultimately reap tangible rewards for you.

How to use this book with the bonus CD and the Internet

The World Wide Web of the Internet was the first mainstream recipient of hyperlinking capability. Hyperlinkning is the capability to automatically link a Web site word, phrase, table, or graphic image to another site on the Internet with the click of a mouse. The site that the hyperlink connects to could be on the same Web page, the same Web site, or to the same computer or server. The hyperlink could also connect to a different Web site or a different computer or server located thousands of miles away. Today, the power of hyperlinking information extends much further (and much closer) than the Internet.

With the arrival of new office suites from Microsoft, Corel, Lotus, and so on, information now links your desktop to files within your computer and even to locations within documents. This book is a practical demonstration of this new capability. We use Microsoft as a complete solution because of ease of use. If you have another program, consult the help files or user documentation that accompanied the product.

Using the power of Microsoft Word 97, the electronic version of this book contains hyperlinks. Clicking on these hyperlinks propels you to the specified location either in this book or to the Internet. Within the electronic edition of this book, use the back arrow on yopur browser to return to the page that you were reading before you clicked on the hyperlink.

For the sake of easy identification, hyperlinked words or phrases in this book are identified as underlined text (which can also be referenced in the glossary). These are words or phrases that you should pay special attention to or may be company names. WWW addresses are identified as underline and in a special `mono` font. Typically, in a Microsoft Word document, the hyperlinks are identified as blue text. To visit Microsoft's Internet Web site, either left-click on the word Microsoft or on the phrase `http://www.microsoft.com`. Either choice will automatically launch your Web browser and take you to Microsoft's Internet domain.

For further convenience, the glossary section of this book is also interactive on the CD. Internet terms and concepts appear as hyperlinks. To link to the interactive glossary, left-click on the red underlined word or phrase such as "hyperlink".

Check the Net!

The *Hitchhiker* graphic will provide a hyperlink to the Netcom Business Center or to other links on the Internet that contain additional topic related information. `http://www.netcomi.com`

Wherever possible we will provide hyperlinked examples or instructions that more fully illustrate our comments or demonstrate a process. As an example, <u>Bell Labs Text-to-Speech</u> lab has a Web demonstration that converts any machine-readable text into speech. We created the following audio (.wav) file using this demo site. `http://www.bell-labs.com/project/tts`

Text submitted: This is the way your office will integrate with your employees and your customers in the 1990s and beyond.

 (Click on the speaker to hear the result of our test.)

Bonus CD

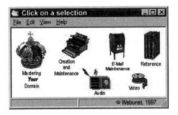

Included with this book is a feature-rich CD that contains the interactive edition of this book, which was produced in Microsoft Office 97 and published using FrontPage 98.

The CD also includes all of the free software, Web site maintenance tools and instructions, graphics, and supporting documentation. The latest version of the Microsoft Explorer 4.0 browser is also included.

 The *NetTip* button graphic indicates that information located beside the graphic is considered an important Internet tip or trick as it relates to Internet design, programming, or marketing.

 The CD button graphic is a hyperlink to additional information located on the Bonus CD.

---

[1] PICnet was one of the first Internet Service Providers to offer Internet access in Dallas, Texas and was acquired by Netcom in August 1995.

Internet: Hype or Hyperlink?

The Internet—The World Wide Web—The Information Superhighway

Since 1994 there has been a relentless outpouring of news (read: hype, noise, confusion) about the Internet and the <u>World Wide Web</u>. The news has been force-fed to us through radio, television, magazines, and newspapers. Yet, the question of the Internet's relevance to small business remains a mystery to many small business owners.

The world of Internet business communication is changing at warp speed. Today, a Web site is one of the most effective communication tools a company of any size can utilize. If strategically produced, properly implemented and managed, a Web site is one of the fiercest global marketing weapons available to small businesses.

By the 21st century, an Internet presence (e-mail address and Web site) will become a mainstream business protocol just as using a telephone is today. As a business owner, you have the option of getting online now or later.

How big is the Internet?

Big! Attempting to tabulate the exact number of Internet users is like trying to count black T-shirts at a Harley-Davidson rally. You know the total number is large, but you'll probably end up counting the same shirts more than once and miss many others.

Although impossible to pinpoint the exact number of users and machines that make up the Internet, suffice it to say that it is very *BIG* and growing larger *every* day. Because almost one-quarter of the households in the United States own a computer and a modem (and one twentieth of the world, for that matter), you can no longer ignore the possibilities the Internet holds for your business. In an effort to explain the dynamics of this medium, consider:

- The number of commercial sites on the Web is doubling every six months. This major expansion in commercial Web sites is a result of the tremendous growth in the adoption of Internet and World Wide Web technologies by businesses.[1]
- By the end of 1997 there will be 82 million PCs hooked up to the Internet and 268 million by the year 2001 according to survey data collected by research firm Dataquest. (www.gartner11.gartnerWeb.com/dq/)
- The top five countries by domain names as of January 1997 in decreasing order: United States, Japan, Germany, Canada, and the United Kingdom.
- By the year 2000, an estimated one billion people worldwide will be plugged in, as the Net becomes less a novelty and more an indispensable business and personal tool.[2]
- According to IDC, nearly 50 percent of all U.S. companies have set up sites on the Web. But the National Federation of Independent Business finds that although 75 percent of small businesses use computers, only 40 percent have Web sites.[3]

Is the Internet a serious tool for business?

The Internet is unquestionably a serious business tool. We emphatically believe in the immediate potential and future promise of the Internet. Consider that just four short years ago, only a small number people even knew what the Internet was. Today, the Internet has become a multimillion dollar electronic communication medium that has redefined communication, is projected to have millions of users, and is home to thousands of business Web sites that cater to the exploding Internet user population.

Four years ago, did you own a modem (or even a computer)? Did you have an e-mail address? Did you know what a URL was? Could you have conceived that in a few short years you would be able to do the following online:

- Buy or sell a car online ?
- Trade stocks with instant execution for a $5 fee?
- Order dinner or buy your groceries and have them on your kitchen table in a few hours?
- Locate a package you shipped this morning?

- Update your software without having a disk or CD?
- Reserve and pay for an airline ticket, choose your seat, order your special meal, book a hotel room, rent a car, or plan an exotic vacation?
- File your taxes?
- Apply for a loan and have a decision hours later?
- Make a long distance call to England at no charge?

The Internet already provides unparalleled opportunities for cost-effective marketing and customer service. A site on the World Wide Web is one of the most powerful and visible means to market your company. Every business with a Web site has the potential to promote itself as an around-the-clock worldwide business. If "perception is reality" and "what you see is what you get," as a business manager in the '90s you need to make the most of what you've got. You need to put your business online and "be seen." Your competitors, if not already there, are planning their appearance.

Should my business be on the Internet?

- If your business relies on communication with employees, customers, associates, vendors, and so on, to remain in business, then your business should be on the Internet.
- If your business relies on profit from sales of a product or service to remain in business, then your business should be on the Internet.
- If your business relies on donations or volunteers to remain in business, then your business should be on the Internet.
- If your business (fill in the blank)_____, then your business should be on the Internet.

Bottom line, if you're in business and want to stay in business, you should be on the Internet.

What are the benefits of having a business Web site?

The benefits of a Web site are numerous. Whether you do business on a global basis or within the confines of a small community, staking your claim on the Internet is important and can be a rich source of supplemental marketing 24 hours a day, seven days a week.

The most obvious benefit is the capability to provide information about your products or services to customers in a graphically pleasing manner. Think about your business' value proposition. You possess information about your products, services, industry, or related industries that a potential buyer is probably interested in learning.

Your Web site can be the source of your specialized knowledge. If the information is organized effectively and listed in Web search engines, Web users can easily find you. Price and product lists can be updated quickly and inexpensively. Requests for information can be received and answered immediately via interactive forms and automated e-mail systems.

A Web site can also be a valuable commerce tool. Products can be showcased in much the same way as a catalog, but in an interactive manner. For example, visitors could check the availability status of a certain product, fill out a form requesting more information, or place an order immediately. As security software becomes more advanced and consumers become more comfortable with online purchasing, Internet commerce will explode and become a part of mainstream purchasing.

Perhaps the most valuable benefit of a Web site is the capability to communicate with customers who can provide invaluable suggestions, opinions, and questions about your products in a manner that is convenient for them.

In relation to the advertising benefits of having your business online, a Web site offers the highest coverage area of any advertising medium in the world (potential web visitors). Because the coverage potential is so high, it follows suit that the reach (actual Web visitors) and frequency (the number of times Web visitors are exposed to your message) will be a percentage of that coverage.

Because most advertising costs are determined by how many people can be reached via a specific medium, Internet marketers have attempted to adopt traditional measuring yardsticks for the World Wide Web as well. Although absolute costs for Web site creation are easier to identify, relative costs where they relate to price comparison of other media vehicles are not as clear cut. For example, print media uses cost per thousand (CPM) as a formula for cost breakdown while broadcast media uses cost per ratings point (CPRP).

Initially, relative cost formulas for measuring Web marketing effectiveness involved tallying the total number of clicks or hits per page (also referred to as traffic) or visits to your Web site. This process was and still is accomplished through such software programs as WebTrends. These programs are designed to automatically log Web site traffic data and create a file for you to reference on a daily basis. Point your browser to the Netcom Business Center to learn more about WebTrends Internet traffic analysis software. http://www.netcomi.com/nbc/partners/#webtrends

As the medium has grown, marketers have included page views (the total number of times a Web page is viewed), ad views (the total number of times that an advertising banner [or link] appears on a specific Web page), and "click throughs" (the total number of times a visitor actually clicks on an ad banner) as other instruments by which to measure Web marketing effectiveness. As Web sites become more divergent, so will the ways of measuring their success.

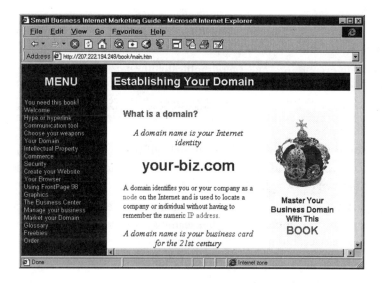

Do I have to be a computer programmer to create a Web site?

No. Since 1994 there have been enormous improvements in software-Internet-integration areas that have simplified Internet communication and Web site creation. Also, small business owners now have the benefit of owning a fully integrated computer system by purchasing software such as Microsoft's Office Suite and FrontPage 98.

How do I determine if my business is right for the Web?

Products that require little or no physical examination have proven to be wildly success-ful on the Web. The most obvious examples include computer-related products, books, music CDs, office supplies, and so on, and services, such as photo processing and travel agencies.

However, don't fall prey to the notion that if your business does not fit into one of these categories that all is lost. On the contrary, products as diverse as antique furniture and swimming pool supplies are also finding a receptive audience online.

To help you decide whether the Web is right for your business, consider the following:

- Would you gain a competitive advantage if you improved customer service and expanded your company's visibility?

- Would customer feedback better help you to meet customer's needs and increase profits?
- Do your products or services require substantial consumer education or after-sale support?
- Would improved communication with your customers help obtain new or repeat business?
- Would you expand into new (geographically unrelated) markets if you could do so cost effectively?
- Does the opportunity to offer your products or services internationally appeal to you?
- Do any of your products have niche market appeal?
- Do you desire to extend database access to your outside staff or partners when they are out of town or away from the office?
- Because the "barriers to entry" are minimal, would developing a Web site permit your company to compete with other leading companies that offer the same product or service, but have large overhead costs?
- As your cost of marketing via traditional channels continues to rise does it have a reciprocal impact on your profits?
- Does the possibility of providing sales and customer service 24 hours a day using no additional personnel sound cost-effective to you?

These questions were designed to make you think about the benefits of using Internet technology. There are no right or wrong answers except how they pertain to your business and your long-term marketing plan.

A rose by any other name. What is the difference between a company that sells millions of flowers on the Internet and your business? What about a company that virtually markets antique furniture, or wine, or CDs, or T-shirts, or office equipment, or automobiles, or plumbing supplies? What makes your business different from others? What do they know that you don't? What steps have they taken that you haven't?

- They have already established a business domain on the Internet.
- They have developed a well-designed, easy to navigate Web site that appeals to their target market.
- They have positioned their Web site properly in most major search engines, portals, and content aggregators.
- They promote their Web site through conventional advertising channels.
- They sell their products online.

Internet security

Internet security is nothing more than risk management. Think about the levels of security we adopt in our daily lives. Our backyard has a locked gate designed to keep the family pet confined, but it can be opened by anyone. Our homes have doors and windows with additional locks, deadbolts, and high-tech security systems. However, our "very important" documents are kept off premise and stored in a bank vault or a safety deposit box.

> *Like any technology, the Internet is ideologically neutral.*
>
> *Neither good nor evil, it doesn't magically foster golden age Athenian democracies and isn't a miracle cure for all that ails us. It's merely a tool that smart folk can put to good use, and that crooks and cranks can put to bad.*[4]

Security on the Internet involves the same reasonable common sense that we apply to other areas of our personal and business lives. On the Internet, static or dynamic Web pages that have no physical link to a company's internal <u>LAN</u> require little or no security. However, you would not connect your corporate network to the Internet without installing a deadbolt on the door and setting up some kind of alarm mechanism. Part of managing a LAN with an Internet connection means adopting more rigorous precautions such as a <u>firewall</u>.

What is a firewall and do I need one?

A firewall (as the name implies) is a means of blocking a threat or an intrusion by an "uninvited guest." A firewall can be a hardware or software solution (or both) and cost a few hundred dollars to hundreds of thousands of dollars. The cost is relative to the degree of protection required weighed against the sensitivity of the data. These factors determine the sophistication of the firewall.

Most small to medium sized businesses that use the Internet as a method to display their <u>brochureware</u>, do not typically need a firewall. The need for a firewall increases however, when that company connects its LAN to the Internet or begins offering <u>transaction processing</u> on its Web site. In either case, it is wise to consult with a knowledgeable network security technician. For additional research on security related matters see a White Paper entitled <u>Securing Your Business</u>, by The Open Group.[5]
`http://www.rdg.opengroup.org/public/tech/security/backgrnd.htm`

Check
the
Net!

As a public service, The Open Group offers <u>security & electronic commerce links</u> to information on topics of mutual interest. `http://www.rdg.opengroup.org/public/tech/security/seclinks.htm`

Should I be afraid of hackers?

In the movies, hacking a computer looks appallingly easy. The "antihero" assumes a determined scowl, punches a few computer keys, and mutters several buzzwords like *backdoor* or *cyber tunneling* and bingo, he's in. We watch over his shoulder while he casually browses the CIA's top secret files or transfers money from the U.S. Treasury to his checking account.

In the movies, this remote computer exploitation looks easy, but real computer hacking is a tad more complex. Fortunately, the majority of dial-up users or people who sit behind a corporate firewall are safe from hackers.

Can I prevent visitors from viewing my Web site HTML code?

Sorry Charlie, but when dealing with *simple* HTML pages the Net doesn't operate that way (today). Internet browsers are designed to read HTML code to display pages. Therefore, hiding the code would defeat the purpose. Although hiding HTML source code makes perfect mainstream business sense, in most cases that level of competitive positioning is unnecessary on the Internet. Although there are ways of hiding code that involves complex scripting of active server page implementations, that discussion is outside the realm of the subject matter of this book.

What do I need to know about computer viruses?

Most of the things you have heard about computer <u>viruses</u> are not altogether true. Generally speaking, the stories are myths perpetuated by the uninformed. Rumors about the danger to your hard drive, world peace, and how widespread viruses are make for great water-cooler conversation. The good news is that the majority of what you have heard is no more dangerous to your computer than e-mail from your mother. Relax, be aware of the potential danger and take the right precautions.

In their truest form, viruses operate like the Trojan horse of ancient mythology. They appear harmless or friendly but can produce programming mischief. Most real viruses (as opposed to rumored viruses) essentially make a program do something it is not supposed to do or something that you were not expecting.

The U.S. Department of Energy's CIAC (<u>Computer Incident Advisory Capability</u>) was established in 1989 to provide computer security services to employees and contractors of the United States Department of Energy.[6] The CIAC Web site states that *"we find that we are spending much more time de-bunking hoaxes than handling real virus incidents."*
http://www.ciac.org/

 To learn more about the facts and fallacies of computer viruses, visit http://kumite.com/myths/ for more myths, hoaxes, urban legends, and the ramifications of computer virus myths.[7]

Does this mean that there is no threat from viruses?

On the contrary, the threat is real, computer viruses *do* exist and there are some that could ruin your entire afternoon if your computer were to get infected. Nearly half of all virus attacks come from the Word.Concept macro virus.[8]

Although the destructive threat from viruses is a bit over-exaggerated, you should still take proper precautions. View computer viruses much like you would a real-world disease like malaria, tuberculosis, or smallpox. To guard yourself against those diseases, you would get an inoculation.

The inoculation to prevent computer viruses from infecting your computer comes in the form of virus detection software. One of the best solutions to virus protection is McAfee VirusScan.[9] http://www.mcafee.com/ VirusScan 3.0 offers the highest level of virus detection rates in the industry. This software monitors your incoming and outgoing mail, your Internet activity, and the files you exchange from your various disk drives. The McAfee Web site provides registered users with DAT file updates that help your program to recognize new viruses. http://www.nai.com/products/antivirus/viruscan/default.asp

What you should know about e-mail security

This is a vast subject that is under constant challenge by users, developers, employers, and software vendors. As it relates to the subject matter of this book, you should view e-mail security in the same way in which you view your FAX transmissions. Security is manageable and acceptable for most of your communication needs, but highly sensitive information requires the use of more established methods of security.

Later in this chapter, we discuss digital encoding but bear in mind that an e-mail message (like a FAX) can be "picked-up" by someone else. Never give *anyone* your password and be careful about retrieving your e-mail using someone else's computer. Some programs can remember your access information.

The U.S. Postal Service is in the process of releasing (and evaluating) new services called Postmark and PostECS. Users will be able to send e-mail via the usual unsecured path to a post office location. The mail will be stamped (postmarked) and forwarded with guaranteed security to the intended destination. The Postal Service's intent is to develop a series of services similar to those of traditional mail. The time and date stamp will represent the electronic postmark. Other planned services will include return receipt requested, certified, and registered, verification of sender and recipient, and archiving services. http://www.usps.gov/news/press/96/96108new.htm

PostECS will ensure the security of legal and other official documents sent via the Internet. Key aspects of the new technology include document encryption, password protection, and real-time tracking and tracing. Additional capabilities that may be tested in the future are public key cryptography, digital signature, and proof of delivery and receipt. Be aware, that like most other Post Office services, there will be a charge for such applications.

What are secure messages?

As more and more people send confidential information via e-mail, it is becoming increasingly important to know that your messages cannot be intercepted and read by anyone other than the intended recipient. It is equally important to know that documents sent by e-mail, such as checks and credit cards, cannot be forged.

Secure messages are those that are warranted to be confidential between the sender and recipient(s). This is accomplished by encryption, or digitally signing an e-mail. By using a "digital ID" with an e-mail client, you can prove your identity in electronic transactions, similar to showing your driver's license when you cash a check. You can also use your digital ID to encrypt messages to keep them private. Digital IDs incorporate the S/MIME specification for secure electronic mail.

How do digital IDs work?

A digital ID is composed of a public key, a private key, and a digital signature. When you send your digital ID to others, you are actually giving them your public key, so they can send you encrypted mail, which only you can decrypt and read with your private key.

The digital signature component of a digital ID is your electronic identity card. The digital signature tells the message recipient that the message actually came from you and has neither been forged nor tampered with. Before you can start sending encrypted or digitally signed messages, you must first obtain a digital ID and set up your mail account to use it. If you are sending encrypted messages, your address book must contain a digital ID for the recipient.

Where do I get a digital ID?

Digital IDs are issued by an independent certifying authority. To obtain a personal digital ID, customers can apply online at the certifying authority's Web site. Before issuing the digital ID, the certifying authority will verify your identity through a confidential process. Different levels of digital ID's are available and provide a specific level of credibility. For more information, read the Help section at the certifying authority's Web site.

You have two search options available to obtain a digital ID of someone who has not yet sent you a digitally signed message. You can search for a person's digital ID through a certifying authority's Web site database or you can search or browse through directory services who catalogue digital IDs along with other properties.

How do I obtain a digital ID and add it to my e-mail account?

As the leading provider of digital authentication products and services, VeriSign is Microsoft's preferred provider of digital ID's. Through a special offer from VeriSign (http://www.verisign.com), Microsoft Internet Explorer 4.0 users can obtain a free trial digital ID which can be used as positive identification when you send or receive encrypted messages from business associates or friends. http://www.microsoft.com/ie/ie40/oe/certpage.htm

Net Tips

To add a business contact's digital ID to your address book or to send an encrypted and/or digitally signed message, refer to the Outlook Express Help section under Security and Advanced Security information in Windows 98.

Are credit card numbers floating around in cyberspace?

No! Credit card numbers that are used to make online purchases have an ultimate destination (a computer server) just as credit card numbers that are used to make purchases at a grocery store or gas station do. Internet users cannot just reach into cyberspace and extract credit card numbers. Nor can Internet users reach into cyberspace and retrieve your entire credit card purchasing history, even though your credit card history does reside on a computer server somewhere.

Bear in mind that credit cards are not just "borrowed plastic money" on which you pay interest. In some cases, what you have purchased and the amount of money you spend annually is just as valuable to mainstream marketing firms as is the interest on your purchases to a financial institution. Although credit card numbers do not float in cyberspace, they do reside on financial databases somewhere regardless whether you have purchased anything online.

The odds that you will win your state lottery and get struck by lightening on the same day are greater than the odds that a cyber thief will hijack your credit card information. Most computer security specialists are amazed at the anxiety the average Internet user expresses when it comes to online credit card transactions compared to the unfounded faith in conventional dealings. Consider for a moment how many people (other than yourself, of course) have called an 800 number for the first time and freely given their credit card information with little thought of any repercussion? The odds may be in your favor, but do be careful and use common sense.

What about dishonest Internet merchants and stolen credit cards?

Getting ripped off in cyberspace is no different than getting mugged in broad daylight. Unscrupulous people can be found anywhere. Just as in the day-to-day world of commercial transactions, if a card is stolen, most major credit card companies have a policy that holds users liable for approximately $50. In some cases, where the credit card company contacts you about increased activity, and you prove that the charges are fraudulent, it may not impose any liability.

Should an infraction occur, call your credit card company and explain the situation. Typically, it will send you a form to complete and return. In most cases, the credit card company immediately credits your account and the burden of proof falls on the merchant. The merchant almost always loses these appeals. In the case of an unethical merchant, this bodes well for the consumer.

Is fraud a big problem on the Net?

Not at all; it may appear that way because it makes such great press and it gives the uninformed public something new to fear which means you probably need to buy a new gadget. Most of the time Internet fraud is more like forgetting to close the garage door when leaving for work in the morning. It's a common sense awareness issue. You should use the same precautions on the Internet as you do when you give your credit card information over a telephone or fax machine while at work. If you think you are the target of an online swindle, visit the Federal Trade Commission's Web site. www.ftc.gov

What about investment scams on the Internet?

Most facets of cyberspace mirror the physical world and include good and bad. Again, common sense and a little background research are your best tools to avoid fraudulent situations. If you do find yourself in a scam situation, the Security and Exchange Commission is now investigating online investment scams and abuses. If you have suspicions about an activity or a public stock, visit the SEC's Edgar database. www.sec.gov/cgi-bin/srch-edgar

Investment Fraud and Abuse. The explosion of commercial on-line services and the rising popularity of the Internet have created new opportunities and new dangers for investors. The U.S. SEC (www.sec.gov/consumer/cyberfr.htm) alerts you to the types of investment fraud and abuse used online and suggests ways to avoid becoming a victim.[10]

BBB to the rescue. The <u>Better Business Bureau®</u> (<u>www.bbbonline.org</u>/) has recently launched a new online consumer protection program. According to the Better Business Bureau Web site, businesses displaying the new BBB online seal "have demonstrated their commitment to a series of strict business standards. When a consumer clicks on a company's BBBOnLine seal, he/she will be provided instantly with a BBBOnLine Participation Report on that company."

What is a secure versus a non-secure transaction?

In the case of a secure transaction, the data being transferred over the Internet is scrambled. The process of producing this unreadable code is called encryption. To unscramble the code, a specific decryption key is required.

As we discussed, there are different levels of security but to "hack" (break into) common code requires a tremendous amount of computing power and knowledge. A criminal possessing these tools and skills would not typically be bothered lifting a credit card from cyberspace. There are much more lucrative opportunities available for people possessing such devious talent.

How do I know if I am conducting a transaction on a *secure* site?

Although you will find some Web sites that claim they process orders via a secure server, this is not always true. To be certain, always look for a visual indicator of security. When using Internet Explorer 4.0, the bottom status bar of the browser window will display a lock to indicate that the page you are viewing is being generated from a secure server.

We began this discussion comparing security on the Internet to the defensive measures we assume in other parts of our daily lives. That common sense approach dictates that a ounce of prevention is *still* worth a pound of cure. Be careful out there, wear your galoshes, cross at the light, remember to lock your door, and be judicious with whom you share private information.

---

[1] International Data Corporation (IDC) and its subsidiary, IDC/LINK, are the world's leading providers of information technology data, analysis, and consulting. http://www.idcresearch.com/

[2] Source: *Trend Letter*, Dec. 11, 1997, published by The Global Network.

[3] Sources: National Federation of Independent Business and IDC Research, July 1997, "Businesses Building Web Sites." http://www.cyberatlas.com/segments/site/businesses.html

[4] Joseph R. Garber, Interhooey, *Forbes* magazine, May 5, 1997. http://www.forbes.com/

[5] The Open Group is an international consortium of vendors, ISVs, and end-user customers from industry, government, and academia. http://www.rdg.opengroup.org/

[6] CIAC is the U.S. Department of Energy's Computer Incident Advisory Capability. (http://ciac.llnl.gov/ciac/CIACHome.html)

[7] Source: http://www.kumite.com/myths World Wide Web site and banner graphics © 1995, 97 Rob Rosenberger; all rights reserved.

[8] Will Rodger, *Inter@ctive Week* magazine article, "More PCs Come Down With Macro Viruses," April 21, 1997. http://www.zdnet.com/intweek/

[9] McAfee is a registered trademark of McAfee Associates, Inc.

[10] SEC Investor Beware sponsored by the SEC Office of Investor Education and Assistance (http://www.sec.gov/consumer/cyberfr.htm)

Using the Net to Help Manage Your Business

There can be no economy where there is no efficiency.
- Benjamin Disraeli

Electronic online commerce (*e-commerce*)

What is the difference between e-commerce and real commerce?

Let's take a side trip for a few minutes to add perspective to the changing environment of doing business in the '90s. We will consider a real-world versus cyber-world analogy of a small business faced with the challenge of increasing revenue and controlling costs.

Starting from scratch, you decide to open a retail store to sell your (world's finest) homemade widgets. You will need to locate a building to rent or purchase that meets your criteria of location, traffic, size, zoning codes, and a host of other considerations that hopefully will meet your proposed budget.

After solving all those inaugural headaches that every small businessperson has faced, you then need to decorate your showroom and arrange your goods in such a way that you can display a short description of the widgets unique features, price, and so on. Somewhere in your facility is a reserve of inventory that you monitor with some type of accounting method that also (fingers crossed) tracks your revenue and receivables.

Cash purchases are somewhat rare in today's world of invisible plastic money so your business will need to become "credit card enabled." To do this, you acquire a <u>merchant bank account</u> and a merchant ID number from a bank. To communicate with the bank that will be processing your transactions, you will also need a device that allows you to process the credit card presented by your customers. This device, called a P.O.S. (Point of Sale) terminal, is equipped with a modem that communicates directly with the financial clearinghouse.

When a sale is made, the credit card is swiped through the P.O.S. device that records the customer's card number. Then you enter your merchant number, the amount of the purchase and hit Send. Before you can say "thanks for shopping at "Widgets R Us," the clearinghouse verifies the card number, the available balance, and your merchant ID and issues an approval code for that transaction. Within seconds, funds have been debited from your customer's credit line and transferred to your merchant bank account. You have just increased your revenue by $29.34 and reduced your inventory by one widget. Business is booming (one live, time-consuming contact at a time).

In its most rudimentary context, the purpose of electronic commerce is to encourage unassisted selling and delivery of useful, decision-making information. The Internet is not so much a place to sell as it is an environment that fosters a reason to buy. The one-to-one relationship generated by the Internet allows a person who is ready to buy your product or service do so immediately.

In its simplest form, e-commerce permits businesses to capitalize on the efficiencies of dealing with routine transactions. However, the definition of electronic commerce today cannot be constrained to such a narrow explanation. Business expansion is a component of online commerce.

Electronic commerce considerations

We point out a number of times in this book how important it is to plan the creation of your Web site. We have seen companies spend tens of thousands of dollars launching a site only to tear it down and start over. In some cases the company may have chosen the wrong operating system or server platform, wrong software, or hardware that could not scale, while others may have chosen a theme that was too incompatible with their corporate message. Regardless of the reason, proper planning in the beginning saves time and money in the long run. The chapters "Creating Your Web Site and "Opening a Business" will help you develop your master plan and answer your other questions about e-commerce.

Automate wherever possible. By automating customer order confirmations and shipping notifications (via online credit card processing, e-mail, etc.), you will save the time it takes to perform these tasks manually and gain tremendous efficiencies. When selecting e-commerce software, keep in mind that some software requires server side configuration in order to operate properly. Make sure your ISP can support the software you decide to use. These are just a few considerations that provide more compelling reasons to choose Netcom as your business Web site hosting provider. Netcom provides the appropriate infrastructure and recommends reliable complimentary software solutions to help ensure your success.

Is e-commerce for real and is it right for small business?

The growing acceptance and success of electronic commerce is not only undeniable, but the fact that it will soon become a standard operating procedure for many businesses is irrefutable. Estimates for the future of online commerce range from the ultra-conservative to the wildly optimistic, but most forecasters predict hundreds of billions of dollars in Web commerce by the year 2001.

According to a report by IDC Research, the amount of commerce conducted over the Web will skyrocket from $2.6 billion in 1996 to $220 billion in 2001. The percentage of users who will buy goods and services on the Net will also climb from 25% to 39% during the same time period, claims IDC.[1]

In another report by Activemedia, "The 1997 Real Numbers Behind 'Net Profits," "…overall movement to online commerce may well swell 'Net-generated revenues to $1 trillion by the year 2001." They go on to say that "Small to medium-sized companies building strong personal relationships continue to nibble away at the shares formerly maintained by large corporation marketing advantages." `http://www.activmedia.com/`

As to the question of online commerce being right for small businesses, the answer lies in the interpretation of "commerce." Too often we narrowly refer to e-commerce as online transaction processing. Period! A customer orders a widget, provides the merchant with a credit card number, funds are transferred, and the widget is shipped to the recipient. If you operate a business such as an office supply firm that stocks commonly used items, then you are accustomed to such dealings. Therefore, the logical progression to expanding your business online will be an easy transition. Many of the early adopters of Internet technology were those kinds of businesses.

Unfortunately, many small businesses cannot squeeze their type of business model into an order, pay, and ship scenario. Their widgets may require customization (build to suit, cut to fit, and so on) or require some type of interaction between the client and the business owner. E-commerce is right for these businesses, too; however, their online store will require customization to meet their specific needs.

Growing your business

Every business reaches a point when it realizes that to survive, it must grow. *Business as usual* will not keep pace with ever-increasing expenses, squeezed margins, and new competition. Growing your business can be done a thousand different ways, and you conclude that you need to reach a larger audience as opposed to increasing the size of your present location. Expanding into new markets with additional stores may not be cost feasible, but reaching those markets via other channels such as direct-mail, telemarketing, or a catalog seems quite attractive.

After weighing the possibilities, you decide to create a catalog of your widgets to reach new customers and those who shop repeatedly at your store. You pull together photographs of the different types of widgets, give each an identifying number, a price, and add some descriptive comments. The catalog will include an order form, but you soon realize that you will need to rely on your customer to calculate the sales tax, add the shipping charges, and total the order correctly.

A moment of panic grips you when you visualize a faceless shopper deliberating, "Is the sales tax applied where my order originates, from where it ships, or the address I am shipping it to? No matter, they'll call if there is a problem. Hope it arrives at my brother's house in time for his birthday or I'll just have to return the order for credit."

The possibility of so great a chance for errors and the potential after-sale support causes you temporary mental anguish, but the need to increase sales demands new marketing techniques and some additional risk taking. The catalog is soon ready for the printer and you are faced with another decision of how you are going to distribute your catalog to potential prospects.

Another frightening thought forces reality into your illusion of financial salvation when you realize that your supplier changes prices and part numbers quite often.

You think to yourself, "That will require frequent reprints of my catalog and cause people to order incorrectly from old brochures. I'll have the same issues when I want to add a new widget or drop an obsolete unit or a slow moving product."

It seems there are a hundred other concerns with your new marketing scheme. Clearing out-of-state checks, chasing low-ticket bad debt, processing phone orders, obtaining the best mailing list, deciding how many catalogs to mail, the increasing costs of bulk mail, and your worry list grows steadily. You lie awake at night tormented that the anticipated increase in sales will not cover your additional costs and that the risks outweigh the return. Surely there must be a better way.

The Web offers a better, less expensive solution

Creating an online store versus producing a direct mail catalog offers substantial savings for businesses of *any* size. Decisions about <u>CPM</u>, choosing the right zip codes, the hassles of bulk mailings, catalog reprints, price or model changes, tax and shipping charges, advertising expenses, and a slew of other problems literally disappear with an online store.

If you were to speculate as to how many people on this planet may be a prospect for your widgets, there is no other feasible means of achieving such potential as the Internet.

- *Imagine* your storefront open to potentially millions of possible shoppers, 24 hours each day, 365 days per year having no employees, no parking problems, no zoning restrictions, or showroom overhead.

- *Imagine* updating or redecorating your *electronic* catalog with a few keystrokes and incurring no additional printing, inventory, or distribution charges.

- *Imagine* being able to deliver personalized sales suggestions customized to the individual buying habits of your customers.

- *Imagine* receiving all of your orders complete with correct calculations for state and local taxes and shipping charges.

- *Imagine* operating a global business from a desktop computer on your kitchen table.

Such is the promise of the Internet and the immediate advantage of an online store. Establishing a showroom on the Internet is similar to preparing a layout for a direct mail catalog. However, besides graphics and descriptions of your widgets, you will also need a merchant bank account and the capability to fulfill (ship) an order.

So, how easy is easy?

Jim Tyler (a.k.a. Diamond Jim) is a part-time magician who lives in Mesquite, Texas. Besides working a full-time job, Jim manages a small entertainment business with one employee—*himself*. Jim worked his way through college performing his sleight of hand at private parties, restaurants, and various corporate functions. Over the years he has performed for companies and organizations as diverse as AT&T, ABC Television, PepsiCo, MBNA, McDonalds, Kraft Foods, and even the Boy Scouts of America.

Despite having an impressive list of references, Jim knows that like any small business he must spend a considerable amount of his time marketing his services to new clients. Jim turned to the Web to solve his marketing dilemma. He applied for his domain, www.diamond-jim.com, and purchased Microsoft's FrontPage HTML authoring program. In a matter of months, he has generated thousands of dollars of new bookings as a result of inquiries received from his online brochure.

How does he do it? Jim's occupation as a magician may be uncommon, but his business and marketing challenges are the same as with any other business. He faces the identical problem of maximizing his time and money to generate new business. When performing his close-up magic routine, he builds rapport with the clients by telling jokes and answering questions. At the end of his performance he distributes his business card and asks that he be considered if ever there is a need to entertain friends or business associates. Jim encourages these "prospects" to visit his Web site,

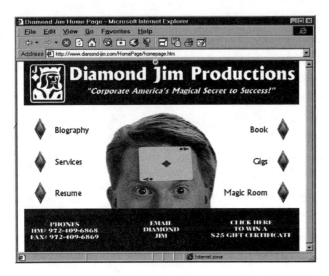

listed on his card, to learn more about what he can do for them.

If you visit Diamond Jim's Web site, you will notice that he advises the viewer to call or e-mail him for additional information. Jim is not peddling widgets, but he is doing a marvelous job of selling his highly specialized services via his electronic brochure. http://www.diamond-jim.com/

What is e-commerce (electronic commerce)?

Is Jim doing e-commerce? Absolutely! Funds do not have to be exchanged "online" for a sale to be attributed to or considered part of electronic commerce. What then, is the definition of electronic commerce? "The conducting of business communication and transactions over networks and through computers. EC also includes all inter-company and intra-company functions (such as marketing, finance, manufacturing, selling, and negotiation) that enable commerce and use electronic mail, EDI (Electronic Data Interchange), file transfer, fax, video conferencing, workflow, or interaction with a remote network."[2]

Diamond Jim Tyler is marketing his services on the Internet the "HTML way." This means that his services are displayed on HTML pages even though inquiries and bookings are channeled through telephone or e-mail requests. In his case, he handles his financial transactions and accounting manually.

In the chapter entitled "Open for Business," we examine the more widely ascribed e-commerce definition: *the buying and selling over the World Wide Web and the Internet, electronic funds transfer, and digital cash.*

Is e-commerce right for my business?

Whether your business is suited to Web commerce as it relates to exchanging funds online (an electronic store versus an advertising storefront) is a decision that only you can make. The value of offering online transactions can only be quantitatively measured by comparing online sales versus expenditures.

Electronic commerce as it relates to an advertising storefront cannot be quantitatively measured. Its value is received in the form of customer goodwill and increased brand awareness.

For the record, however, many product retailers have received a receptive audience on the Web. Early product successes were products and services that required little or no touchy-feely from a buyer. Products such as CDs, software, flowers, books, specialty foods, wine, and so on, made an easy transition to Web sales. Many department stores and specialty stores, such as Macy's, Ross-Simon, and L.L. Bean have also been successful with online sales. As for successful services on the Web, travel agencies, employment agencies, airlines, and so on, have not only been successful on the Web, but are redefining their business model.

Like Diamond Jim, there are a growing number of businesses selling services, advice, advertising, club memberships, etc. on the Web. There are even businesses that host online wagering. *(For the record, we do not endorse or condone using the Internet for illegal purposes.)* Our point is that as the use and popularity of the Internet increases, so too will the diversity among the types of businesses that will incorporate e-commerce.

To better help you identify the criteria to use in making a decision, consider asking yourself:

- Does my product require physical examination?
- Does my product require specific customization?
- How will I satisfy the shipping and handling of my product or delivery of my service?
- Will shipping and handling charges exceed the customer's perceived cost of my product or service?
- Does my product or service require much explanation or consumer education?
- Does my product or service offer a convenience benefit to consumers who order online?
- Is my product or service one that lends itself to repeat sales or reorders?
- Are my margins sufficient enough to absorb increased product returns?

For additional reference regarding e-commerce considerations see the chapters entitled "Creating Your Web Site" and "Open for Business."

Can anyone host my online store?

That depends on your store (Web site), the software you use to build it, and what features you are offering to your customers. Obviously, you will need some place to store your Web pages, *or host your site*. Just be aware that there are different ways to host your Web site when implementing a commerce solution. This is another good common sense reason to trust your business site to a company experienced in this area, Netcom.

"HTML" sites, like Jim's, do not require special software since he does not actually sell products online or process credit cards or bank drafts. However, if you want to conduct business online and be open 24 hours a day, you need a service provider with a reliable network, infrastructure, and backbone. You don't want your host provider's server to crash because three customers tried to place an order simultaneously.

After all, some hosting service providers require that your domain actually reside on their "virtual mall" server for you to offer Web commerce. In some instances, when you host with these companies, your URL is identified as a directory behind their domain name. Instead of seeing www.your-biz.com, a customer would see something like:

```
www.somehostingcompany.com/your-biz/widgetstore/order.html
```

Also, some hosting companies may own and control the commerce application programming on the server where your online store resides. This is important to note because if you ever decide to move your site to another hosting company, you may find that your Web site no longer functions the way it was designed. The reason the Web site won't work is because the programming functions remain on the original hosting company's server.

Furthermore, some hosting companies require that you host only with them to process real-time credit card authorizations. The reason for this may be because the mechanics for the transaction process are tied to the hosting company's servers. Some companies house their own transaction servers, while other companies route your domain to a third-party transaction service located off premises. Either way, this type of hosting service may mean that you will pay a higher service fee. After all, the commerce host must either cover the high cost of implementation for a transaction server or cover the extra mark-up percentage needed to do business with the third-party service.

Netcom and its strategic partners provide the hardware/software explanations discussed in this book. Netcom offers some of the most efficient, cost-effective solutions available for small business.

Information intoxication

It has been said that the knowledge base of the human race is doubling every eight to ten years. The Internet's frenzied pace makes this seem like it's happening every few weeks. Just trying to keep up with software revisions and plug-ins can be an intimidating task. Imagine the difficulty in attempting to keep abreast of all the new information being posted every second of every day on the Internet. Evelyn Wood couldn't teach you to read that fast.

So, how do you locate specific information on the Internet? And more specifically; how will someone locate your Web site?

Search engines and search services

One of the most mysterious occurrences on the Internet is the technology of <u>search engines</u>, software programs called <u>robots</u> and <u>spiders</u>. These invisible robots and spiders scramble their way from URL to URL feeding on new or updated Web page content. Ideally, their mission is to visit every Web site on the World Wide Web and index the information from each page. While some search engines are designed to record an entire Web site indexing every word to its database, others track only specific data. Even if you have never registered your Web site with a search engine, the robots and spiders will eventually find your Web pages.

Thanks to the advent of search engines, Internet users can access a variety of Web search services and research information by keywords, phrases, titles, domain names, URL addresses, individual names, links, images, sound, and so on. Visualize yourself visiting one of the world's largest libraries. If you wanted to find information on the subject of "zoology," you would not start at section "A" and work your way to "Z," reading every title of every book. You would go to the card catalog (computerized database) and search under "Z" for zoology. In essence, you would use the library search engine. Internet search engines are vaguely similar in concept to a library's database.

For those of us who attempt to apply some degree of logic to our thought processes and believe in the power of words, perhaps the most frustrating misconception regarding the Web is the overuse of the words "search engine." Although search engines supply the technological edge to major search services, such as Alta Vista, Excite, Hotbot, Infoseek, Lycos, Webcrawler, and others, not all major search services are search engines; most notable is Yahoo!

As a side note, most search engine services today are strategically positioning themselves as portals and offer on-site content such as news, weather, sports, financial information, and a host of other customized services and options. By forming partnerships with other content-specific aggregators, search engine services are building value in their own service offerings. As for the Web searching public, portals offer a multitiered value in relation to time management. You only have to go to one Web site to start your online session, to access personal information such as e-mail, news, financial updates, and to perform a Web search. Imagine, everything you need under one roof!

For business owners who want to increase their chances of getting found by search engines and being found in Web search results, refer to Chapter 12, "The Key to Success."

What is the difference between browsing and searching on the Web?

A few years ago when there were only a few thousand Internet Web sites (referred to as a home page back then), browsing or surfing the Web was the way many people stumbled on fascinating Web sites. The Internet was new to the general public and it was entertaining to see what people were doing with this new technology. Today, however, the <u>World Wide Web</u> is host to tens of millions of Web pages and it would be ridiculous to expect to surf your way to everything you wanted to see.

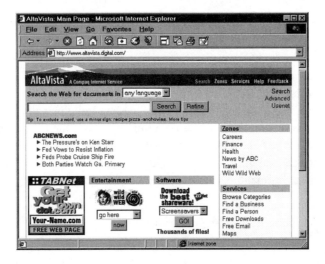

"The magnitude of information available on the Internet is nothing short of astounding. From the correct spelling of a computer-hardware term to a detailed demographic analysis of computer users, the Internet has now replaced traditional library resources as a starting point for research."[3]

Using search engines

If you're using Microsoft's Internet Explorer to browse the Web, then searching the Web has been made a little easier for you becausethe browser offers a Search icon that automatically opens a search frame on your current Web page. If searching the Web still seems confusing, however, then fear not!

The following is a brief overview of seven popular and useful Web search services and basic "how to search" tips. Although the screen captures may drastically change in appearance and layout, chances are the basic functionality of each will remain as is or become easier to use. At the risk of repeating ourselves, this is the Internet, and Web sites do change daily. So, don't be alarmed if a URL has changed or the search service has changed its name because some media giant has acquired the company. After all, it's the Internet—anything is possible!

Alta Vista is designed to search the Web and/or Usenet and provides headline news and a variety of free services and zones by which to find specific information. The service offers a pull-down menu of 25 languages for Web page searching. Simple search features enable you to search for a keyword(s) or a phrase. The site also has a "fancy" search feature that offers the option to search only for text in a Web page title, text in a URL, links to a URL, and more. Advanced Web search features rely on Boolean operator commands known as AND, OR, NOT, NEAR, and ( ) parentheses or brackets. For detailed information designed to help you maximize your Alta Vista search, refer to the Help link on the Web site. `http://www.altavista.digital.com/`

Net Tips

- A query typed in lowercase text will find "all" pages containing the queried keyword or phrase.

- A query typed in UPPERCASE text will find only those pages where the queried keyword or phrase appears in uppercase.

- If you are searching for an exact phrase, use " " (quotation marks) before the first word and after the last word in the phrase.

- To make sure that a word in a phrase is definitely included in your query results, use a + plus sign directly in front of the word(s) in your phrase when you submit your query.

- To make sure that a word in a phrase is not included in your query results, use a – minus sign directly in front of the word(s) of the phrase you do not want to see in your query results.

- To broaden your search results when searching for a keyword, type an * asterisk at the end of the word to find words that begin the same as your word but may have a plural or different word ending.

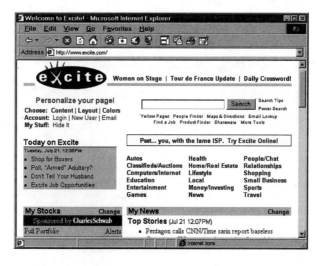

Excite is designed to search the Web and selected Web site listings and Usenet postings. The service also offers a variety of topic-based selections, free services, headline news, and customized sports and stock market information. General search features of this Web site enable you to search for ideas and concepts instead of a keyword match. So, make a special note to use more than one word in your query. Advanced search options include using " " quotation marks, the + plus sign, the – minus sign, and Boolean operators, AND, OR, AND NOT, and ( ) parentheses.

Be aware that when using Boolean operators in an Excite query the concept-based search mechanism will be disengaged. Therefore, your Boolean query will only find exact word results. As an added benefit, Excite also provides a Power Search feature that offers explicit pull-down menus to help you refine your Web search query. For detailed information designed to help you maximize your Excite search, refer to the Help link on the Web site. http://www.excite.com

Net Tips

- For best results, use very specific words to describe your query ideas.

- As you review your query results and find a selection that best satisfies your search needs, click on the hyperlinked words "Search for more documents like this one" located at the bottom of the description. Excite then uses that document as the basis for a new search.

- To compress your search results page, click on the hyperlinked title "Show Title only" if you want to hide the Web site descriptions, or click on the hyperlinked title "List by Web site" if you only want to review how many relevant documents are contained in each Web site.

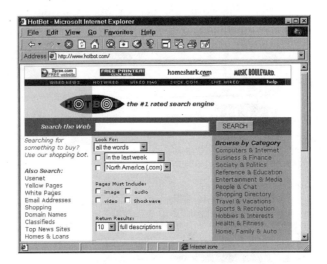

Hotbot is designed to perform Web based searches using keyword queries. By selecting the onsite Usenet link, you can also perform a quick search of Usenet postings. For Web users who enjoy browsing, various other Web site services, subject categories, and collections can also be accessed from the Hotbot Web site. To help you refine a simple Web search, Hotbot contains several pull-down menus and buttons. Additional web searching capabilities (additional pull-down menus and buttons) may be found by selecting the "More Options" button on the simple search results page. Advanced search features include using Boolean operators such as, AND, OR, NOT, and ( ) parentheses, using query modifiers such as, " " quotation marks, the + plus sign, and the – minus sign, and using Meta words with prefixes such as, domain:, depth:, feature:, linkdomain:, linkexe:, newsgroup:, scriptlanguage:, title:, after:, before:, and within: for achieving a power search. For detailed information designed to help you maximize your Hotbot search, refer to the Help link on their Web site. http://www.hotbot.com/

- Hotbot's pull-down menus enable you to select predefined options such as "Search the Web" for: all the words, any of the words, exact phrase, the page title, the person, links to this URL, and Boolean phrase.

- Hotbot also allows you to select pre-defined time line search options such as in the last week, the last 2 weeks, the last month, the last 3 months, the last 6 months, the last year, and the last 2 years.

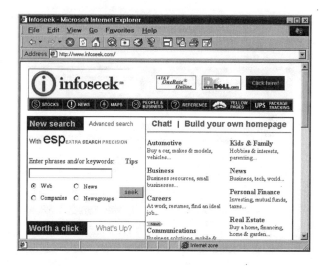

Infoseek is designed to search the Web, selected news information, selected company information, and Usenet. The service also offers various headline hyperlinks for searching such subjects as, Stocks, News, Maps, People & Business, Reference information, Yellow Pages, and UPS Package Tracking. Subject categories are also available on the site for browsing. Other features on the Infoseek Web site include the option to view headline news and the option to personalize a variety of news selections using keywords that appeal to you. To perform an Infoseek search, type a phrase or keyword query in the appropriate box and click on the "Seek" button. The Infoseek Advance Search screen is a very detailed pull-down menu designed to refine your search query with ease. For detailed information designed to help you maximize your Infoseek search, refer to the Help link on the Web site. http://www.infoseek.com/

- When searching for a topic of interest, make sure to type all the keyword(s) that apply to your search—be specific.

- If you are searching for an exact phrase, use " " quotation marks before the first word and after the last word in the phrase.
- To make sure that a word in a phrase is definitely included in your query results, use a + plus sign directly in front of the word(s) in your phrase when you submit your query.
- To make sure that a word in a phrase is not included in your query results, use a – minus sign directly in front of the word(s) of the phrase you do not want to see in your query results.
- When searching for proper names, make sure to capitalize the first letter in both the first name and the surname.

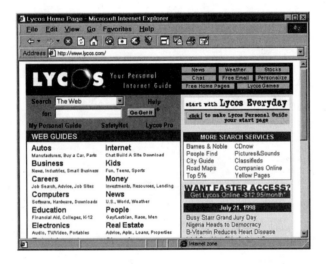

Lycos is designed to search the Web using keyword(s) and phrases and offers a pull-down menu that includes additional search sites such as Web Site Reviews, Personal Homepages, Message Boards, Reuters News, Weather, Cities, Dictionary, Stock, Music, Books, Pictures, Sounds, Downloads, and Recipes. The service also provides selected Web guide topics for browsing, various other online services for searching, and selected free services for Web users. Daily headline news can be found on Lycos as well as links to Lycos Web services such as shopping and travel. Advanced search options are available by selecting the "Lycos Pro" hyperlink. The advance search page consists of a variety of predefined pull-down menus and buttons for your review. For detailed information designed to help you maximize your Lycos search, refer to the Help"link on the Web site. http://www.lycos.com/

- When searching for a topic of interest, make sure to type all the keyword(s) that apply to your search—be specific.

- If you are searching for an exact phrase, use " " quotation marks before the first word and after the last word in the phrase.

- To make sure that a word in a phrase is definitely included in your query results, use a + plus sign directly in front of the word(s) in your phrase when you submit your query.

- To make sure that a word in a phrase is not included in your query results, use a – minus sign directly in front of the word(s) of the phrase you do not wish to see in your query results.

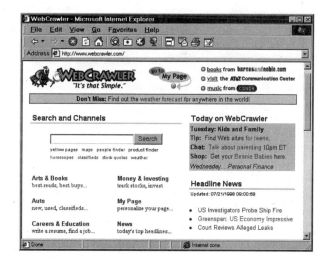

WebCrawler is designed to search an index of the Web and provides headlines news, a daily toolbox, and selected categories for browsing. It offers onsite hyperlinks such as Yellow Pages, Maps, People Finder, Product Finder, Horoscopes, Classifieds, Stock Quotes, and Weather. The service also contains a page where you can personalize information that you want to receive in relation to news, stock market information, reminders, horoscope information, sports scores information, weather, and TV listings. Basic search features rely on keyword(s) or phrases. Advanced search features use Boolean operators such as, AND, OR, and NOT, and the + plus sign, the – minus sign, and ( ) parentheses. For detailed information designed to help you maximize your WebCrawler search, refer to the Help link on the Web site. http://www.webcrawler.com/

Net Tips

- Because WebCrawler is designed to search for any or all of your keyword(s) queries, Web sites that contain all of your query words appear at the top of your search results page.

- On the search results page, you can choose to view a short or detailed format. The short format provides you a list of Web site titles. The detailed format provides descriptive summaries along with the URL and relevancy ranking scores.

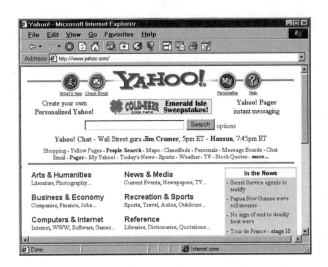

Yahoo! is designed as a searchable index guide to the Internet. The service maintains a custom-made database of Web sites and categories and offers you the option to search its database or browse their subject categories. In relation to full-text Web page searches, Yahoo! relies on Web pages indexed by Inktomi, one of its strategic partners, who use the search engine to index every Web page that it can find to answer your search query. The Yahoo! Web site offers subject categories, headline news, free services, additional hyperlinks for searching the Web, and online entertainment. For detailed information designed to help you maximize your Yahoo! search, refer to the Help link on the Web site. http://www.yahoo.com/

Net Tips

- If you are searching for an exact phrase, use " " quotation marks before the first word and after the last word in the phrase.
- To make sure that a word in a phrase "is" definitely included in your query results, use a + plus sign directly in front of the word(s) in your phrase when you submit your query.
- To make sure that a word in a phrase is "not" included in your query results, use a – minus sign directly in front of the word(s) of the phrase you do not wish to see in your query results.

How do I locate someone's e-mail address on the Net?

Locating someone's e-mail address can be a daunting challenge. How would you locate a person whose e-mail signature is *3876d,qw4zm@acme-cyber-provider.net*? Fear not, help is available. There are a number of Web sites that specialize in collecting and cataloging e-mail addresses. (Don't worry, inclusion in these directory listings is voluntary.)

With Microsoft Internet Explorer 4.0, finding someone's e-mail address is easy. To find an e-mail address, click the **Find People** icon the Outlook Express **Edit** menu.

A dialog box appears that offers you several different directories from which to choose, including:

Bigfoot	http://www.bigfoot.com/
WhoWhere	http://www.whowhere.com/
Four11	http://www.four11.com/
Switchboard	http://www.four11.com/

Select a site to search, type the name of the person for whom you are searching, and click the **Find Now** button. After you find the person you need, you can click the **Add to Address Book** button for later use.

The dark side of the Net

Is it true that pornography is rampant on the Net?

Yes and no. Just as every city has its "dark side," the Internet is no different. If you want to view pornography, there is plenty to see, but like any dark side of any city you must go looking for it. Pornography Web sites do *not* automatically appear on your Web browser. With the possible exception of unsolicited SPAM that may include a hyperlink to an adult site, pornography *is not* thrust in front of your eyes as some people would have you believe. However, a seemingly innocent search for information may reveal pornographic sites based on the criteria of your search. Even though you can choose not to access this content, it may still be presented to you. You could also be subjected to ads if the advertiser bought certain key words.

Is there any way to minimize this exposure?

Regardless of the terminology, pornography, "adult entertainment," or better yet, "First Amendment freedoms," there are screening utilities that work with your browser to filter these sites and block access from children or employees. As the owner or manager of a business you do have the option (and possibly a legal responsibility) of limiting your employees access to these sites. In all likelihood your employees' job description does not include such provisions as on-the-job free time to explore adult-oriented Web sites.

The Internet can be a tremendous aid to your business, or it can be an absolute waste of your employees' time.

The decision is yours.

SURF WATCH SurfWatch service available through Netcom enables you to block World Wide Web, FTP, Gopher, IRC, and other sites likely to contain objectionable material. Customers are kept up-to-date with a monthly service that automatically updates the blocked site list. http://www2.netcom.com/personal/surfwatch/index.html#advantage

SurfWatch (http://www.surfwatch.net/) SurfWatch Professional Edition can provide your company with a powerful, easy to implement server-level approach to managing your employee's Internet usage. Designed to run on the leading Proxy Servers, SurfWatch allows you to control access to Internet sites ranging from sex and violence to sports and chat—a total of more than 100,000 sites from more than 20 categories. SurfWatch is an award-winning, easy-to-use filtering software solution that parents, educators, and employers can use to screen the Internet, providing a unique technical alternative to government censorship. Since creating the market for Internet filtering technology in May 1995, SurfWatch has shipped more than 7.2 million copies of the software and has become the industry-standard tool for blocking access to unwanted materials on the Internet.[4]

Check the Net!

CYBERsitter offers free daily updates, ease of installation, and overall effectiveness in filtering and monitoring Internet activities. CYBERsitter gives the employer (or parent) the capability to limit access to objectionable material on the Internet. You can choose to block, block and alert, or simply be alerted when access is attempted to objectionable areas.[5] http://www.solidoak.com

Net Nanny, according to their Web site, is the only software program that allows *you* to monitor, screen, and block access to anything residing on, or running in, out or through your PC, online or off. It's two-way screening in real-time.[6] http://www.netnanny.com/

Push versus pull

What is "Push" technology?

Ideally, with *Push* technology, you won't need to scour (Pull) the Web for specific information, Push technology delivers information to your desktop without searching. The reason is the way in which *push* assembles targeted information in a timely fashion and delivers it directly to you in a format that you choose. Using intelligent agents with predefined search criteria, information is filtered and customized individually.

Internally, a company could configure its own corporate channel using an intranet server and push company information such as product schedules, company events, etc. This is currently being done by some large organizations.

"Push leverages the Internet's greatest fundamental asset—a universal network—to mitigate the unfortunate byproduct of its own overwhelming success-access to too much information."[7]

In some cases, you may need special software, which is usually free and can be downloaded from various Web sites. The technique used to deliver content varies quite a bit. It can range from timely e-mail notices to screensavers with video clips.

The idea of Push, originally developed by PointCast, was a screensaver that displayed news, sports, weather, stock prices, and advertisements when your computer used its screensaver routine. Although the screensaver concept is still quite popular, the future of Push is trying in the hands of the browser engineers. Unfortunately, history is once again being repeated in that there are few standards in place and the browser behemoths are trying to jockey for the number one position.

Push also works best if you have a "dedicated" connection to the Internet (ISDN, T-1, and so on). If you are a dial-up user, you can only receive information if you are online. Although, you can program your computer modem to dial up periodically for updated information, that is generally less thrilling than information that appears magically on your screen as in the case with a permanent Internet connection.

Should I consider using *Push* technology to reach my customers?

"No matter what you call it—Webcasting, netcasting, channelcasting, pointcasting, direct deliver—push is the future of the Internet."[8]

The keyword in the above prediction is "future." *Push* technology *may* play a big part in the Internet's future. However, embracing this technology before the wrinkles have been ironed out may be acceptable for bleeding edge media companies with big budgets. For the rest of us, the potential rewards may not be worth the investment of time and resources.

Until the dust settles, what should you do while you wait for the industry to agree on standards? Exercise patience and use e-mail and/or a Listserv service to reach your customers. In the interim, Microsoft Explorer 4.0 offers channels that you can incorporate in your business.

What are channels and what can I do with them?

Essentially, a channel is a Web site designed to deliver content from the Internet to your computer. Channels are an example of Internet Explorer's use of *push* technology. Technology that will notify you automatically when your selected favorite Web sites have been changed or updated.

As we mentioned, Push is a paradox of how the Internet has traditionally functioned. Typically, users go out to the Net for information and pull it down via their browser. With Internet Explorer 4.0 you can tell a Web site when to send (push) information to you. An entire Web site can be delivered to your computer to read at your convenience, or when you are not connected to the Internet and want to <u>browse</u> offline.

Net Tips

From a guerilla marketing intelligence viewpoint, imagine being alerted every time your competitor changes its pricing pages or adds new products or services.

Where do I find a list of available channels?

To view a list of channels visit the Microsoft Web site at `http://www.iechannelguide.com/guide/en/en_us.asp` or select the "View Channels" button located on the desktop taskbar, or select **Go + Channel Guide** on the toolbar of Internet Explorer 4.0.

You do not have to <u>subscribe</u> to a channel to view it. However, you can subscribe to a channel as you add it to your channel bar. The channel bar displays all of the channels installed on your computer, whether you subscribe to them or not.

How much do subscriptions cost?

That's part of the good news, subscriptions today are free (for now). Internet Explorer 4.0 has a built-in Web crawling agent that will monitor any Internet Web page or Web site that you subscribe to. After you subscribe to a Web page, Internet Explorer 4.0 will automatically monitor the page, notify you whenever it changes, and deliver the updated content when it is most convenient for you.

How do I subscribe to a Web site?

To subscribe to a Web page, your browser must first be connected to the page you're interested in. Then, simply choose Add to Favorites from the "Favorites" button on the menu bar. You can subscribe to any standard Web page and to as many pages as you want. The page that you subscribe to does not have to be a Web site's main page.

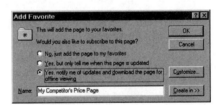

The subscription process allows you to decide when your selected site should be monitored, how often it should be monitored, and whether you want to be notified of the changes through e-mail. Typically, when one of your selected sites has changed, the browser will add a "gleam" to the site icon located in your "Favorites" menu. Imagine, no more wasted time combing through a site just to see if it has changed.

Also, you can take advantage of this subscription feature any time you decide to add a site to your Favorites list. Choose the third option, "Full subscription: download for offline reading." Internet Explorer 4.0 has the capability to check a Web site for changes since your last visit and *download* any files that have changed. You can schedule downloads for off-peak hours (saving connect time and money) or have Web content delivered on demand.

By choosing to schedule downloads for offline browsing, you can download an entire Web site including graphics and all page components in a fraction of the time it would take you to read them online. Once the pages are on your computer, you can read them at *your* convenience.

Net Tips

For laptop users, downloading your Web site or related competitive information is a great way to make offsite multimedia presentations.

How do I browse offline?

| Work Offline |
| Close |

All the text, graphics, and multimedia files on the Web site that you select to download will be transferred to your hard drive. To browse offline or read the pages, select **File** + **Work Offline** from the menu. Then open any page on your machine by typing the URL of the site you've selected as a favorite. Even though you're not connected to the Web, Internet Explorer 4.0 recognizes the address and retrieve the page from your computer's memory.

Business productivity links

A small to medium-sized business has the need, but seldom the infrastructure in place to perform the duties of a legal department, human resource department, travel department, and so on. Finding help or information on virtually any subject is only a mouse click away on the Internet.

The Net offers a plethora of resources on demand. The following links are included as *starting points*. They may not necessarily be *the* definitive or authoritative information sources to solve all your business needs, but they will give you a head start to finding a solution. Your best resource is almost always a well-defined search query using one of the major search engines.

Remember, this is the Internet and things change virtually overnight. These links can disappear or move to another location in the blink of an eye.

Books and Magazines

Amazon.com—Earth's Biggest Bookstore.[9] `http://www.amazon.com/`

Barnes and Noble—The world's largest bookseller online.[10] `barnesandnoble.com`

The Electronic Newsstand—Links to more than 2,000 magazines. The most comprehensive site about magazines on the Web. `http://www.enews.com/`

Entrepreneur Magazine Online—A free membership and tons of useful business links, tips, strategies, and information targeted to the small business. `http://www.entrepreneurmag.com/`

SmallOffice.Com—Sponsored by Home Office Computing and Small Business Computing Magazines. `http://www.smalloffice.com/`

Macmillan Computer Publishing—The world's largest computer book publisher offers more than 150 full-text references for your review, including the latest technologies. `http://mcp.com`

Inc. Online—If you're in business, you know Inc. magazine. Inc. was recently named Best Online Magazine in Folio magazine's 1996 Editorial Excellence Awards. `http://www.inc.com/`

In Touch Networks—Provides unabridged "audio versions" of articles from more than 100 newspapers and magazines nationwide. You need to install the RealAudio Player. `http://www.tstradio.com/intouch.html`

Communications

FaxSav Incorporated—Lets you use your Internet connection to fax from your desktop, from anywhere to anywhere. `http://www.faxsav.com/`

Internet News Bureau—A service that sends out a comprehensive e-mail to 1,200 media professionals who specifically asked to be notified of such events, more than 2,000 outlets in all. `http://www.newsbureau.com/`

Electronic News

CMPnet—Offers free e-mail newsletters. You can subscribe to one or more of their free e-mail newsletters for the latest technology features, financial updates, and news headlines. `http://www.cmpnet.com/delivery`

The Red Herring Direct—The leading magazine on the business of technology specializing in high-level business information on technology and entertainment. `http://www.herring.com/`

San Jose Mercury News—The Good Morning Silicon Valley Morning report delivered to your e-mail box. `http://www.sjmercury.com/`

InfoWorld—The technology weekly for 25 years, this source will give you the latest on industry news and products. `http://www.infoworld.com`

Wired News—The leading online news source for the latest reports on how technology is changing your life. Available in text or HTML versions. To read the HTML version of the Wired News front page, you must use a Web-based e-mail service such as Outlook Express. `http://www.wired.com/news/`

Human Resources

Benefits Link—A free link to information and services for employers sponsoring employee benefit plans, companies providing products and services for plans, and participating employees. `http://www.benefitslink.com/`

Career Mosaic—Encourages employers to post jobs to the JOBS database directly online. Learn of recruiting events in cyberspace, salary information, links to related sites around the world, and more. `http://www.careermosaic.com/`

Human Resource Store—A good reference site offering free documents discussing many of the HR issues you face every day. `http://www.hrstore.com/`

Monster Board—A popular job placement and posting site where you can post your jobs to attract top candidates and conduct a resume search to find your next employee. `http://www.monsterboard.com/`

TrainingNet—Looking for the right solution to your Training or HR issues? Then, look no further than their PowerRFI mechanism. From a single form you can send a Request for Information to the most respected solution providers in the industry. `http://www.trainingnet.com/`

U.S. Department of Labor—A Web site that makes information about the Department, its programs, and the laws and regulations it administers widely available and easy to access. `http://www.dol.gov/`

Insurance

Quotesmith Insurance—Where you can obtain instant quotes right now from 328 leading insurance companies and request an application online, *without having to speak to any insurance salesmen!* `http://www.quotesmith.com/`

Quicken InsureMarket—Lets you receive real-time quotes, obtain information, connect with agents, compare quotes, and purchase policies from the nation's leading insurance companies. http://www.insuremarket.com/

InsWeb—Offers insurance shoppers a convenient way to get accurate quotes from many companies in a secure, pressure-free environment. http://www.insWeb.com/

Insurance News Network—Presents unbiased facts about auto, home, and life insurance, including Standard & Poor's ratings. http://www.insure.com/

Internet Help

eRetail.Net—News and Information for Internet Retailers. http://www.eretail.net/

VirtualPROMOTE—Guest tutorials by invitation. http://www.virtualpromote.com/guest.html

Marketing Tools—A magazine for information-based tactics and techniques. http://www.marketingtools.com/

SupportHelp.com—A one-stop-shop for locating contact information for hardware and software manufacturers. Technical support telephone numbers, e-mail addresses, and direct Web site hotlinks. http://www.supporthelp.com/

Webmonkey—Part of the Wired Digital family, an online help site for most things Internet. http://www.hotwired.com/webmonkey/

Web Site Garage—Will perform a 5-point checkup to diagnose common mistakes in Web sites. http://www.Web sitegarage.com/

ZDNet—An all-in-one Internet help site also covering software, hardware, games, and so on. http://www.zdnet.com/zdhelp/

Legal

The Business Law Site—Federal and state statutes, cases and agencies! Legal research sites! Business and high-tech law! Tax forms! http://members.aol.com/bmethven/

Legaldocs—Allows you to prepare customized legal documents directly online. Fill in the form, "submit" and instantly obtain a completed will, estate plan, contract, or other document. http://legaldocs.com/

Intellectual property law server—Provides information about intellectual property law including patent, trademark, and copyright. Resources include comprehensive links, general information, and space for professionals to publish articles and forums for discussing related issues.[11] http://intelproplaw.com/

KnowX—The most comprehensive source of public records on the Web. http://www.knowx.com/

Living/Health

Achoo Healthcare Online—Lets you search or browse through an extensive listing of healthcare information on the Internet. `http://www.achoo.com/`

healthfinder™—Is a gateway consumer health and human service information Web site from the United States government. This site can help you locate selected online publications, databases, support, self-help groups, and other government agencies and not-for-profit organizations that produce reliable information for the public. `http://www.healthfinder.gov/`

MedicineNet—Offers information about diseases and treatments, a pharmacy medical dictionary, an "Ask The Experts" section, First Aid, poison control centers, and more. `http://www.medicinenet.com/`

Money

Bloomberg—Offers a broad range of financial services in a single Web site. `http://www.bloomberg.com/welcome.html`

CBS Market Watch—Recently rated by Barron's (http://www.barrons.com/) as one of the top Web sites for investors, the DBC Online Web site now takes a giant step by joining forces with CBS News to create the new financial supersite.[12] `http://cbs.marketwatch.com`

The Final Bell—Information from how to pick stocks to playing investment simulations, hot stories, and links to many investment related sites. `http://www.sandbox.net/finalbell/`

Financial Calculators—HSH Associates is the world's leading publisher of mortgage and consumer loan information. `http://www.hsh.com/`

The Motley Fool—A company that aims to educate, amuse, and enrich the individual investor. To prove to you that the best person to manage your money is YOU. `http://www.fool.com/`

The Red Herring magazine—The leading magazine on the business of technology. `http://www.redherring.com/`

TheStreet.com—An outstanding Web site with areas for the public and members only. You can register to get two weeks of free, unlimited access including the Daily e-mail Bulletin every morning. `http://www.thestreet.com/`

Wall Street City—From its slick Java tickertape to its thorough and intuitive menu, Wall Street City provides several services that are FREE as well as a huge selection of useful and powerful tools at monthly rates from $9.95 to $34.95. `http://www.wallstreetcity.com/`

Office Supplies

Inktec—Offers ink cartridges and refills at discount (50%) prices for your inkjet printer. You can save money by replacing or refilling your cartridges. `http://www.ink-jet.com/`

Office Depot—Next business day delivery at no charge on orders of $50 or more within local trading area. U.S.A. & Canada orders only. `http://www.officedepot.com/`

OfficeMax On-line—Buy office products from your keyboard, and your order is delivered free directly to your door the next day. `http://www.officemax.com/`

Staples, Inc.—Everything for your office. `http://www.staples.com/`

Viking Office Products—See more than 500 office products priced to save you up to 69%. America's favorite name brands delivered overnight almost anywhere, or same-day in 10 cities, free! `http://www.vikingop.com/`

Online Commerce

Charge.Com—In addition to accepting credit card orders, you can accept checks by phone (or fax or e-mail) with no set-up charge with rates as low as 1.55%. `http://www.charge.com/index.html`

CyberCash—Wallet is a key component of the CyberCash Secure Internet Payment System that enables users to securely purchase products and services from Internet merchants.[13] `http://www.cybercash.com/`

First Virtual—Says that all you need is a valid Visa or MasterCard, a private e-mail account, and for a $2 annual fee, you can become one of the hundreds of thousands of people shopping on the Internet through today."[14] `http://www.firstvirtual.com/services/`

ZDNet—ZD University's online courses will help make your e-business a roaring success. `http://www.zdnet.com/products/ecommerceuser/tips.html`

Package Tracking

Airborne Express—Airborne is the third largest and fastest-growing air express delivery carrier in America. We deliver time-sensitive documents, letters, small packages and freight via same-day, next-day, next-afternoon, second-day, and other service options.[15] `http://www.airborne-express.com/`

DHL—Its extensive global presence enables DHL to provide unmatched worldwide services from its offices in every country.[16] `http://www.dhl.com/`

Federal Express—InterNetShip[SM] is the way to ship packages via the Internet to more than 160 countries from the U.S. `http://www.fedex.com/`

United Parcel Service—With services tailored to meet the needs of today's growing companies. No matter what you ship or where you send it, UPS has the right service for you.[17] `http://www.ups.com/`

US Postal Service—Offers services that include Express Mail tracking, and changing your address on line. `http://www.usps.gov/`

Printing/Faxing

Deluxe Printing—A longtime provider of business checks, form supplies, and related services to consumers and small businesses. `http://forms.deluxe.com/`

Printovation—A printing service for Microsoft Publisher and Word delivers high-quality, full-color printing from orders you place via modem. Printovation's software allows you to submit your print order electronically, 24 hours a day. Get a free starter kit. `http://www.printovation.com/`

WebRecord—Developed by Canon. Enables you to print entire Web site complete with complex images, page backgrounds and a table of contents. Select specific pages to be printed and arrange them in any order. WebRecord is optimized for Microsoft Internet Explorer 3.0 or higher or Netscape Navigator 2.0 or higher. `http://www.ccsi.canon.com/Webrecord/`

Wink Photo Services—Will scan your images, to any format from basic "Raw Scan" to "Full Image Restoration." `http://www.tiac.net/users/winkfoto/`

Reference

AT&T Toll-Free—Internet Directory. `http://www.tollfree.att.net/dir800/`

Bartlett's Quotations—A collection of passages, phrases, and proverbs traced to their sources in ancient and modern literature. `http://www.columbia.edu/acis/bartleby/bartlett/`

Dictionary/Glossary—OneLook Dictionaries has 844,463 words in 197 dictionaries now indexed. `http://onelook.com/`

U.S. Census Bureau—U.S. Census Bureau data. `http://www.census.gov`

U.S. Patent and Trademark Office database—The starting point for the USPTO's free patent databases U.S. patents issued from 1976 to the present. `http://patents.uspto.gov/`

Calendar Land—Provides lunar and sky calendars, holidays, holy days, festivals celebrations, global indexes, ancient calendars, Chinese, Mesoamerican, Japanese, Mayan, Catholic, Persian, Jewish, and more. `http://www.juneau.com/home/janice/calendarland/`

Write your Congressperson—Send a telegram to an entire Congressional committee. `http://www.voxpop.org/zipper/`

Zip Code Finder—Zip Codes, City, State, Population, and Distance Information.
http://link-usa.com/zipcode/

Software

CWSApps—According to them, is the ultimate one-stop download site for the latest and greatest software on the Internet. Comprehensive file listings, ratings, and extensive reviews for the hottest Windows 3.x/95/NT applications are just a few of the many goodies to be found here. http://cws.internet.com/

Download.Com—By CNET, this is one of the most extensive computer software sites on the Internet. http://www.download.com/

Jumbo Download Network—The largest collections of software and downloadable files on the Web. http://www.jumbo.com/index.htp

Shareware.Com—Another one of the many Internet help and entertainment sites owned by CNET. You can search for software by name, category, arrival date, and so on. http://www.shareware.com/

Windows Users Group Network—A complete resource center for top quality shareware, a new Windows Tip Center, and more. Each week WUGNET and Microsoft feature a shareware pick demonstrating the highest standards available today in shareware for Windows 98. http://www.wugnet.com/

Windows95.com—A popular destination for 32-bit Shareware, Drivers, Tips, and Information. http://www.windows95.com/

Taxes

Ernst & Young—The largest provider of tax services in the U.S. and around the world. http://www.ey.com/tax/default.stm

H&R Block—The country's largest tax preparation firm, serving 17.4 million taxpayers in nearly 9,700 offices in the United States. http://www.hrblock.com/

Internal Revenue Service—The IRS' home on the Web where you can download forms or use the TaxFax service from anywhere in the world. http://www.irs.ustreas.gov/

Tax Prophet—Deciphers the Internal Revenue Code for U.S. and foreign taxpayers. http://www.taxprophet.com/

The Tax Foundation—A nonprofit, nonpartisan policy research organization that monitors fiscal issues at the federal, state, and local levels. http://www.taxfoundation.org/

There are thousands of travel related sites on the Internet with more being added every day. It is estimated that travelers will book more than one billion in on-line air travel in 1997.[18]

Travel

Most small business people typically don't travel as much as the corporate road warrior types but are usually more sensitive to fare prices. The Web offers a huge advantage to anyone willing to do a bit of research to save some money.

You might want to check out Arthur Frommer's Web site (`www.frommers.com`). You'll find his "Vacations for Real People" (a daily news magazine), a comprehensive encyclopedia of travel information, unique message boards, and more, as well as his multitude of books on every travel destination imaginable.

Before heading out on your next adventure, your very first stop should be **weather.com** (`http://www.tiac.net/users/winkfoto/`). The Weather Channel on-line is actually better than its cable clone in that you can select the information you want to see without having to wait for the programming to cycle.

After you've learned how to dress for your destination, you might want to make a note of some ATM machines that will be near your hotel. **ATM Locator** (`http://www.visa.com/`) by VISA Worldwide will give you the location of the nearest ATM machine by city, road intersection, zip code, and so on. Detailed maps are included with the results.

When you get to where you're going, **MapBlast**, by Vicinity Corp. (`http://www.mapblast.com/`) will provide you with door-to-door, turn-by-turn driving directions with maps in metropolitan areas nationwide.

Additional Travel Related Links

American Airlines—Travel planning offers fare quotes, flight schedules and you can earn bonus AAdvantage miles by booking via the Web. `http://www.americanair.com/`

American Express Travel—Offers real-time airline information, hotel information, reservations, ticket booking and last minute travel bargains. `http://www.americanexpress.com/travel/`

Biztravel.com—Promotes itself as the Internet company for frequent business travelers. Among other services, bizAlerts deliver critical travel information to you via your alphanumeric pager (if you have an e-mail paging address for your pager). `http://www.biztravel.com/V4/newhome.cfm`

Delta Airlines—Real-time connection to schedules and fares for cities within the U.S. and SkyMiles account information. `http://www.delta-air.com/`

Microsoft Expedia—Lets you use an Expedia travel agent, step-by-step wizards for booking flights, hotels, and rental cars and receive timely e-mail notification of low fares to your favorite destinations. `http://expedia.msn.com/`

Southwest Airlines—Home gate, the home of Southwest Airlines offers ticketless travel online. `http://www.iflyswa.com/`

Travelocity—Offers the access the power of easySAABRE, plus the vast destination and entertainment databases of Worldview Systems. Flight Paging comes directly to your alphanumeric pager with national access. `http://www.travelocity.com/`

Web Promotion

The Global Information Infrastructure Awards—GII is the independent awards program that recognizes and promotes best practices and new models in the use of Internet and network technologies. Their program has been described as a cross between the Oscars and the Baldrige Awards. `http://www.gii.com/`

Award-It!—A one-stop award registration service. Submit their form to have your Web site reviewed by all of participating members of Award-It!. They don't guarantee your Web site will qualify for an award, but you'll never know unless you try. `http://www.award-it.com/`

Top 5%—Operated by the editorial staff at Lycos. The Top 5% makes no distinction between commercial, public and personal sites. Excellence is their only criterion. `http://www.lycos.com/help/top5-form.html`

Yahoo's—Listing of Web Site Awards. Submit your site. `http://www.yahoo.com/Computers_and_Internet/Internet/World_Wide_Web/Best_of_the_Web/Awards/`

Miscellaneous Business Links

Kelly's Blue Book—Offers free reports for 1998 new car pricing and free reports for used cars—both Retail and Trade-in values. `http://www.kbb.com/`

MapBlast!—A free mapping service available from Vicinity Corporation.[19] Using Vicinity's dynamic GeoEnabled[tm] technology, MapBlast! allows you to create, customize, and save easy-to-read digital maps pinpointing almost any location within the United States. You specify the location and MapBlast! makes the map. After you've customized the map to meet your needs, you can embed it on your Web page, or e-mail it anywhere in the world. `http://www.mapblast.com/`

MapQuest—Lets you add interactive mapping, routing, and trip planning to Web sites. GeoSystems is the world's leading supplier of geographic information products and services for the information publishing industry.[20] `http://www.mapquest.com/`

Rent.Net—A free database of apartments, temporary furnished suites, international rentals, self-storage facilities, truck, furniture, and relocation-related services in more than 1,500 cities! `http://www.rent.net/`

1800flowers.com—For that business or personal gift that you just don't seem to have the time to buy. After you open a FREE account, there are a number of benefits that include a gift reminder program, access to your purchase history, special offers and more. `http://www.1800flowers.com/`

Microsoft Support Links

For reasons mentioned a number of times prior, we have recommended a Microsoft centric solution to meet the challenges of Internet site design, authoring, and related technology. The following links provide additional support, information and many free extras from Microsoft.

FrontPage 98—Support, answers to common questions, resources, tips, and tricks. `http://www.microsoft.com/frontpage/support/default.htm`

Best of the Web—An easy-to-use, comprehensive guide to everything that most people want to do on the Web. Be entertained, learn something new, and communicate with others. `http://home.microsoft.com/exploring/exploring.asp`

Build an Intranet in One Hour—With Office 97, FrontPage® 98, and Microsoft's new 60-Minute Intranet Kit. Build a customized information-sharing solution for your team. `http://www.microsoft.com/intranet/default.htm`

Internet Explorer—Tips and tricks and getting more from the Internet, `http://www.microsoft.com/magazine/internet/ie/ie.htm`

Site Builder Network—A "members only" organization that anyone can join by answering a few questions to determine which level you can qualify for. Basic membership can be gained just by including the *Get Microsoft Internet Explorer* logo on your site. As a "Premier Web consultant," you can receive a tighter working relationship with Microsoft to help you accomplish your goals. `http://www.microsoft.com/sitebuilder/default.htm`

The Gallery—The one-stop place to get tools, images, sounds, information on dynamic html, data source objects, scriptlets, and more. `http://www.microsoft.com/gallery/default.asp`

Images—Offers a variety of images that you can download for **free**. These include rules, buttons, backgrounds, bullets, icons, clip art images, and photographs. `http://www.microsoft.com/gallery/files/images/default.htm`

Typography Web site—For type users and type developers where you can download free fonts for use with Windows and Apple Macintosh computers. `http://www.microsoft.com/truetype/fontpack/default.htm`

Word 97 free stuff—An assortment of wizards, templates, and add-ins. `http://www.microsoft.com/OfficeFreeStuff/Word/`

Windows 95—Support, training, free software, technology updates, and everything Windows 95. `http://www.microsoft.com/windows95/default.htm`

Windows 98 Home Page—`http://www.microsoft.com/Windows98/`

---

[1] Source: Ben Elgin in ZDnet article on electronic commerce. http://www.zdnet.com/products/ecommerceuser/intro.html

[2] Source: http://wagner.princeton.edu/foldoc/cgi-script?electronic+commerce

[3] Source: Cynthia N. James-Catalano, Internet World Magazine, May 1997, (http://www.internetworld.com/) article "In A Hurry For Info," e-mail: jamcat@jamcat.com

[4] Spyglass, authors of SurfWatch provide software and services that help make a variety of devices that work with the World Wide Web. http://www.spyglass.com/company/whatis.html

[5] Source: Solid Oak Software, Inc. Web page. http://www.solidoak.com/

[6] Source: NetNanny Software International Inc. Web page. http://www.netnanny.com/home.html

[7] *Internet World* magazine, May 1997, Planning for Push article by Whit Andrews.

[8] Jesse Berst, Editorial Director, ZDNet AnchorDesk, quote from the Berst Alert for Monday, April 21, 1997. http://www5.zdnet.com/anchordesk/

[9] Amazon.com, Inc. http://www.amazon.com/exec/obidos/subst/misc/copyright.html

[10] barnesandnoble.com is owned and operated by barnesandnoble.com inc. http://www.barnesandnoble.com/include/disclaimer.asp?userid=221K0TF6S7

[11] Source: Intellectual Property Law Server Web site located at: http://www.intelproplaw.com/index.shtml

[12] MarketWatch.com L.L.C., (jointly-owned by CBS and Data Broadcasting Corp.) http://cbs.marketwatch.com/press_room/www.htx

[13] CyberCash is a trademark of CyberCash, Inc. and the CyberCash logo is a registered trademark. http://www.cybercash.com/cybercash/wallet/faq/shortfaq.html

[14] First Virtual, VirtualPIN, and 1 Virtual Place are trademarks of First Virtual Holdings Incorporated. http://www.firstvirtual.com/

[15] Airborne Freight Corporation Web site http://www.airborne-express.com/about/whoair.htm

[16] DHL International, Ltd. Web site located at: http://www.dhl.com/

[17] United Parcel Service of America, Inc. Web site: http://www.ups.com/

[18] Source: USA Today, March 25, 1997, Business Travel Bonus Section. http://www.usatoday.com/

[19] Source: Vicinity Corporation, 1135A San Antonio Road, Palo Alto, CA 94303 http://www.vicinity.com/

[20] GeoSystems is the leading supplier of geographic information products and services to the information publishing industry. http://www.geosys.com/

Internet Marketing

The success or failure of every business enterprise is traceable to one source, and one source only, namely somebody's mind, for no one has yet invented a machine that can think.

- Henning W. Prentis Jr.

Marketing definition

Perhaps the best way to begin this chapter is to first define marketing. Although many business people define marketing as selling or advertising, those two aspects of marketing only scratch the surface. The <u>American Marketing Association</u> defines marketing as: "The process of planning and executing the conception, pricing, promotion and distribution of ideas, goods and services to create exchanges that satisfy individual and organizational objectives." `http://www.ama.org/mngraphics/sixtieth/eighties.htm`

So, what does this mean to you? It means that marketing your business depends on four interdependent on-going processes. The blending of these processes make up the marketing mix which is identified by marketing professionals as the four P's (Product, Price, Placement or Distribution, and Promotion). Each process is essential to business success and must be developed, implemented, and monitored. For the sake of clarity, business success is achieved through "exchanges that satisfy individual and organizational objectives." The term "exchanges" may be interpreted as the transfer (sale) of your product, service, or idea to a customer who, in return, gives you something of value (money).

In business, the value of whatever you receive (revenue) must be in excess of the time and money (expenses) that you invest in your product, service, or idea. Otherwise, your business will not produce profit. And profit is, in all probability, the major reason you started your company or went into business for yourself.

Although this information may seem rudimentary, it still serves well to remind yourself that it takes more than entrepreneurial enthusiasm to remain competitive in business. As a business owner, you must continually develop, implement, and monitor the four P's of marketing your company.

1. **P**roduce a solution that "meets a need" or "solves a problem." (Develop your product, service, or idea and identify a target market.)
2. **P**rice your product, service, or idea competitively. (Determine a price for your product, service, or idea that is acceptable to your target market.)
3. **P**lace or distribute your product, service, or idea. (Make your product available in the right place for your target market.)
4. **P**romote your product, service, or idea. (Promotion includes making decisions about advertising, public relations, sales, and sales promotion.)

By now, as a small business owner, you have completed all the necessary steps to marketing your business at least once. Therefore, if you're reading this book, chances are that you are monitoring steps three and four and have questions on how best to place and promote your business online.

How is Internet marketing different from conventional marketing?

The introduction of Internet marketing is the dawning of a new age in marketing communication that provides companies with a powerful tool to reach new audiences. The most exciting aspect of this technology is that it provides the ability to target select groups of potential buyers. Once you identify your target market, you can develop and continue on-going, inexpensive, interactive communication with that group.

Most conventional marketing is essentially one-way communication to a relatively large audience with varied buying interests. Unlike Internet marketing, conventional marketing does not foster the opportunity to develop an intimate relationship with your customers.

The Internet is information on demand: information that is pertinent to your customer's precise needs and desires. Whereas, conventional marketing is more time sensitive. After all, business owners answer inquiries and sell products or services during standard business hours, not 24 hours a day. Therefore, the expensive "one to many" marketing avenue is no longer the only channel to reach your target audience.

Online advertising and public relations overview

Inasmuch as most small business can't afford to hire an experienced PR firm, we asked John Weekley, president of Weekley/Group/McKinney, a successful Dallas-based public relations, advertising, and public affairs consulting firm, to share his professional expertise with you. John's firm was one of the first in Dallas to embrace Internet technology and he knows firsthand what is takes to communicate effectively online.

One of the critical challenges for business communications today is selecting and tailoring your advertising messages through an economy of words and images so that they are relevant and meaningful, and then presented in such a way that they stand out.

Simply stated, your task is to chose—from all of the possible messages and ideas associated with your business—only the most important. Then, prioritize and transmit your messages in the right way *matched* to the right audience—your target market.

Therefore, get organized by taking stock of the important messages you currently attach to the varied aspects of your business, and give some thought to the image(s) and ideas you would like to project.

If you currently market one or more products, consider these basics for your online advertising:

- Photo(s) of items
- Model # or style identification
- Utility or use of item
- Price(s), including applicable taxes, shipping options, and charges
- Expected (and accurate) delivery times
- Payment method
- Brief description of item linked to more detailed description
- Warranties or guarantees
- Full description of accessories available
- Information about manufacturer
- International restrictions or conditions of sale
- E-mail address and telephone number for more information
- Return policy and instructions
- Service information, locations, and policies
- Disclaimer, product liability information, and so on
- Special prices or conditions for government or nonprofit groups
- Downloadable order blank or other information

If your business is service oriented, then consider including the following in your online advertising:

- Name or title of service
- Brief description with link to complete description
- Utility of service
- Value(s) of service
- Information about your company and length of time in business
- Price(s) of service (including any applicable taxes)
- Endorsement or satisfied customer list
- Conditions of service or legal contract language
- Distinctive competencies of your company
- Service delivery dates or expectations
- Online forms for requesting service or stating problems
- Contact e-mail addresses and telephone numbers for more information
- Special pricing for ordering services online
- Map to service location (if applicable)
- Conditions of any government imposed requirements of service

It is certainly expected that your public relations, advertising, and marketing efforts tell your side of your story, and cast your business and its wares in the best possible light. However, one of the first rules of good business communication is absolute honesty and factual representation. If the laws in your state require that you disclaim warranties or print warning labels applicable to certain products, then use good common sense and include this information on your Web site under an appropriate heading.

 As you begin to plan your online communications strategy, you should always keep in mind that your Internet advertising, public relations, marketing, and promotions should integrate and be coordinated with those same activities already a part of your Business Plan.

For small business, the Internet has proven to be a perfect Public Relations medium because Public Relations is the business of inducing various "publics" to have understanding for and goodwill toward a person, firm, or institution. While Public Relations may be interpreted to cover a very broad range of communications specialties, often included in the list are: media relations, employee relations, vendor relations, market relations, customer relations, stockholder relations, governmental relations (and/or public affairs), labor relations, regulatory relations, industry/trade relations, corporate communications, crisis management, Total Quality, and strategic planning.

The Internet easily allows you to feature important announcements on your Web site, display previous news stories about your company or its employees, create a special media section for your news releases, and post copies of your newsletters.

Through the use of e-mail, you can send news releases to media organizations, answer customer inquiries, publish electronic reports or bulletins, and electronically send them to customers and/or employees, and stay in touch with public officials important to the success of your business or industry.

The tools needed to assist you in your public relations efforts are plentiful on the Internet. One of the most useful of these is the PR Newswire, http://www.prnewswire.com/, a news release distribution service used by many professional public relations firms and businesses. Although PR Newswire is a leader in the field of Public Relations, there are many other companies on the Web that specialize in distributing news releases to news outlets. Many of these organizations offer e-mail gateways and are discussed later in this chapter.

The Public Relations portion of a well-organized small business Web site might include:

- Employee of the Month recognition
- History of the company
- Copies of the company's newsletter(s)
- Photos of the company's building or offices
- Customer service surveys and response areas
- Password protected areas "for employees only" about benefits and pensions
- Map(s) to the company's offices or store locations
- Links to organizations with whom the company is affiliated (such as the local BBB, Chamber of Commerce, and so on)
- Job openings and qualifications
- Emergency contact numbers (for some specialized businesses)
- Online general brochure about the company
- Fact sheets, FAQS, or Q&As about the company or industry
- Information about the company's favorite charity or its civic involvement

In addition to these, many publicly held companies have also found it advantageous to place their quarterly and annual reports on the Web...with appropriate notes and legal disclaimers, of course.

Finally, do not neglect the many opportunities of sponsorship available on the Internet. If your business sponsors an area Little League team, then you might want to also consider sponsoring its Web site. Many civic groups and charitable institutions are just now discovering the value of having a presence on the World Wide Web, but many lack the financial resources to establish and maintain a sophisticated Internet site. Sponsorship is an excellent opportunity for your business to receive positive exposure, is often tax deductible, and is an ideal example of how businesses can partner with the non-profit sector for the benefit of the community.

As more and more companies establish a Web site and even more consumers get online, the Internet will continue to help redefine the publics expectation of customer goodwill. As consumers adopt the Internet as a normal part of their daily business and personal routines, small and large businesses alike will increasingly use their domain as a Public Relations platform.

 Make sure to include your e-mail address and your Web site URL in all of your news releases. If a news reporter considers your announcement especially newsworthy and has further interest in your story, he/she may very well decide that your company deserves additional media coverage. So, why not make it easy for them to research your company and contact you.

For additional public relations marketing information, you may access a limited version of The Weekley Group PR Notebook for Small Businesses at `http://www.weekley.com/prnotebook/`.

Online marketing tactics

Conventional press releases

The announcement of a new Web site is a newsworthy event for most relevant publications. What's relevant? Obviously the local newspaper will be more interested in McDonald's Welding Supply's leap into cyberspace than would the *Wall Street Journal* or the *London Times*. A successful press release should be newsworthy and targeted to the proper publications.

Nonconventional press releases

There are a number of companies who specialize in fee-based online press release placements. These companies will usually permit you to choose appropriate industries, and which publications or media outlets will receive your release. Typically they will deliver your press release via e-mail.

One such company is PressPromoter™, an online marketing resource that will submit your press release to targeted publications and media whose audiences you feel would most likely be interested in the information you are submitting. `http://presspromoter.com/`

Press release distribution via e-mail can be an important tool for Web site promotion, marketing and public relations. According to their Web site, they *"maintain up-to-date databases consisting of more than 10,000 editors. The PressPromoter™ system helps you select which editors to submit your press release to by presenting your options using a logical 'drill-down' approach.* Our online resources will take you by the hand and step you through the process. What makes an effective press release? How and why press releases can be worth more than their weight in marketing, promotions and public relations gold to your business. Our Tips, Hints and FAQ's should answer most of your questions."

They also offer a free Templates-based Press Release Generator and some excellent tips and tricks, guidelines for writing press releases and FAQs on their Web site.

If your business happens to be focused around the computer industry, a company called <u>NewsTarget direct</u> could be a great fit. However, even McDonald's Welding Supply could get a story picked up if it had a unique twist to its service or were using the Web in a creative *(newsworthy)* manner.

NewsTarget direct is an Internet based service that performs like your personal, in-house marketing department. They have compiled a list of more than 200 industry publications like PC Magazine, Computerworld, Network Computing, Windows Sources, and others that will receive your release.[1] http://www.newstarget.com/

"One of the most cost effective ways to get the word out to the media about an event is by using the <u>Internet News Bureau</u> service, which for $225 sends out a comprehensive e-mailing to 1,000 online media outlets that specifically asked to be notified of such happenings."[2] http://www.newsbureau.com/

Internet News **Burro** is a news service designed for those who want to announce their Web site to over 1,200 journalists, but don't have the need (or perhaps the budget) to issue a full press release for only $55.00. http://www.newsbureau.com/order/orderburro.html

What if I just don't have time to distribute a press release?

The fact that you are online is a positive statement by itself. It implies that your company is a progressive firm and is interested in providing additional service to your customers. By Webutizing your business, you are assisting your customers 24 hours each day, 365 days each year. You are providing additional convenience for your customers.

How do I deliver my advertising message on the Web?

The Web offers you (and your customers) an opportunity that no other advertising or promotion medium can deliver. You are providing an environment where you can *fully explain* a product or service with demonstrations, color charts, specifications, question and answer areas (<u>FAQs</u>), brochures on demand, special events, contests, testimonials, tips, competitive comparisons, instructions, and links to related information, *(whew)*!

Reciprocal link free for all

LinkExchange The <u>LinkExchange</u> advertises itself as "the Web's largest advertising network." If you would like to increase your Web site's exposure, LinkExchange is a good way to advertise yourself through banner ads without spending any money. http://www.linkexchange.com/welcome/

Talk it up! Tell everyone you meet that your company has a Web site and that they need to come visit and tell others.

Will I be able to charge others to advertise on my site?

The future of online advertising in the U.S. is expected to swell from $305 million in 1996 to more than $5 billion (*that's Billion with a "B"*) by the turn of the century. What's in it for you will be impossible to predict. Obviously, advertisers look for (*and pay for*) opportunities to present their story to targeted audiences.

No other medium can segment an audience like the Web. If your site produces enough traffic, to a particular group of visitors, a noncompetitive manufacturer or service provider may be interested in placing banner ads on your pages. How you will price that Web real estate will be determined by the market as it comes to terms with a model that offers measurable results vs. traffic.

Should I list or advertise with a city-specific service?

You should definitely investigate this as an option. Chambers of Commerce, entrepreneurs, local newspaper, TV and radio stations, search services, and ISPs in every city offer local content online, and some are better than others. Many of these listings are free or low-cost and offer a local business additional opportunities to appear on lists that cater to local clientele. Many of these services have developed strong local followings because they are promoted and updated well. You may also want to consider your own "co-op" of products and services and share the cost with another store owner. This is very effective when people are moving to new areas (for example, listings of restaurants, dry cleaners, mechanics, and so on).

What about positioning my Web site in an online shopping mall?

Because the effectiveness of such a tactic has yet to be consistently proven, this is a difficult call. The landlords or *cyber-lords* of these malls boast great things, but their claims are too often focused on the number of "stores" in their mall, not merchant successes or traffic counts. While some malls have been in existence for years, there have been some casualties in a very short time. IBM's World Avenue Cybermall closed its doors in less than one year of operations.

"In the online world, solid-looking strategies that model traditional, successful marketing concepts frequently fail."[3]

When the Web was still new and search engines were not as commonly used, there was a strong argument for positioning your "store" in an E-mall (electronic mall). The thinking was that an E-mall in cyberspace would function in the same way as does a shopping mall in Peoria. Shoppers would "browse by" while looking for red-tag specials and other bargains and *stumble* upon your store.

Today, with tens of millions of Web pages on the Net, the casual bargain hunter may be difficult to snare. As we discussed earlier, Internet users now shop for specific items by conducting Web searches. Browsing is something people do while listening to a telemarketing pitch for why they should change their long distance company. If Internet shoppers had the time or inclination to browse, they probably would not do their shopping online.

So, if you are interested in test marketing your site with an online mall and the price is right, try it for a while and monitor your results. Certainly, any time you put your company name in front of people you stand an opportunity to profit. Like anything else in business, if it doesn't work, move on and try something else.

How do I use the Web for sales promotion?

To encourage Web activity and motivate people to visit your Web site, you should offer incentives to customers who visit the site. Examples include price discounts, special bonuses, drawings, discounted delivery, and so on.

Newsgroup marketing

Using newsgroups to promote your Web site

A newsgroup is an electronic bulletin board open to the worldwide public. People of similar interests can post messages and dialog with others who share their interests. If properly executed, posting to a newsgroup can generate tremendous activity. If done incorrectly, you can make a whole bunch of enemies very quickly. You must observe your Netiquette when posting to a newsgroup.

Before you commit your energies to a newsgroup marketing campaign, it is always a good idea to "lurk" in that newsgroup for a while and observe what is going on. The best advice for selecting a newsgroup(s) is to target those groups that primarily concern themselves with your subject matter and determine if the newsgroup accepts postings.

When you submit your posting, provide useful advice or information, without making your contribution a blatant advertisement for your business. You can soft-pedal your expertise by ending with a comment such as:

> "…also, I have additional information regarding this kind of service on my Web site. I invite you to visit http://www.your-biz.com/"

When you want to first introduce your Web site to the world, you are encouraged to use one of the announcement newsgroups. These newsgroups are designed for new Web site announcements. If there is sufficient interest in your subject, you may want to consider creating your own newsgroup.

How do I create a newsgroup?

Unfortunately, there is no short answer to this question. To do this correctly, refer to the complete instructions found at http://www.indiana.edu/ip/ip_support/ usenet_guidelines.html. These guidelines have been generally agreed on across

USENET as appropriate protocol for creating new newsgroups in the "standard" USENET newsgroup hierarchy.

Also, to gain a better understanding about creating your newsgroup, the guidelines, can be found in the periodic posting "How to Create a New Usenet Group" in news.announce.newusers, or FTP to `ftp.uu.net`; change directories to:

usenet/news.announce.newsgroups and download the file named "guidelines." Another great source of information is NetGuide's Newsgroup FAQ.

`http://www.netguide.com/server-java/NGPage/KnowhowNetcoachNewsgroups`

What do I do if someone attacks my company in a newsgroup?

Life is too short to involve yourself in a newsgroup flame war, especially considering that in war there are *no* winners. A disgruntled customer, a competitor, or former employee who takes the time to produce (libelous or slanderous) postings will jump at the chance to dispute any statement you make. Your best response to this kind of behavior is to issue *one* statement presenting the facts and ignore any further articles. Additional involvement on your part would probably just escalate the war and call undue attention to the matter.

Effective e-mail marketing

Suggestions

Always include your electronic signature with all e-mail correspondence. A no-cost, yet highly effective method of generating interest in your Web site is to use a "signature file." A signature file is the footer information that most e-mail programs will add to the bottom of an outgoing e-mail message. You can usually configure one or more signature files and select which one is most appropriate to append to your e-mail.

You may want to create one file to use when writing to friends or relatives and another for business use, and so on. To emphasize the importance of a sig file, would you omit your telephone or fax number from a product brochure, your business card or an advertisement? The same holds true for your outgoing e-mail correspondence, Always include your sig file. An example of a business sig file:

> Your Biz Incorporated
> Doing Business Your Way
> Bus: 1-888-yourbiz
> Fax: 972-555-1212
> WWW: `http://www.your-biz.com/`

Net Tips

The subject line of your e-mail message determines whether it will get read or treated as junk mail. You will discover that the differences between your postal (snail) mail and your e-mail will blur—junk mail gets discarded and is seldom read. Use the subject line as a teaser for what is discussed in the body of your message.

Ask for a referral with every e-mail. Consider using a postscript at the end of your message soliciting referrals and/or feedback.

> PS: If you are pleased with our service, please recommend us to a friend. If you are not 100 percent satisfied, please let me know. Thank you.

What is automated mail (autoresponder or autobot)?

Another important attribute of electronic communication is automated mail service-<u>autoresponders or autobots</u>. This service is similar to interactive voice response or fax-back services. Automated mail servers can be programmed to immediately respond to e-mail messages 24 /7. Typically, these servers are activated by certain keywords contained in the body of an e-mail message or a keyword contained in the e-mail header.

Automated mail servers can be configured with any information you want to make publicly available. The most common application is product and service marketing. For example, a potential customer may send your business an e-mail message that contains the words "product information" or "price list" in the subject line or body of the message and within minutes receive an automated response or reply.

Besides the obvious benefits of e-mail, perhaps the most valuable aspect of automated communication is the increased potential for customer goodwill. By giving your customers an additional channel for communication, you establish your business as one who values the customer's time. Today's consumers have more choices than ever before. They do not appreciate waiting in line, whether in person or on a telephone, to ask a simple question. If you cannot assist them at their convenience, they may find someone else who will.

Automated mail also increases the potential for better time management. Your employees no longer have to be physically in the office to meet all of your customer's requests. A customer who wants information about your products or services needs only to send an e-mail message to your autobot address, such as <u>info@your-biz.com</u>, to receive your compelling marketing message.

Produce an e-newsletter

Your electronic newsletter can be in the form of a periodic e-mail or published on your Web site. Although producing an e-newsletter will require a large amount of your time and energy, it is an ideal way to maintain contact with your customers and cultivate future business. You can solicit Web site visitors to register for the e-newsletter so that they will receive information about your product updates or specials as they become available. Your e-newsletter can be handled via a <u>Listserv</u>.

Direct e-marketing (electronic direct mail)

Although we do not recommend spamming, some companies do send messages in e-mail or HTML format; solicited and unsolicited. Beware, sending unsolicited e-mail can set you up to get flamed or bombed on the Internet, and even prosecuted in a court of law. If you are interested in electronic direct mail, there are companies that offer to e-mail your message to people who have agreed to receive unsolicited e-mail.

What are automated mailing lists (listserv)?

Not to be confused with an autoresponder, an automated mailing *list* or discussion group is another form of streamlined electronic communication. These (membership) lists are designed to be subject or topic specific, and participation is on a voluntary basis. They consist of a series of e-mail <u>threads</u> that are periodically compiled and sent out to subscribers. Because mailing lists are comprised of people with like interest, the threat of being flamed for your opinion (as long as it is in context to the discussion) is remote.

It is estimated that there are some 70,000 mailing lists that cover almost every topic you can imagine. Before you decide to provide such a service to your customers, we recommend that you experiment with this concept first by subscribing to some lists in areas that are of interest to you. One of the best sites on the Net to search for mailing lists is the archive at <u>Liszt, the mailing list directory</u>. `http://www.liszt.com/`

Unlike autoresponders, managing an automated mailing list will demand much more participation on your part. <u>Listserv4</u>, commonly associated with mailing lists, is a popular e-mail program that is used to create and maintain these mailing lists or discussion groups. Other programs that support mailing lists are <u>Majordomo4</u> and <u>Listproc5</u>. Reviewing these Web sites will give you all the information you need should you decide to sponsor a mailing list.

For more information on Web marketing, you might want to consider reading *Net Results: Web Marketing that Works* published by Hayden Books. It reveals the successful strategies and tactics that have been used to create winning marketing campaigns for Avon, Bristol Myers Squibb, Macromedia, Time Inc., and Women's Wire.

---

[1] Functional Concepts, Inc. (FCI) is the distributor and operator of NewsTarget direct. http://www.newstarget.com/aboutus.htm

[2] According to the New York research firm of Jupiter Communications, Inc. http://www.jup.com/index.shtml

[3] Copyright © 1997 CMP Media Inc., By Kathryn M. McGrail and M. Trouble Sample, with contributions from Daniel Akst and Kevin M. Savetz. http://techWeb.cmp.com/ng/home/

[4] Majordomo is community-supported free software. Great Circle Associates—http://www.greatcircle.com/—is the home for Majordomo releases and mailing lists, but does not offer any technical support for Majordomo.

[5] CREN's ListProc (ListProcessor), is a powerful mailing list agent that keeps track of thousands of people subscribed to any number of mailing lists. CREN—http://www.cren.net/—a founding organizational member of the Internet Society.

Choose Your Weapons

Don't build me a watch, just tell me the time.

– Charlie McCarthy, COO, Tetley USA

What you will need to start today

If you speak with 20 Internet savvy people, you will get 20 different and sometimes torrid opinions about which are the best software tools on which to standardize. After the smoke has cleared, the opinions are usually no different than the "Ford versus Chevrolet" discussions in which we have all participated. One gets you there faster, one more comfortably or more economically, but they both get you there.

Because we want to make your online trip fast, comfortable, and economical, we recommend that you upgrade or purchase Windows 98. Along with that, we encourage that you invest in Microsoft Office 97 and Microsoft FrontPage 98. We firmly believe that the complete integration of the operating system (Windows 98/NT) and the desktop (Office 97) with the browser (Explorer 4.0) and the Web publisher (FrontPage 98) is a powerful computer solution for small businesses.

Why you should buy or upgrade to Microsoft Office 97

Every business needs the basic functionality that comes with the office suites mentioned previously. Few businesses could operate without a word processor, spreadsheet, or database program. The Microsoft Office 97 Small Business Edition suite delivers this and a host of other functions that will make your transition to the Internet more productive and rewarding.

Microsoft's Office 97 Small Business Edition provides everything you need to master the tasks you do every day. Whether you're creating documents, assembling and analyzing information, communicating with customers, or publishing marketing materials, you'll find all of the essential tools in this easy-to-use, integrated office suite. Discover an integrated desktop where you can organize and manage your e-mail, calendar, contacts, tasks, and files in one place.

The following features of **Microsoft Office 97 Small Business Edition** and **FrontPage 98** were borrowed form the Microsoft Web site. To see a complete review of these products, click to http://www.microsoft.com/.

Microsoft Office 97.2 Small Business Edition

Publisher 98 makes it easy to create professional-quality newsletters, business cards, brochures, Web sites and more. It gives you all-new professional designs and flexible wizards.

Financial Manager lets you harness the valuable business information contained in your accounting package. Its wizards make it easy to create dynamic and customizable reports.

Direct Mail Manager a new internet-based application in Office 97 Small Business Edition, is designed to make it easy for you to create and manage successful direct mail programs.

Expedia Streets 98 mapping software gives you the capability to quickly locate the addresses of key customers, clients and vendors. Generate maps of your Outlook Contacts and copy maps into marketing materials created in Publisher 98 and Word 97.

Microsoft Outlook manages e-mail, calendars, contacts, tasks and to-do lists, and documents or files on the hard drive.

Microsoft Excel 97 brings core spreadsheet functionality to the surface to make it more accessible to all users.

Word 97 simplifies common word-processing tasks with built-in intelligence. Helpful wizards are there to walk you through creating everything from letters and memos to brochures and Web sites.

How can I justify the cost of Office 97?

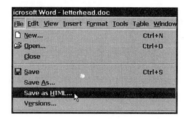

The "**Save as HTML**" feature of the Office 97 program suite is almost enough by itself to justify your investment. Imagine being able to open your legacy (preexisting) documents, spreadsheets, presentations, databases, and so on and save them as HTML files.

Also, Office 97 will import (read) most files from other office suites and convert them to Office 97 files. Example: The document pricelist.wpd could be imported and saved as pricelist.doc. This will greatly simplify the process of creating your Web site and your internal intranet if that is your desire.

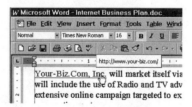

The hyperlinking capability of Office 97 documents is another impressive reason to take the plunge. These *smart* links will permit you to integrate your office files, Web site, and your intranet seamlessly.

The "cursor over" function which prompts the hyperlink to indicate "to where it links" is a terrific timesaving and navigational aid.

What about exchanging documents between Office 97 and earlier versions?

Although backward compatibility (reading documents that were created in a previous Office software version) may have caused some difficulty in the past, Office 97 provides a resolution.

Microsoft issued a Service Release (SR-1), that solves this and some other software issues. Office 97 SR-1 includes a Word 6.0/95 binary converter for Word 97, Outlook 97 enhancements, Access Snapshot technology, and MMX support. To download the patch, go to `http://www.microsoft.com/officefreestuff/office/dlpages/sr1off97.htm.`

Microsoft Internet Explorer 4.0

Of all the software components that embody the total Internet experience, the browser is the easiest program to use; yet it is evolving as the user's most powerful application. On the surface, the browser is a program that combines text, graphics, sounds and video to present an interactive multimedia presentation, a Web page.

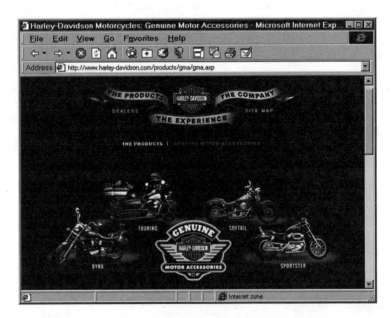

Today, the browser orchestrates tasks that used to be performed by many standalone client programs. With the release of Microsoft's Internet Explorer 4.0, that integration now includes your PC's desktop and hard drives, your LAN, your Intranet and the global Internet. The browser affords one convenient interface to the many worlds of personal communication, entertainment, and education.

Most users require little or no explanation of how to use the browser in its standard configuration. This is the world of "point and click." Point and click is the process used to select a hyperlink. Once a hyperlink has been selected, the user is propelled to a new location on the Net or can initiate an action such as a file download or e-mail inquiry. Hyperlinks are used for a variety of reasons and are usually self-explanatory.

Internet Explorer 4.0 delivers an easy, consistent, and organized way to navigate the Internet (and your own computer or LAN). It installs itself automatically, is ready for use immediately, and offers extensive selections for customization.

The vast majority of users seldom take advantage of all the capabilities built in to today's browsers. Most users add URLs to their Favorites list, use the Search button or tweak a few options (**View + Internet Options**), but rarely use the program to its full potential.

We recommend that users examine the bundle of new features in Internet Explorer 4.0 and customize the browser to their personal preference. Some of these features include:

- New navigational options involving the *Search Bar* that lets you keep your search results visible (in a window) while you select sites from the results list to view individually in another window. You no longer have to click the back-arrow button to return to a search results list.

- The *History Bar* tracks Web site addresses that your browser has visited, helps you track where you've been, and the *Favorites Bar* helps you organize your favorite Web site addresses for future reference.

- Set up content ratings to warn you of questionable or offensive sites and customize security levels and privacy options. (On the menu bar click **View + Internet Options**, then click the **Content tab + Enable** in the Content Advisor block.)

- For convenience of Internet shopping, add your credit card and personal information to the Internet Explorer 4.0 Wallet. Your confidential information is stored securely on your PC and accessible when you are purchasing goods from an Internet site that supports the Wallet program. (On the menu bar click **View + Internet Options**, then click the **Content tab + Payments button + Add.**)

- Watch videos, view Active Channels, listen to real-time broadcasts, and play interactive games on the Internet thanks to Internet Explorer 4.0's extensive support of key Internet standards.

- As you browse the Web, send an associate an actual Web page embedded in an e-mail message without launching your e-mail program. (On the menu bar click **File + Send + Page By Email.**)

- Discover how AutoComplete automatically completes addresses of Web sites you have already visited when you enter the first few letters of the Web site in the address bar. When the name appears, press Enter.

- Add items to the links menu bar by dragging the icon from the address bar or dragging a link from a page. Also, you can rearrange items on the links bar by dragging them to a new location on the bar.

- Customize your desktop, how you view files, your browser's fonts, colors, hyperlinks, how you read mail and browse Newsgroups, and much more.

- Conduct real-time meetings online with NetMeeting.

- Hold a conversation with another participant.

- Use the *whiteboard* to draw illustrations and make notes.

- Collaborate on a document with another participant during a meeting making edits visible to all.

- On the menu bar click **Go** + **Internet Call**.

See Internet Explorer 4.0 Tips and Tricks in Chapter 13 "Web Site Toolbox."

Microsoft continually releases software updates and third party add-ons to Internet Explorer 4.0. Visiting the Internet Explorer 4.0 Download Area will let you review your installed components and select other programs to include with your browser. http://www.microsoft.com/ie/ie40/download/

Why do I need FrontPage 98?

Microsoft FrontPage 98

Microsoft FrontPage 98 gives you powerful tools to create rich content and manage your Web site effectively. Microsoft FrontPage 98 is a quick, effective way to create and manage professional-quality Internet or intranet sites without programming. It makes it easy for new users and professional Web developers alike to build and maintain great-looking, professional-quality Web sites in no time. Create great-looking Web sites and manage your Web sites your way. Integrate with what you already have.

Easy-to-use, leading edge features let you create professional Web sites without programming. Produce <u>WYSIWYG</u> frames pages and draw HTML tables in the WYSIWYG FrontPage Editor. Add sophisticated, interactive functionality using FrontPage components, and there's no need to write code.

Innovative imaging tools and intelligent design assistance make it easier than ever to build great-looking Web sites. Add rich, dynamic graphics to your sites using Microsoft Image Composer, Microsoft GIF Animator, and more than 2,000 image samples.

With FrontPage 98, you can easily include powerful Web functionality in your sites by adding Java™ applets, ActiveX™ controls, and browser plug-ins. Support for databases and Active Server Pages allows you to include database content in your Web pages easily and lets users perform dynamic database queries on your site over the Web, giving them direct access to the information they need.

WYSIWYG tables: Draw and erase tables with the same ease that you use a pencil and paper. Insert rows and columns, and then select the borders of table cells and drag them to the positions you want.

Wizards: Make creating new pages or entire Web sites easy. Just answer a few questions, and wizards will do the rest for you.

Templates: Generate Web sites or pages from predefined formats. Simply replace the generated content with your own words, images, and ideas.

FrontPage components and Save to E-mail: Eliminate the need to write your own programs by providing drop-in commands for adding sophisticated, interactive functionality to your Web sites. Submit form results over the Web to an e-mail address or file of your choice, or easily add full-text searching capabilities to your Web sites.

Themes and Themes View: Give your entire site a high-quality, consistent look. Choose from more than 50 professionally designed thematic templates that include backgrounds, fonts, page headers, and navigation buttons, or assign a Theme to any individual Web page to vary the look of that page only.

Graphical bullets: Easily specify custom images to use in place of the bullets normally found on Web pages. Either apply a Theme to a page to add its matching graphical buttons, or choose any image to be used as the new bullet.

Banner Ad Manager and Dynamic HTML support: Select from several easy options that handle rotating information in your Web site, or easily add dynamic Web content such as text that "flies" onto your page from off-screen!

Java™ applet, ActiveX™ controls, and browser plug-in support: Include powerful Web functionality in an intuitive WYSIWYG environment.

Import Wizard: Easily import existing files or entire folders of information into your FrontPage Web sites, and now import Web content directly from the World Wide Web.

Database Region Wizard and Active Server Pages support: Leverage Active Server Pages functionality to include dynamic database content directly in your Web pages, or connect to OBDC-compliant databases to allow users to perform dynamic database queries to your site over the Web.

Text over images and hover buttons: Easily add text directly over images, making graphical button creation a snap. Then, effortlessly create cool animation effects on your button-shaped images, so that when a user "hovers" over or clicks on the button, it changes color or shape, or animates the way you have chosen.

Automatically generate your navigational links in this printable view by using it to build your Web site's key navigational structure—ensuring easy site-wide navigation and intuitive site organization.

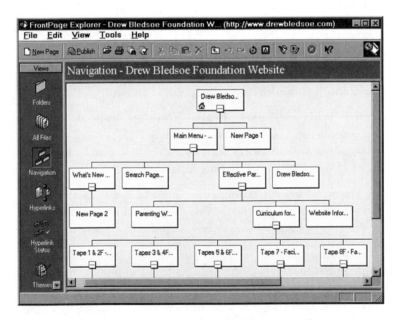

View your site's entire layout. The Hyperlink View provides hierarchical and graphical representations of your site's structure, including all pages and hyperlinks, so you can see just how easy it is for a user to discover your content.

Graphically display all hyperlinks between pages, with arrows indicating the direction of each link. Position your cursor over any icon in the view to call up its related attributes.

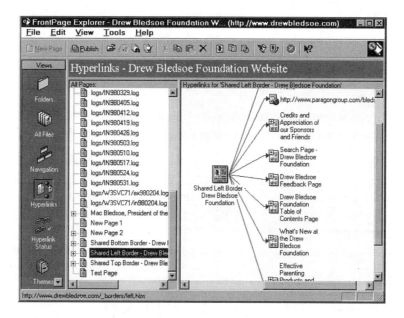

To learn more about Microsoft <u>FrontPage 98</u>, visit them on the Web at: `http://www.microsoft.com/frontpage/default.htm.`

Are you connected?

You are just a few clicks away from getting yourself and your business online and productive.

 Netcom On-Line Communication Services, Inc. is a leading international Internet Service Provider. By joining Netcom, you'll receive:

- Fast, reliable, and affordable network access
- All the internet software you'll need
- A world class technical support organization
- Access to a whole host of flexible solutions and added features tailored to your individual internet needs

Netcom offers a variety of service plans tailored to fit your business. To review these options, please visit the "<u>Web Hosting</u>" section of the Web site for more information or call **1-800-Netcom1** for personal assistance, or visit them on the Web at: `http://www.netcom.com/offer/index.html.`

Signing up is quick and easy. You can sign up for an account and get everything you need to be up and running in a matter of minutes. NETCOMplete software, nominated for the 1997 RetailVision Internet Product of the Year, is designed to enhance your Internet experience. It quickly installs and configures all the software necessary to connect to the Internet. The <u>NETCOM Software Download Page</u> is also where you will be able to get new versions of software as they become available. `http://www.netcom.com/about/index.html.`

You'll find everything you need to make your Internet experience more productive and enjoyable—from up-to-date custom news, to the most sophisticated online support in the business.

 If you already have Internet access through another ISP, it is not imperative that you change. However, there are significant advantages to considering Netcom as your ISP of preference. To find out more about how Netcom can put the "Net to work for you" visit the Web site at: http://www.netcom.com/joinus/index.html.

Defining your connected office

What hardware should I buy, what do I really need?

When you shop for a PC, buy more than you need and as much as you can afford. Believe it or not, this advice will actually save computer purchase dollars in the long run. You *will* outgrow your system regardless of how powerful it is today. Microprocessor speeds double every 12 to 18 months at the same price point. This trend is predicted to continue indefinitely.

Therefore, as a benchmark of today's processor options, at a minimum, consider nothing less than a Pentium 200 Mhz computer with a 3+ gigabyte hard drive, 32 MB of RAM minimum, video card with 1 (or 2) MB on board RAM, and a 33 kbps modem (56k recommended). These computers are currently priced in the $1,000 "sale" range (minus monitor). Once again, the Internet offers many resources that can help simplify the decision making process when shopping for a new computer.

Computer sources

Check the Net!

Compaq Computer Corporation lets you build your own Presario system solution or upgrade your current system online. `http://www.compaq.com/`

Dell Computer Corporation lets you build your own custom computer online. `http://www.dell.com/`

Gateway 2000 Inc.[1] (the computer company in cow country) will take your custom order over the Net. Three-year limited warranties, a 30-day money-back guarantee and <u>24 x 7</u> toll-free telephone technical support. `http://www.gw2k.com/`

NetBuyer.Com is Computer Shopper's[2] online catalog that lets you to shop, compare, and buy any computer or peripheral from hundreds of sources. `http://www.netbuyer.com/`

TechShopper, an online guide from <u>CMP Media Inc</u>., with a database of 4,000 PCs can help you find the PC system that's right for you. The site includes product reviews archives and weekly feature reviews on hardware and software.[3] `http://www.techWeb.com/shopper`

What software will I need?

The software that we recommend and discuss in this book specific to creating, maintaining, and viewing your Web site is Microsoft Office 97, FrontPage 98, and Internet Explorer 4.0.

How do I connect to the Internet?

Connectivity options continue to advance (and get more confusing) every day. Your decision as to which type of access is best suited for your business will depend on factors such as:

- How many employees require simultaneous access?
- Will most of your usage be browsing or sending and receiving e-mail?
- Do you have a need to exchange large files (contracts, brochures, and so on) with clients and suppliers on a regular basis?
- Will you be providing outside access (for salespeople, vendors, suppliers, and so on) to an internal server (Intranet or Extranet)?

How you answer these questions will determine if you need an industrial strength "pipe" (ISDN or T1) or if your needs can be met using an inexpensive dial-up solution. A brief overview of available access alternatives is discussed in the next section.

Getting wired—connectivity options

Modems

As with most everything associated with the Internet, there are few simple explanations or answers. Modem choices and connectivity options offer no exception. The following is a short overview of options available today and a brief mention of what's on the horizon.

What is a modem?

The word modem is an acronym for *mo*dulator-*dem*odulator. A <u>modem</u> accepts a digital signal from a computer and converts it to analog that can then be transmitted over a telephone line. The process of encoding, transmitting and decoding these signals is called modulation. A modem will modulate an outgoing binary bit stream to an analog carrier and demodulate an incoming binary bit stream from an analog carrier. Got that?

Modems transfer data at different rates (speeds). Although it is possible to exchange e-mail and view the Web at slower speeds, the bare minimum modem speed you should consider today is a 33.6 kbps. Fortunately, unless you are using an older computer, most new computer systems purchased today include an internal 56 kbps modem.

What are the differences between modem speeds?

The Need for Speed! In the case of the Internet, *speed thrills*. Few things are more exasperating than waiting for a single Web page to appear on your screen. Without deciphering or debating the exact scientific interpretation about bits per second transfer rates (kbps), error correction, line loss, and so on, the following explanation provides a nontechnical approximation of modem speeds.

A **14.4k** modem receives and transfers data at 14,400 bits per second over standard copper phone lines. A **28.8k** modem is approximately two times as fast as a 14.4k. A **56k** modem is twice as fast as a 28.8k and four times as quick as a 14.4k modem. Using the same mathematical formula, it figures that a **128k** modem (<u>ISDN</u>) is eight times speedier than a 14.4k, four times as snappy as a 28.8k and double the rate of a 56k modem. Still with us?

Industrial strength Internet pipes are <u>T-1</u> speeds and higher (T-3, and so on). Chances are that if you require this kind of connectivity, you are already (or need to be) talking to a professional networking engineer. T-1 circuits require special wiring, equipment and system configuration. If you intend to provide full Internet access to a large group of employees, you will need to have a professional analyze your requirements. To receive an online quote from Netcom, see `http://www.netcom.com/offer/index.html`.

In keeping with our multiplication explanation above, a **T-1** is 12 times swifter than 128k, 27 times quicker than 56k, 53 times more rapid than a 28.8k modem and 106 better than a 14.4k modem. *Whew!* A **T-3** is faster than a speeding bullet and few companies can justify the five-figure monthly expense of such a connection.

<u>Connectivity</u> options don't end with this confusing narration, there are new technologies being developed that will add more choices (and confusion) to the modem menu. Some of these new services are being test marketed in selected areas of the country today.

33.6 kbps modems are now sold by most manufacturers and offer a slight improvement over 28.8 modems. Although 33.6 modems offer potentially better connectivity, if you plan to purchase a new modem, go for the 56k. Prices are now competitive with slower offerings. If you have a 33.6 modem, most manufacturers are promising upward compatibility with the emerging 56 kbps standards.

56 kbps (K56 flex is <u>Rockwell's</u> patented technology) `http://www.nb.rockwell.com/mcd/` `K56Plus/` is a new modem technology that permits connections at rates up to 56 kbps over standard copper lines. Be aware, however, that the sending capability is approximately 28.8k while the receiving capability is 56k. This may evolve into a great alternative choice between a standard dial-up 28.8 modem and Integrated Services Digital Network (ISDN). Although industry standards have yet to be universally adopted, Rockwell assures their customers that the 56k chips are compatible. Most 56Kbps modems shipped in the past year will almost certainly require an upgrade to be "standards" compatible.

ISDN (<u>Integrated Services Digital Network</u>). A telecommunications service that integrates voice, video and data services into one cohesive digital network. ISDN service has been available for many years. However, its availability has not been widely promoted by the TELCOs. In spite of the technojoke that ISDN is an acronym for "**I**t **S**till **D**oes **N**othing," it is gaining wide popularity in certain areas of the country. As ISDN costs continue to decline, it may well become the new telecommunications standard for residential and business service.

Because ISDN does not use the same kind of wiring that your existing telephone system uses; it requires installation of a new circuit. Unfortunately, local telephone company installation costs vary from city to city depending upon availability. An ISDN connection also requires the purchase of a "special" digital modem that ranges in price from $250 to $500. Residential ISDN customers can also expect to pay between $100 to $300 for monthly service.

Cable Modems. Theoretically, the wire used by cable TV companies is an ideal networking cable. The cable is capable of transmitting data at speeds of 500 kbps to 30 mbps downstream and 96 kbps to 10 mbps upstream. Also, cable modems operate differently than telephone modems. A cable modem is always online and has no dial-up requirements.

Unfortunately, the major obstacle with cable, in the United States, is the cable infrastructure itself. The cable infrastructure is a one-way medium and the Internet is a two-way medium. Furthermore, the high costs associated with upgrading the infrastructure are enormous and depend on complex technology issues that have not yet been fully resolved. Although isolated test are being conducted in various parts of the country, cable is not a viable widespread access option today.

Frame Relay. Viewed more as a <u>LAN</u> solution for businesses with moderate to high traffic demands, frame relay is another source of connectivity. Frame relay offers transfer rates from 56 kbps to 512 kbps. Although equipment can be leased or purchased from your local telephone company, installation can be expensive. Also, besides monthly service, you will incur a by-the-mile charge for the digital line between your business and the nearest TELCO central office. Currently, most local ISPs do not support frame relay.

ADSL (<u>Asymmetric Digital Subscriber Line</u>). A new technology that permits data to be transferred over existing copper wires (<u>POTS</u>) at rates several hundred times faster than today's analog modems. The major benefit of ADSL is that your existing telephone wiring can be used to provide ADSL. Also, filters that split the ADSL signal from the telephone line signal ensure that service will not be interrupted if the ADSL line or equipment fails. For pricing and availability, contact the business office of your local telephone company. ADSL and other xDSL solutions including HDSL (High Speed Digital Subscriber Line) are still in the trial stages, yet considered very promising.

Wireless Modems. Although much is promised for the not too distant future, wireless Internet access options are somewhat limited. Cellular modems will permit access to the Net from anywhere within your cellular coverage area. Expect to pay $250 to $350 for a 28.8 PC card but don't expect to connect at speeds greater than 14.4 (go figure). As for monthly service, expect to pay per-minute usage rates and additional miscellaneous charges.

Another wireless option, for consideration, is packet radio modems. Packet radio modem technology relies on one of the nationwide two-way data networks by companies such as <u>Metricom</u>. This option can be less expensive than cellular because users are invoiced for system usage only. Presently, per-minute usage fees are not an additional charge in the monthly billing process. A connect rate of 19.2 kbps will be about the best you can expect to achieve from a 28.8 PC card modem. `http://www.metricom.com/`

Satellite Access. Internet access via satellite may prove to be a cost-effective solution for people other than just rural Netheads. Today, <u>Hughes Network Systems' Direct PC</u> is about the only choice, but it requires expensive equipment and is basically a one-way solution. Although information can be received at 400 kbps, transmission requires a conventional dial-up account. For most small to medium sized businesses, this is not an optimum solution. However, great progress is planned for satellite service in the very near future.[4] `http://www.hns.com/`

The FCC recently approved Sky Station International, a scheme to provide T1-level service (1.5 mbps) to your laptop via giant "weather balloons." (Really!) The FCC also approved Teledesic's plan to put hundreds of satellites into low orbit by the year 2002. Originally founded by billionaires Bill Gates and Craig McCaw, the company recently received an investment of up to $100M from Boeing, which will also be the prime contractor.

For additional information about wireless Internet options:

Check the Net!

Advanced Radio Data Information Systems. The world's first and largest nationwide wireless data network offering a packaged wireless Internet solution. `http://www.ardis.com/`

RAM Mobile Data. Offers a product, the Inter@ctiveTM Pager that will permit you to access databases, Intranets and query a Web site. `http://www.ram-wireless.com/`

Is it true that a modem can be difficult to use?

Using a modem is easy, having everything work between your keyboard and the Internet can be the difficult part. Consider for a moment what is involved when you initiate a dial-up Internet session from your computer. For the sake of our example, we'll assume that:

- Your modem is working
- Your computer recognizes your modem
- The initialization string of your modem is correct
- The stop bits and parity are set properly
- The communications port has been identified
- Your phone line is plugged into the correct socket
- You did not mistype your user name or password
- The telephone company has done their part, and
- Your ISP is awake and open for business (*if Netcom, relax!*)

You click `Connect`to begin the dial-up process.

Then, in a matter of seconds, your call is processed and you are connected to the Internet. To reach this point, however, your call:

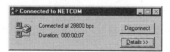

- Had to travel over telephone lines (where quality is affected by the weather and the temperature)
- Pass through the telephone company's central office that forwarded it to your local ISP POP (Point of Presence) where
- It was greeted by a host of various manufacturer's modems connected to portmasters that communicated with an authentication server (to verify that you are you) before returning an acknowledgement that you were now indeed, connected to the Internet.

As a society, we are quite spoiled when it comes to most standard methods of communication. We pick up a telephone handset and expect to hear dial tone 100 percent of the time. We take for granted the common household appliances that we use everyday. We drop bread into a toaster and out pops toast, first time, every time. We have been conditioned to demand such performance from any technology or modern convenience.

Unfortunately, the Internet and its related technology are not like a toaster. The Internet is not entirely "plug and play," in many cases it's more like "plug and *pray*." Things can, and sometimes do go wrong. Sometimes, it's a marvel that the entire integration process works as well as it does. If any of the variables of the connection process are less than favorable, you could end up spending the evening watching C-SPAN.

Modem summary

In short…buyer, inform thyself. The only problem (and it can be a problem) with choosing any of the <u>POTS</u> connectivity solutions in excess of 33.6 kbps is that both ends of the communications link *must* be compatible. This means that your Internet service provider must offer the same service. If you have a 56k modem and dial in to an ISP that is using 28.8, you will connect at 28.8 or a slower speed.

Although some local ISP's promote new services such as, XDSL and others, it may be a while before most providers jump on the bandwagon. With the costs of upgrading a nationwide infrastructure and the standards issues mentioned above, many ISPs will wait to see which technologies best meet the needs of the general public.

The best way to determine your "wired" needs is to fire-up an inexpensive 33.6 (or 56K)modem and visit the Netcom Web site. To find the perfect solution for your business, take a couple minutes to complete a personal Internet solution profile. By answering only 10 questions, Netcom will be able to tell you which solution best fits your needs. <u>http://www.netcom.com/profiler/profiler_welcome.html</u>

To track the progress of new modem technology and get Internet user's opinions, conduct a <u>Deja/News</u> search to locate the best Newsgroup. <u>http://home.microsoft.com/access/allinone.asp</u>

---

[1] CMP Media Inc., 600 Community Drive, Manhasset, New York 11030. http://www.techWeb.com/info/publications/publications.html

[2] Rockwell is a leading developer, manufacturer, and worldwide supplier of semiconductor technology.

[3] ZDNet (Ziff Davis Publishing) AnchorDesk, Monday, May 12, 1997, Jesse Berst, Editorial Director. http://www5.zdnet.com/anchordesk/story/story_914.html

Mastering Your Domain

You know, I'm all for progress, it's change I object to.

- Mark Twain

Establishing your domain

What is a domain?

In terms of Internet networked computers, a <u>domain</u> is a location on the Internet. Identified by a domain name and an IP address, a domain physically resides on an Internet-based network server.

What is a domain name?

A domain name is your Internet identity. A domain identifies you or your company as a <u>node</u> on the Internet and is used to locate a company or individual without having to remember the numeric <u>IP address</u>. A domain name is your business card for the 21st century.

The domain *name* is the alpha identity of your Internet address. The location of a domain relies on its numeric counterpart, an IP address, for complete identity. Domain

Name Service (DNS) is a critical component to the addressing (routing) operation of the Internet. DNS is simply a table of names called domain names.

What is an IP address?

An IP address is the numeric identity of a domain. Most of us are quite comfortable calling each other by name whereas machines prefer using a sequence of ones and zeros to talk with each other. DNS translates the naming convention of a domain (microsoft.com) to the actual numeric IP address (207.68.156.52). In other words, typing http://207.68.156.52 or http://www.microsoft.com will both take you to the Microsoft Web site. You decide which is easier to remember.

What is a domain classification?

A domain classification is that part of the domain address that follows the *dot*—as in your-biz **DOT** com. A domain classification identifies the type of organization or entity that owns the domain. Domain classifications, in the United States, are currently categorized as:

Commercial organizations	.com
Educational institutions	.edu
U.S. government	.gov
U.S. military	.mil
Network providers	.net
Nonprofit organizations	.org

The InterNIC is the registering agency for .com, .net, .org, and .edu. The Center for Electronic Messaging Technologies (CEMT) oversees .gov and the Department of Defense Network Information Center administers .mil Their servers update to the InterNIC servers.

Domain classifications of .com, .net, and .org are the most popular for businesses and organizations and are easily obtained through the domain name registration process. There are restrictions and qualifications for the classifications ".gov", ".mil", and ".edu". Only four-year colleges and universities can use .edu, .gov is limited to U.S. federal agencies only, and .mil is restricted to U.S. federal government military entities. Policies for the use of Country Code domain names (.CA, .FR, .UK, and so on) vary and are regulated by the governing agency for each country.

Due to the tremendous demand and growth of the Internet, there are several proposals to add additional domain name categories. Some of the new proposed Top Level Domains (TDL) are:

business and commercial enterprises	.firm
retail establishments	.shop
organizations emphasizing activities related to the Web	.Web
cultural and entertainment	.arts
recreational and entertainment	.rec
informational services	.info
personal nom de plume	.nom

There is still a lot of controversy surrounding the implementation of new Top Level Domains and the underlying infrastructure necessary to implement them. In January 1998, the Department of Defense issued *A Proposal to Improve Technical Management of Internet Names and Addresses —Discussion Draft 1/30/98* (Green-Paper) that outlines a policy framework for the governance of the Internet calling for stability and reliability as it continues to grow in the commercial arena. http://www.cmcnyls.edu/public/misc/dnsdraft.htm

What does this mean for you? The domain name issue is evolving and at the time of this writing there is no consensus for the new proposed TLDs and registration procedures. You may be asked to commit money to "preregister" domain names, but be aware that until decisions and policies are established you may not get your name or your money returned. Your best course of action is to work with a reputable and trusted Internet Service Provider who deals directly with the registry organization.

What is the advantage of owning my domain?

The key word is *"owning."* You will own the rights to your Internet identity. Therefore, you don't have to worry about future Internet address changes. The marketing potential for owning your domain is comparable to owning a toll-free 800 number that spells your company's name. Equally important, you and your employees can establish e-mail addresses that identify you as members of your organization. As an example, your employee Mary can have an e-mail address of

mary@your-biz.com

This is much more impressive and easier to remember than

3876d,qw4zm@acme_cyber-provider.net

As with anything (your letterhead, business cards, and so on) you do not want to disconnect your Internet identity from your business. Utilizing a unique address provides that connection.

Every domain name is unique. There is only one "mcdonalds.com" or "goodyear.com," and there is only one "your-biz.com." Once your preferred domain name is registered with the InterNIC, no one else may use that domain name. `http://www.internic.net/`

Now is the best time to reserve your domain name and ensure that your business will have an address that is easy to find and remember. *Thousands of domains are registered every day!* Has your business registered its domain?

How do I obtain a domain name?

Internet domain names are granted and managed by a company called Network Solutions Inc. (NSI), the InterNIC. However, dealing directly with NSI requires a degree of technical expertise. Because the InterNIC does not provide a hosting service, many businesses register their domain name through an ISP, such as Netcom, who works directly with NSI on the customer's behalf. `http://www.netcomi.com/cbc/domain3.html`

Are there any rules about domain names?

Domain names may contain a total of 26 characters. However, you are only allowed to choose 22 of the characters because four of the characters will be the .com, or .org, or .net portion of the domain name. The 22 characters that you choose must be letters or numbers or hyphens. However, a hyphen may *not* appear at the beginning or the end of a domain name. Also, domain names may *not* contain any blank spaces or underscore marks. If you choose two or more words, separate the words with a hyphen, such as acme-painters. If someone already owns the domain name you wanted, consider using initials. Initials may also serve you well if the domain name you want exceeds the 22-character limit.

What if someone has already taken my domain name?

In the physical world, Acme House Painters and Acme Auto Repair can coexist peacefully; there is little chance of the two being confused. However, on the Internet there is only one "acme.com." Generally speaking, whoever registers a domain name first gets it. If you find that the domain name you wanted is taken, you have two options.

- Get creative and choose an alternative domain. Consider a domain using the initials of your company, or a word that describes your company, or a word that is used in your company slogan, or a word that is important to your mission statement, and so on. Make sure, however, that you do not get so creative that people can't make the connection.

- Read the Domain Name Dispute Policy that the InterNIC has published at `http://rs.internic.net/domain-info/nic-rev03.html`. Although the InterNIC outlines specific steps to take to resolve such issues, they are not responsible for solving domain name disputes.

What does it cost to register my unique domain name?

Currently, NSI charges an initial one-time $70 registration fee (this includes the first two years of registration). After the second year, NSI will charge an annual $35 renewal fee.

What will it cost to activate my domain name?

In addition to the NSI registration fee, most ISPs charge an additional fee for account set-up and registration. The Netcom one-time service fee to set up and register your domain will depend upon the type of hosting package you choose and will range in price from $25 to $350 per month (some may or may not require a set-up fee). If you already have Internet access, visit the <u>Netcom Hosting Web</u> site for more up-to-date information. There, you can search the online NSI database of assigned domain names and immediately reserve your domain request. `http://www.netcomi.com/`

 To take advantage of the Special Offers associated with this book, you *must* register in accordance with the process outlined in the software installation chapter.

Virtual domains versus dedicated domains

As recently as 1994, there were only two ways to host a commercial Internet domain. One way was to purchase and maintain a dedicated computer server equipped with a dedicated telephone circuit (<u>ISDN</u>, 56k, <u>T-1</u>, and so on). The second way was to park your dedicated server at an Internet provider's facility. Both options were expensive and resource intensive. Today, the majority of domains are hosted on "<u>virtual servers.</u>"

A virtual server is a computer that houses many domains. This allows organizations A, B, and C to exist together "virtually" on the same network server. Virtual servers reduce the costs associated with domain hosting and make it possible for small businesses to compete effectively online with Fortune 1000 companies.

What should I consider when choosing where to host my domain?

As with most important business decisions, look to an industry leader with experience. In the case of Internet hosting, network infrastructure and integrity are vitally important. Industry analysts predict that 95% of the ISPs in business today will disappear within two or three years.

> *"It's common knowledge that Internet service providers (ISPs) are in trouble. And common wisdom says we're going to see an industry shakeout—a serious one. The only disagreement seems to be over how many of the 4,000 or so ISPs out there will be left standing when the dust settles."*[1]

This is not as much of a "buyer beware" environment as it is a "buyer, inform yourself" scenario.

Why should I choose Netcom to host my domain?

Experience and value. Netcom hosts thousands of business domains that range from Fortune 1000 companies to one-person operations. The automated "Netcom Business Center" is an industry first and is one of the primary reasons for this success. The NBC includes a fully automated domain registration process with immediate IP assignment and the ability to upload files within minutes of applying for a domain name.

The <u>Netcom Business Center</u> provides a full array of tips and tools that small business and home business owners find indispensable. These are accessed through the Maintenance Sections at <u>http://www.netcomi.com</u>.

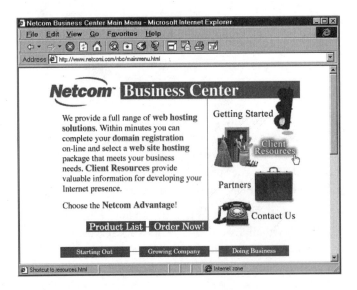

The NBC allows you to add password-protected directories to your site, publicize your URL, and update the InterNIC for changes to billing or administrative contact information. All hosting products support FrontPage extensions.

The online e-mail maintenance area, permits a business to perform a number of e-mail functions that include adding, deleting or changing passwords, forwarding mail, and creating auto-responders. Maintenance is performed online in real-time through the convenience of a Web browser. This offers users control of their e-mail maintenance tasks any time they need it.

Library: Online programming tutorials, <u>HTML</u> and graphics design tips, royalty-free samples of HTML, <u>Shockwave,</u> <u>CGI</u> and <u>Java</u> scripts, and royalty-free graphics to incorporate into your Web site. Also included is a comprehensive dictionary with search capability.

Toolbox: Over 30 valuable software tools to assist with the creation and maintenance of your Web site. Selections include browsers, <u>plug-ins</u>, HTML editors, traffic statistic tools, and other unique cutting-edge software applications. Instructions on how to download, install, and use the programs are included.

Help: Read an online <u>FAQ</u> and find help about how to configure your e-mail and <u>FTP</u> programs for your new domain.

E-mail maintenance: Real-time management of e-mail accounts; add, delete, or change user names and passwords anytime.

Traffic statistics: Get vital marketing information about whose server visited your site, which pages they viewed, and how long they stayed.

Incremental services: Need additional disk space, e-mail accounts, CGI access? The Netcom Clients Resource Maintenance section allows you to immediately add these features.

Submit It!: A software program that helps businesses publicize their Web site to a choice of hundreds of search engines and directory listings. This is an automated process that permits the user to fill out a series of fields describing the Web site's products and services therefore saving countless hours of completing this information for each search engine. **Submit It!** is available at a discount through the Netcom Business Center Maintenance section.

Virtual WebTrends: Analyzes individual log files and provides customers with valuable information about their Web site traffic. These reports can be generated as HTML files that can be viewed by any browser. They include statistical information as well as colorful graphs that illustrate trends, usage, and much more.

What if I already use a different Internet Service Provider?

You do not have to be a Netcom access subscriber to host your business Web site with Netcom. However, few Internet Service Providers of any size can offer the network infrastructure, experience, and support that can be found with Netcom. In December 1997, Netcom was recognized as the Number One Web Hosting Provider by the Ultimate Web Host List. The following press release says it all.

NOTE

Netcom Ranked No. 1 Web Hosting Provider by the Ultimate Web Host List!; Netcom Rated Top Web Hosting Provider over 6,000 Web Hosting Companies

BusinessWire, Thursday, December 11, 1997 at 06:16

SAN JOSE, Calif.—(BUSINESS WIRE)—Dec. 11, 1997—Netcom On-Line Communication Services, Inc. (NASDAQ:NETC) has secured the number one position as top Web hosting provider, according to The Ultimate Web Host List!, the only professional directory of Web hosting companies on the Internet. Netcom's Web hosting services were independently reviewed by www.Webhostlist.com and compared to 6,000 other Web hosting companies from around the world.

"Netcom is a company that helped usher in the age of Internet. As such, it has some unique insight into the technologies and issues around Web hosting. Netcom's services are extremely broad. Virtually every available requirement can be met," reads the review by The Ultimate Web Host List!

"The Netcom experience shows in their step-by-step instructions for new hosting users, and pre-defined templates to help new users get up and running quickly. For more experienced users, Netcom offers easy ways to change account levels. Add to all this Netcom's excellent customer support, and it's easy to see why Netcom ranks number one."

Netcom has consistently been awarded high marks in The Ultimate Web Host List! since its inception and has moved from the number two position secured in September, October and November 1997 to become the number one Web hosting provider for December 1997 in this independent evaluation.

Netcom's ranking in each of the five categories: value, quality, support, flexibility and miscellaneous were extremely high, ranging from 90 to 96 percent out of a possible 100 percent.

Definitions of the five criteria are as follows:

Value: Measured by the amount of features the Web host company provides for the cost of their services;

Quality: Measured by the ease, speed and reliability of connectivity and service;

Support: Measured by early notification of and rate of responsiveness to system problems, updating as to status of problem resolution, and knowledgeability of technical support staff;

Flexibility: Measured by ease of construction and manipulation of Web site, ability to upgrade and choose between a wide variety of value-added services, timeliness of changes taking effect;

Miscellaneous: Any aspect of the Web host provider not covered by the other categories.

"We are delighted that The Ultimate Web Host List! has given Netcom top honors due to the expertise we offer in the development and support of a full array of Web hosting services, as well as the overall ease-of-use and flexibility of our products," said Tom Heatherington, General Manager of Netcom's Web Hosting Group. "We believe our success in Web hosting is attributed to responding directly to our customers' needs for scaleable, value-added solutions that allow them to establish and maintain their own distinctive on-line presence."

About Webhostlist.com

Webhostlist.com is wholly-owned and operated by Sumo, Inc., a leader in the development and operation of cutting-edge Internet business models. The Ultimate Web Host List has been honored with five out of five stars in the June 1997 issue of PC Computing, as well as making Information Weeks Site of the Week and NetGuides Site of the Day.

The Ultimate Web Host List! concept, copy, and graphics are copyrighted and a product of Sumo, Inc. Additional information on the company can be found at http://www.Webhostlist.com/.

Registering your domain

This section illustrates the domain name selection process as performed via the NBC and how to choose the Netcom hosting product best suited to your business.

Complete instructions as to how you can choose and register your exclusive domain name are fully explained on the www.your-biz.com Web site. http://www.your-biz.com You will be guided through the process by easy-to-follow instructions as shown in the following illustration.

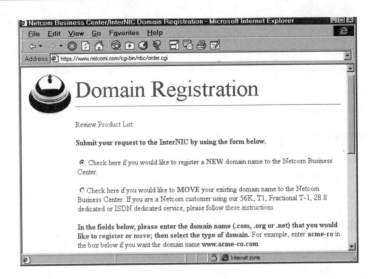

Additional domain reference information

American Association of Domain Names—The AADN works to provide information and advocacy services for domain name holders, briefings on current events, and issues of interest, and all possible support.[2] http://www.domains.org/

---

[1] Source: Nick Lippis, Pres. of Strategic Networks (Rockland, MA) article from Data Communications Magazine, May 1997. E-mail: lippis@snci.com

[2] American Association of Domain Names works to provide information and advocacy services for domain name holders. http://www.domains.org/

The Net as a Communication Tool

One of the best ways to persuade others is by listening to them.

- Dean Rusk

The Net as a communication tool (e-mail)

E-mail, *"Killer App"* of the Internet

Although it may not be the ultimate, standalone, do everything "killer app," e-mail still accounts for the majority of traffic on the Internet (it's even surpassed telephones as the primary communications tool). Even with the hype and potential surrounding the World Wide Web, e-mail remains the number one reason people use online services. As business people, we all have a need to communicate and e-mail affords benefits not available using conventional communication methods.

The use of electronic mail has evolved into an indispensable communication link to associates, customers, vendors, and suppliers. E-mail will soon become (if it is not already) as rudimentary to your business as your fax machine is today. E-mail is as essential to conducting business online as your telephone is to operating your existing business.

What is e-mail netiquette?

<u>Netiquette</u> is a combination of the words Net and etiquette. It is the proper manner by which you should conduct yourself on the Internet. Netiquette involves some conventional do's and don'ts about writing e-mail messages and posting to newsgroups. Some of the basic e-mail commandments include:

Thou shall not SHOUT	Shouting is done by WRITING IN ALL CAPS
Thou shall not flame	Use offensive words and caustic messages to insult someone in a newsgroup
Thou shall not SPAM	Send unsolicited mail to large groups of people or newsgroups
Thou shall not attach large files to e-mail messages	Remember that not everyone surfs the Net behind a T-1 connection
Thou shall not use text formatting options in your programs e-mail	Many e-mail programs offer text formatting such as **bold**, *italics*, and so on. However, few recognize + another program's formatting commands. The result can appear as %looks% like% this% (or worse).

Emoticons, although not necessarily an element of netiquette, can be used (and over-used) to express emotions in e-mail. The <u>Unofficial Smilie Dictionary</u> lists dozens of variations of the basic emoticon smiley ☺ face. `http://isip00.isip.msstate.edu/ fun_stuff/emoticons/emoticons.text`

A few mainstays include:

:-) Smile	:-(Frown	;-) Wink

Additionally, as you become more familiar with the Internet, you will also discover a form of Internet shorthand used in newsgroups, chat rooms, and e-mail that is presumably cosmically understood. In an effort to combine some levity with brevity, someone decided that the following abbreviations should be universally recognized and committed to memory by all users.

<g> or **<G>**	grin or ***BIG*** grin
AFAIK	as far as I know
FAQ	frequently asked questions
FYI	for your information
BTW	by the way
IOW	in other words
IMHO	in my humble opinion

OTOH	on the other hand
LOL	laughing out loud
ROTF	rolling on the floor
ROTFL	rolling on the floor laughing
ROTFLOL	rolling on the floor laughing out loud *(You get the idea.)*

Help is just a mouse click away—a real world example

In March 1997, I purchased a software upgrade to CorelDRAW! 7.0 and experienced some difficulty installing the software. After numerous unsuccessful attempts, I visited the Corel Web site and posted my problem in the CorelDRAW! discussion area. Within hours, I received responses from people offering suggestions. The first e-mail message that solved my problem was from a person in Poland and our correspondence is reproduced here.

E-mail message posted to the Corel Support Forum

Corel 7 (upgrade) Install problem. I have attempted to install
>Corel 7 many times with same result. Install goes smoothly until
>the last few minutes then the screen freezes and it never
>completes the install. I have a P-200 Toshiba Infinia 7200w/ 3
>gig HD, 32 meg RAM and have had no problem when installing
>other programs on this new machine.
>After I "un-freeze" my machine by rebooting, Corel is loaded and
>for the most part works ok. The problem is that it will not let me
>save or open any file. I can only create a new CDR, but can't
>save or export it.

The response from Poland:

Return-Path: <Name-Removed@pipeta.chemia.pk.edu.pl>
From: " ***Name-Removed*** " < Name-Removed@pipeta.chemia.pk.edu.pl>
To: "Tom" <theather@ix.netcom.com>
Subject: Re: Corel 7 Install Problem
Date: Sun, 9 Mar 1997
        08:10:31 +0100
X-MSMail-Priority: Normal

Ave Tom !

I had the same problem like you. The solution is very simple. You have to start Windows in safe mode (I'm using 95—I don't know if it helps with NT) and run installation setup in this mode. But there is a little problem, in safe mode you can't read CD so you have to first of all copy whole CD on your HDD, run WIN in this mode and run setup from disk (You will have to make space on disk, about 650 megs; 450 for copy of CD and rest for installation). Or run WIN in safe mode with network support and install from network.

I hope it will help you.

This is a marvelous example of how the Internet is expanding (shrinking) our world and can help address your customer service issues. Additionally, bear in mind that obtaining this one-on-one personalized support from a local computer consultant could have cost me hundreds of dollars.

The best feature about e-mail is its immediacy. One of the primary reasons that e-mail has been so warmly received by users is that e-mail provides instant gratification. There is no waiting for the post office to do their job nor is there the expense of overnight delivery. You want it when?

What is "SPAM?"

Unfortunately, SPAM (or j-mail or electronic junk mail), is a growing Internet nuisance. Similar to its snail mail counterpart, SPAM is unsolicited junk mail. The primarily reason for its use is direct e-mail advertising. Although netiquette does not condone such practice, certain individuals and groups seem to confuse intrusive carpet-bombing tactics as appropriate guerilla marketing. In its most basic form, SPAM is harmless; the real problem is the signal-to-noise ratio that it creates.

Most Internet purists get extremely upset when they receive unsolicited, commercial e-mail and will flame anyone who violates their mailbox or newsgroup. Although not designed as a governing body, the InterNIC does provide some suggestions about dealing with e-mail abuse and unsolicited SPAM. http://rs.internic.net/nic-support/nicnews/archive/july96/spam.html

Unfortunately, most SPAMmers are a creative and desperate bunch. The "Reply To" address on their e-mail messages is never a true return address. Consequently, when you reply to a message whose subject line promises "Unimagined Wealth, Happiness, and Acne Cure for only $29.95," your message will be bounced (returned to you) as undeliverable. Therefore, it's often a futile attempt to try to remove your e-mail address from their mass marketing lists. However, recommendations to help streamline incoming mail are made in the section entitled "Microsoft Outlook Express."

What is the best e-mail program to use?

This could be another one of those Ford versus Chevrolet debates. There are many good (some great) e-mail programs available that range from freeware to expensive proprietary programs.

Our recommendation is that you use the new Outlook Express that Microsoft includes free with Internet Explorer 4.0. Outlook Express is a powerful e-mail client containing innovative features that compete with e-mail programs that retail for hundreds of dollars. On the following pages you will learn how to set up and configure Outlook Express with your new domain.

Microsoft Outlook Express (Domain e-mail setup)

Open Outlook Express by clicking the **Outlook Express** icon located on the taskbar next to the Start button.

Next, you will need to add the appropriate Internet e-mail account(s) from which you intend to send and receive mail. As an example, you can pop mail (send and receive) from your existing Netcom "ix" account and/or from your new domain account and/or from any other personal e-mail account.

To add your e-mail address(es), click the **Tools** menu item and select **Accounts**.

This window displays a list of all of the accounts you create.

Select the **Mail** tab and click **Add**. From the list of options, choose **Mail**.

At the screen entitled "Your Name," enter your real name, or the name you commonly use, in the blank field. This is the name that others will see when they receive e-mail from you.

Click **Next**.

 If you accidentally click **Cancel**, simply begin the process over.

On the next screen, enter your e-mail address using the following format: you@your-biz.com.

This address is considered your return e-mail address. It is the address that people will use in response to your e-mail messages. Again, this address can be your existing Netcom e-mail address, your new domain e-mail address, or any other personal e-mail address.

Click **Next**.

 If you accidentally click **Back**, simply click **Next** to advance the screen.

 If you obtained your domain name from the Netcom Business Center and you are configuring **Outlook Express** to send and receive mail from your newly obtained domain (your-biz.com), you must also add that e-mail address and password to the "E-Mail Maintenance" section of the Netcom Business Center. See the NBC e-mail maintenance section of this book for directions about adding or deleting e-mail accounts, changing passwords, and forwarding e-mail from one account to another.

At the "E-mail Server Names" screen, select **POP3** from the drop-down box.

Then in both the **Incoming** and **Outgoing** mail server fields, enter your domain name using the following format: your-biz.com.

Click **Next**.

At the "Internet Mail Logon" screen, click on the **Log on using**: radio button (a dot will appear in the circle).

At the POP account name field, enter your account name. This is the name you used to establish your ISP account or domain account.

At the Password field, enter the password you normally use with the above account name.

Click **Next**.

At the "Friendly Name" screen, insert a friendly name in the **Internet mail account name** field. The name you enter will identify this particular account. It can be any name you choose, for example, your-biz, My Domain, and so on.

Click **Next**.

The last step at the "Choose connection Type" screen is to select the method you use to connect to the Internet. Click on the radio button of your choice.

Click **Next**.

That's all there is to it. You can now begin using Outlook Express to send and receive Internet e-mail.

Outlook Express Mail is an Internet standards based e-mail and news reader. To read e-mail with Outlook Express, you must be using a mail system that uses SMTP and POP3 or IMAP protocols. At this time, you cannot use Microsoft Outlook Express to access your e-mail account with any of the following services: MS Mail, cc:Mail, The Microsoft Network (MSN), with the exception of the MSN "Metro" (MSN 2.5) beta release, CompuServe, America Online (AOL), or Microsoft Exchange Server prior to version 5. If you don't know whether your system uses these services, contact your administrator or your Internet service provider and ask if they support SMTP/POP3 or IMAP mail clients.

Using filters to block SPAM or unsolicited e-mail

Most e-mail programs today offer some form of e-mail <u>filtering</u>. This is a process by which incoming messages are placed in predefined folders instead of cluttering up your main Inbox. These filters will examine your incoming mail for keywords or other attributes that you specify in advance. As an example, you could identify keywords such as "Get Rich," "Secret," "Millionaire," "Multilevel," and so on and have those messages trashed before they ever appear in your Inbox.

A word of caution: Any message that contains the filter words that you selected will receive the same unceremonious processing. Unfortunately, if a friend sends you a message that reads "Secret Birthday Party," it will be treated the same as a SPAM message that reads "Secret Cure for Premature Hair Loss."

To set-up e-mail filtering in Outlook Express, follow these simple steps:

When you receive e-mail from a person or organization that you do not want to receive e-mail from again, highlight the return address of the sender and copy to the Clipboard. To copy to the Clipboard, either choose **Edit** and **Copy** from the menu bar or press the **Ctrl** and **C** keys on your keyboard.

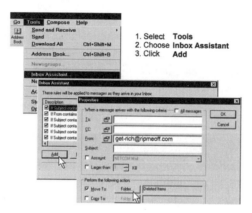

At the **Properties** screen, press **Ctrl+V** to paste the address in the **From** box. On the same menu screen, select or check the **Move to** box, then click the **Folder** button and choose the **Deleted Items** folder. In the future, e-mail that meets the filtering criteria will be disposed automatically.

How do I attach or send a document, spreadsheet, or graphics file with an e-mail message?

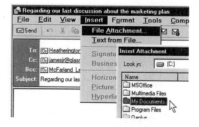

If you are creating an e-mail message in Outlook Express and decide you want to attach a file to that message, do the following:

Select **Insert** and **File Attachment**. At the Insert Attachment dialog box, a list of files on your hard drive will appear. Highlight the folder you want to open and then highlight the file you want to send and click the **Attach** button. You may also drag and drop your file onto your message from Windows Explorer.

> It is always a good idea to add a comment in the body of your e-mail message that a file is attached. That way the recipient will not overlook the attachment.

- Do not attach more than one file with each e-mail message. Some on-line services will accept *only* one incoming file at a time.
- Always use a compression utility (such as <u>WinZip</u>) when attaching or sending any graphics file. By their very nature, all graphics files are large.
- Never use fancy fonts in the body of your message unless you know that the recipient is using the same release of the same e-mail program as you. Otherwise, the message will contain embedded codes and characters that make your message difficult to decipher and annoying to read.
- Review the <u>e-mail commandments</u> in the section entitled "The Net as a Communication Tool (e-mail)."
- To confirm that your e-mail was actually sent, highlight the **Sent** folder. If the message you were concerned about is there, then it was sent.
- Outlook Mail is programmed to ensure that all of your e-mail gets delivered. When you create a message offline and click **Send**, the message is stored in the Outbox and will be queued for delivery the next time you log on. If you close Outlook Express with e-mail in the Outbox, you will be asked if you want to send the mail before you exit.

Outlook Express keyboard shortcuts:

Open a message, select it, press Enter or	**Ctrl+O**
Print a message	**Ctrl+P**
Delete a selected message, press Delete or	**Ctrl+D**
Mark a message as **read**, press	**Ctrl+Enter**
Mark a message as **unread**, press	**Ctrl+Shift+Enter**
To **view** the **first message** in a list, press	**Home**
To **send** or **receive** mail, press	**Ctrl+M**

> Most of the tips and tricks listed here <u>also</u> apply to **Internet News** found in Outlook Express. Internet News is the newsreader for newsgroups.

Always remember to back up your Address Book data. To locate that file on your hard disk, use the Windows Find File feature. To start this process select **Start** from the taskbar, then select **Find**. At the next screen, the first option to choose is **Files or Folders**.

At the **Find: All Files** screen under the field entitled **Named:**, type *.wab. Then select **Find Now**. The file extension .wab denotes "Windows Address Book." You can then copy the file to a floppy disk for future reference or move the file to another computer.

How to add/delete e-mail accounts (users) to your new domain

As the "Master of your Domain," you have the power to create, change, delete or choose what addresses and passwords will reside under your domain. In the e-mail maintenance area of the <u>Netcom Business Center</u>, you can perform all of these tasks and more—24 hours a day, 7 days a week.

Now is a good time to launch Internet Explorer and navigate to the <u>Netcom Business Center</u>. `http://www.netcomi.com/nbc/mainmenu.html`.

On the next few pages we will illustrate how easy it is to add or delete e-mail accounts, create new <u>autoresponders,</u> and forward e-mail to another user.

E-mail configuration using the Netcom Business Center

On the main menu of the NBC, click on **Client Resources**. A window will appear asking you to enter your **U̲ser name** and **P̲assword**. This is the same information you chose when setting up your domain.

Netcom will use your complimentary *Admin account* to communicate with you. This account is in addition to the e-mail accounts included with your Hosting Package. For your convenience, you can forward messages sent to the Admin account directly to your primary e-mail address or another e-mail account you choose.

The Admin username *cannot* be changed.

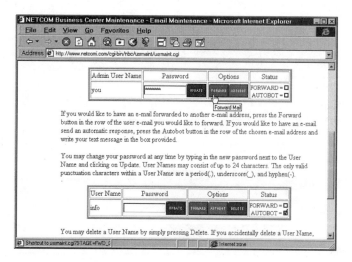

You can change any other password any time by typing in the new password next to the User Name and clicking **Update**. User names can consist of up to 24 characters.

The only valid punctuation characters within a user name are:

. (period)

_ (underscore)

- (hyphen)

You can delete a user name by simply pressing **Delete**. If you accidentally delete a user name, you will need to re-enter the user name and password.

- To have *any* e-mail forwarded to another e-mail address, select the **Forward** button in the row next to the user e-mail you intend to forward.
- To send an automatic response, select the Autobot button in the row next to that e-mail account.

You can select any e-mail address to perform as an autobot. Before you activate this feature, you should first create some intuitive e-mail address names that can be easily recognized by your customers and prospects. Some examples include:

- info@your-biz.com
- service@your-biz.com
- pricing@your-biz.com

When you select **Autobot** under the **Options** column, a new screen appears instructing you to enter the text for your autobot.

Delete the example text inside the scrolling text box and enter the message you wish to have as an automatic response to all messages sent to this account (no HTML please).

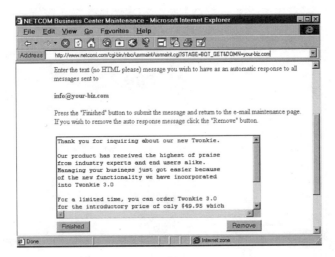

Press the **Finished** button to submit the message and return to the e-mail maintenance page. If you want to remove the auto response message click the **Remove** button.

After you have **Finished** your autobot text message and returned to the e-mail maintenance screen, note that the **Status** column will indicate that this function has been activated with this particular e-mail address.

You can repeat this process for as many e-mail addresses as you deem necessary. Using an autoresponder is like having an employee that gets paid no salary.

Audio and video Web site communication

The way companies compete is changing. Delivery of information is often more important than the actual product or services you sell. The companies that will succeed in this new environment are the companies that deliver business-critical information more rapidly, cost-effectively, and efficiently than their competition. More and more companies are beginning to use Internet broadcasting to deliver business critical information, quickly and efficiently, directly to customers, shareholders, and employees.

What are the benefits of Internet broadcasting?

- Provides cost-effective interactive message distribution
- Reaches an untapped, captive online business audience
- Allows immediate or on-demand access
- Eliminates time-zone and distance barriers
- Enhances your Web site with cutting-edge technology
- Drives traffic to your site with effective promotion

broadcast.com A turnkey Internet broadcasting provider (such as
FORMERLY AUDIONET broadcast.com inc.) can deliver an event by distributing it to the widest possible audience. Broadcast.com inc. delivers all the services and support you need to broadcast live or on-demand programming to global or targeted audiences on the Internet. You organize the event or seminar and they can deliver it to the audience you want to reach—anywhere in the world.

What are some applications for Internet broadcasting?

- **Conferences, Tradeshows, and Seminars**—Trade show organizers and planners can broadcast keynote addresses, daily tradeshow coverage, and business seminars to Web audience members.
- **Investor Relations**—Investor Relations departments can hold annual shareholder meetings and quarterly earnings announcements to reach stockholders, potential investors, and analysts who otherwise could not attend.

- **Public Relations and Marketing Communications**—Broadcast press conferences, product launches, and other public announcements immediately to a mass audience around the globe.
- **Internal Corporate Communications**—Address your employees with broadcasts of company meetings, sales force meetings, and internal corporate announcements.
- **Distance Learning**—Create a virtual classroom offering continuing education credits. Extend the reach of your academic and professional training.

How does it work?

What an Internet Broadcast Provider can do for companies, small and large alike.

broadcast.com inc. delivers more live and on-demand broadcasts with more viewers and listeners than any other company in the world. Their site receives a daily audience of over 300,000 listeners and viewers.

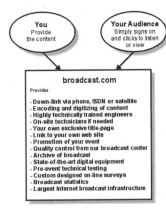

They have broadcast large and high profile business events such as Gartner Group ITEXPO, Michael Dell's keynote at Fall Internet World, Dr. Andrew Grove at E3 Expo and shareholder meetings for AT&T, Genzyme, Intel, and many more.

broadcast.com inc. has the most experience of any broadcast provider on the Internet. They have hosted 3,000+ live broadcasts. broadcast.com inc.'s unparalleled distribution network, which utilizes both unicast and multicast delivery, can support the largest simultaneous multimedia audience on the Web.

broadcast.com inc. is committed to customer support. Their Broadcast Operations Center is open 24 hours, 7 days per week, staffed with trained engineers who will monitor your broadcast and answer every e-mail support question.

Although there have been enormous strides made recently in streaming technology, audio and video broadcasting is still bandwidth intensive. Until bandwidth throughput increases and higher speed access is the norm, this type of communication is mostly suited for business to business applications.

If you would like to investigate the possibilities of incorporating audio or video with your Web site we recommend that you get the book WebsiteSound by Patrick Seaman and Jim Cline. It can be ordered online (ISBN: 1562056263) from Macmillan Computer Publishing at http://www.mcp.com/

Creating Your Web Site

We learn to do neither by thinking nor by doing; we learn to do by thinking about what we are doing.

- George D. Stoddard

Plan your work

Now the fun really begins! At this point, we suggest that you put on your thinking cap and open Microsoft Word or grab a pen and pad of paper to make notes as you plan your Web site. Although designing and creating a Web site may not be rocket science, it will prove more challenging than programming your VCR.

It has been said, "You only get one chance to make a first impression." A visitor to your Web site can decide to go away faster than you can yell *"Fire!"* A misleading headline, a busy background, a hideous text color, an offensive graphic, or even typographical errors can damage your chance to convert a prospect into a customer. Remember, on the Web, "perception is reality."

Because Internet users can afford to be impatient and disappear with a mouse click, make sure to fire your biggest guns first when designing your Web site. If you save the field artillery in reserve, or bury it too deeply in your site, your visitor might not stay around long enough to watch the fireworks.

Although Web site benefits are many and the race is on to get online, companies still need to identify their goals and objectives in order to recognize and reap the benefits. Like all good things, companies should not hastily produce a Web site in blind terror of being left behind.

The content and graphical layout should be just as carefully planned as other marketing communication material. Action items that need to be considered include:

- Set a goal for your Web site.
- Decide on the amount of time and resources (money and personnel) you're willing to dedicate (set aside) to maintain your Web site.
- Develop a strategy to achieve your goals, with time lines.
- Prepare the message or central theme.
- Prepare the layout, design, copy, and navigation that fits within your budgets (of both time and money).

Define your Web site goal(s)

Before you sit down and decide to build a Web site, decide what you want your Web site to do. Whether your goal is to increase public awareness, or establish an additional communication channel, or expand your channel of distribution, an effective Web site can successfully meet any or all of these goals through innovative content arrangement and management. Remember though, be realistic with your goals. If you set goals that are unrealistic, you will be disappointed and less energized about maintaining your Web presence.

Develop a Web site strategy

An Internet strategy should identify specific business objectives designed to help you reach your goal. Since you now have a goal in mind, focus on "how" you are going to meet that goal and what part of the marketing mix (Product, Price, Placement, Promotion) you want to include.

In relation to advertising, will you design your Web site to:

- Offer banner advertising or establish a link-sharing cooperative?
- Offer sponsorships linking your offerings with industry leaders?

In relation to public relations, will you design your Web site to:

- Encourage community involvement?
- Build customer goodwill by providing information that is not readily available, or make it easier for customers to contact you, or make it easier for customers to purchase from you?
- Communicate and drive awareness?

In relation to sales, will you design your Web site to include a compelling call to action by offering:

- A link to a retailer or a "call to action" to go to a local retailer?
- A fax number for Web visitors to call to place an order?
- A 1-800 number for Web visitors to call to place an order?
- An online order form that Web visitors can print and mail through the U.S. mail?
- Online e-commerce which offers online purchasing in real-time?

In relation to sales promotion, will you design your Web site to offer:

- Online demonstrations
- Samples
- Coupons
- Premiums
- Rebates
- Contests/sweepstakes
- An Internet bonus buy program
- Referral programs
- Internet discounts

How do I determine what content I should include in my Web site?

The solution here is to determine who your target market is and tailor your site to meet their needs, as well as communicate your company message. For many of you the solution may mean referring to your business plan or marketing plan. For others, we recommend that you identify your target market by creating a customer profile. To get you started, we have included a list of questions.

- What motivates your prospect customer to purchase one of your products?
- Are your prospect customers male or female?
- Are your prospect customers single or married? Do they have a family?
- What is the age range of your prospect customer?
- What is the income level of your prospect customer?
- What level of education has your prospect customer attained?
- What types of occupations are your prospect customers employed in?
- What geographic area do your prospect customers reside?
- Do your prospect customers own or rent his home?

- What is the personality type of your prospect customers? Is he introverted or extroverted? Is he prudent or impulsive?

- What type of lifestyles do your prospect customers live? How do they use their spare time? What do they value?

- What are your prospect customers' physical needs? His emotional needs? His intellectual needs? His spiritual needs?

- What are your competitors doing (or not doing) to offer their products?

- Do you want to sell direct, sell offline, act as an intermediary?

- What is the nature of your product (does it require significant explanation and product literature, is it an impulse or long-term purchase, does it build on other products, and so on)?

- How easy do you make it to be instantly enticed and motivated to buy now?

After you identify your target market, include the assessment information in your Web site plan so you can better decide what content to include in your Web pages. Consider starting with only one of the motivations, and then address others once you get the first stage of your Web site marketing strategy under control.

If you're still unsure about what types of pages to include on your Web site, consider the following basic pages:

- Include a site directory (or searching capability)

- Include a company mission statement and background information (including perhaps some of the employees if you believe that they may have weight in legitimizing your business)

- Include a product description and price list (with comparisons to your competition, if appropriate)

- Include contact information (e-mail, telephone number, fax number)

- Include news or press releases

- Include a detailed map to your physical location

- Include answers to frequently asked questions (FAQs)

- Include a job posting section

- Include business affiliations

- Include customer testimonials or references

- Include any information that favorably sets you apart from the crowd

- Include a clear way of receiving feedback from those who want to provide it (e-mail, a form, and so on)

Planning your Web site layout

Think theme.

When designing the layout of your Web site, lead your visitors through the Web site in an easy-to-navigate fashion. To best plan this phase ask yourself, "Is it important for visitors to be able to access myWeb site quickly?" If you answered "Yes," which many small business owners do, then strive to keep complex graphics to a minimum to shorten the download time of your pages.

The "less is more approach" is always preferred when dealing with an audience who will primarily access your site via a dial-up connection. If for some reason your specialized site demands that you use huge graphics (i.e. schematics or wiring diagrams that must be viewed in great detail), you will have to weight this against the additional work that will be required of you.

If you feel that you must have such a section in your Web site, you can solve this problem by offering a "low road/high road" alternative. This way your visitors can choose to navigate a site that downloads quickly (low road) or one that incorporates your large graphics (high road). Obviously, offering the two-road option will mean twice the amount of work for you.

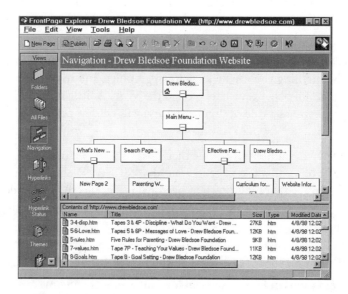

How big is a "page?"

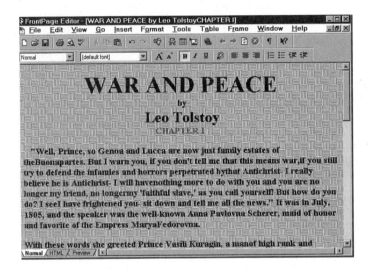

Theoretically, a page on the Internet can be infinite in length because your computer does not know where to end a page until you insert a page break. So, the unabridged version of *War and Peace* could be published on one *l-o-n-g*, continuous scrolling Web page.

Since there is no official answer to how big a page is, conventional wisdom says a page is a page. That is, anything you can arrange (text, graphics, and so on) on a standard 8.5 × 11-inches piece of paper translates well to the Web. A little more or less is fine, but use the 8.5 × 11 size as a rule of thumb and you will get few complaints about page length.

Although some HTML authors will argue that a page should be one "screen view" or that it is acceptable to scroll a text page forever, don't worry! Web page length is a subjective Internet topic that boils down to personal preference. When in doubt, you may want to ask your customers! Put up a design, then ask the people looking at your site what they think.

Why are graphics so important to a well-designed Web site?

Graphics evoke emotions in people and can implant a concept and make a stronger impact than words alone. No matter how compelling your story, the left side of the brain registers the words, and the right side of the brain registers the pictures where the visual impact is made. Graphics can inspire a prospect to read everything you have to say. Imagery appeals; words fill in the blanks.

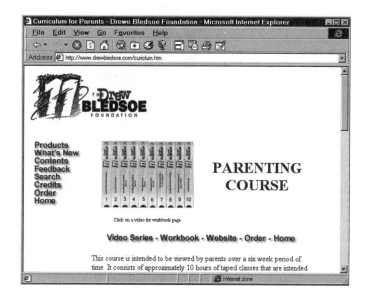

Should I include links to other sites?

You must carefully consider your strategy when deciding whether to incorporate hyperlinks to other sites. Obviously, when you provide that capability, you are in effect sending a potential customer away from your Web site. There are a couple of schools of thought as it relates to including links in your Web site.

Links that are relative to your business or support your site in general can add great value to your Web site. Also, a Web site that has been designed as "an industry authority" with a great number of business related links, may find that Internet users consider that Web site as a good launch pad.

If you are going to include hyperlinks to other sites, consider positioning them at the end of your Web presentation or design your link pages using frames to keep users onsite. In all cases where you include hyperlinks, request a reciprocal link from the other site.

Who knows, you may want to charge for them.

Web site maintenance considerations

As the last step in planning your Web site, it is imperative to consider a long-term Web site management plan. To properly plan, make sure you begin with manageable objectives. Otherwise, big daydreams may lead you to find that the time and resources to keep the site updated are too costly for your business and you end up with a Web site that is stagnant. Because the Web can provide up-to-date information at a speed that rivals other media, Internet users expect to find the most current information all the time. Companies must keep their sites updated constantly or risk losing repeat visits. A good Web site will provide valuable content to users in a timely manner so they will keep coming back to the site. A good site also does this without needing attention 24 hours a day, seven days a week. Successful Web sites need dedicated resources planned for them ahead of time.[1]

Web site design considerations

Try to maintain a "you" storytelling perspective throughout the site. Tell visitors what your product can do for them, not what your product does; emphasize benefits, not features.

When creating Web page copy or text, remember (in the words of the old sales adage) to sell the "*sizzle*," not the steak. You are providing an "experience" for the visitor. Think and decide how you can best "infotain" or "edutain" them.

Each page you create, every sentence you write should have one purpose. It should produce some type of responsive action from the Web site visitor. The action may be as simple as to scroll down to the next paragraph, click through to the next page, answer a question, or request more information.

Avoid humor as it can always backfire. Remember that the Internet is global and few jokes are universally funny. An amusing remark that makes one person laugh may be offensive to another.

Web site design recommendations

The following ideas are recommendations to consider when designing the content and layout of your Web site.

- Web site content should be organized into logical sections that are easy to navigate. A general rule of thumb is that a visitor should not have to travel more than three or four levels into a site to access pertinent company or product information (no more than three clicks to content).

- Remember that a large part of your Web audience may not be able to download plug-ins and helper applications. Many major corporations will not permit software downloads through their firewall. Thus, we recommend that you design your Web site with a minimal amount of new high-tech bells and whistles.

- Offer a call to action (register, buy, receive, whatever) as often as your audience will allow without sending them away.

- Design the look and feel of your Web site to compliment your existing marketing material. Otherwise, the visitor may experience a mental disconnect from their perception of your company. If you are trying to create a "new" company image, then disregard this recommendation.

- Include a comment, response, or Webmaster link (comments@your-biz.com) on every page or, at least, in every section of your Web site. You will find that visitors will tell you what is missing on your site by the type of questions they ask. They will also inform you of errors they discover on your Web pages, such as inactive links, misspelled words, and so on.

- Include an acknowledgement autoresponder to your comment or response links. This way your Web site visitor will automatically receive a thank-you note for submitting his comments.

- Offer an incentive to Web visitors to encourage them to leave their name and e-mail address so you can build a prospect list. Think about providing a free service or monthly drawing for visitors who participate in an online survey or register their product online.

- Include customer support information on an easy-to-locate Web page. If your products or services require a significant amount of after-the-sale support, incorporate the follow-up solutions, advice, or answers on your Web site.

- Perform a thorough Web search and make a list of industry related sites, trade organizations, and so on, from which you can request reciprocal links.

- Offer Web visitors the option to download an electronic product or service brochure.

- Invite your visitors to return to your Web site regularly by reminding them to bookmark your site.

Things you should *not* do when building your site

- Do *not* use annoying background music (MIDI, WAV, or AU files).

- Do *not* build your Web pages as if everyone has a T-1 Internet connection (huge graphics, heavy frames, and so on).

- Do *not* use "under construction" graphics or phrases on a page. If a section of your Web site is not ready for viewing, do not promote it.

- Do *not* overdo the use of scrolling text, animated banners, and marquees (especially on a single page).

- Do *not* use outdated information on your Web site or permit information to remain online when it becomes dated.

- Do *not* mistake your InterNIC invoice as a challenge to use every interactive bleeding-edge capability and proprietary plug-in known to the software industry on your Web site

Web site—ready, set, go!

By now you have a plan of how you want your Web site to look and you're ready to start building Web pages. So, let's review a few basic steps and you're on your way.

As you input your Web site text, make sure you:

- Use headlines, text colors, and bold and italic type judiciously. Since everything you have to say is important, it is easy to overdo it.

- Judiciously choose your background and text color choices. When in doubt, black text on a white background has served us well for centuries. Just because you now have the capability to combine every color of the rainbow doesn't mean that you should. If you want to use a colored or textured background with colored text, select something **nontoxic** that is complimentary and easy on the eyes, such as the colors and textures used on the Drew Bledsoe Web site. `http://www.drewbledsoe.com/`

- You may want to just keep the information in sound bites, and link users to more detailed information if they so choose.

- Watch the length of your sentences and paragraph structure. Too many short sentences will make your paragraphs look and read choppy. Too many long sentences can confuse the reader and make your ideas hard to follow. A one-word sentence can add perceptible emphasis to your remarks. *Absolutely!*

- Validate your company or product's claims sufficiently. If needed, add substance by using supporting statistics, charts, competitive analysis, or testimonials from a list of satisfied users? Proven results have a far greater impact than "biased" opinions.

- Spell check your Web site and then *do it again. Every* time that you make a change or add new content (text or a graphic) to your Web site, use the spellchecker feature.

Copying text and graphics from other resources

Net Tips

You can **copy**, **cut**, and **paste** text, tables and graphics from one program to most any other Windows program. If you are not aware of how to do this with your browser, this little tip can save you hours when creating your Web site. This is especially beneficial if you are collecting data from many different sources, for example, Word documents, graphics programs, the Internet, and so on.

Let's assume you want to quote a phrase from the Constitution of the United States. In your browser window, place your cursor in front of the text that you want to copy. Left-click and hold the mouse button down while dragging the cursor to the end of the text you wish to copy. As your cursor moves down or across the page, the selected text will become highlighted. After your selection of text has been made, press the **Ctrl** key (and hold down) while pressing the **C** key (**Ctrl+C** = copy). The text you highlighted is now stored on the clipboard or your computer's RAM memory.

To paste the stored text in the body of an e-mail letter, a FrontPage document or any other program, place your cursor where you want to insert the text and press the **Ctrl** key (and hold down) while pressing the **V** key (**Ctrl+V** = paste).

To capture a graphic image in your browser window, select the image by right clicking on the picture and select Copy with the left mouse button from the dialog box that appears. The image is now stored in memory. Follow the pasting directions as explained previously. As awkward as this may sound, this copy technique will become second nature.

Windows 98 offers a number of other ways to import, copy, or move text and graphics in the same document or program. A variation on the above cut and paste procedure is to highlight the text you wish to move, then hold down the mouse button and drag the selection to its new location.

Another copying and pasting trick within the same document, is to use drag and drop (with a twist). Highlight the text you wish to move, while depressing the **Ctrl** key and drag the selected text to the spot in the same document where you want it to be copied. When you release the mouse button and Ctrl key, a duplicate of your selected text will appear.

Using Spike instead of "cut and paste" (*Microsoft Word only*)

When working in Microsoft Word, if you have a need to use the same graphic or text over again, you should use **Spike** instead of the copy and paste technique. Here's why.

If you copy (**Ctrl+C**) a selection to the clipboard without pasting it and then cut or copy something else, you will lose your first copy/cut selection.

Another benefit of using Spike comes when you need to remove two or more items from nonadjacent locations and then insert the items as a group in a new location or document. The selected items will then remain in the Spike so you can insert them repeatedly. If you want to add a different set of items to the Spike, you must first empty the Spike's contents.

To move an item to the Spike, select the text or graphic you want, and then press **Ctrl+F3**. You can repeat this step for each additional item you want to move to the Spike.

Click where you want to insert the Spike's contents.

To insert the Spike's contents and empty the Spike, press **Ctrl+Shift+F3**.

To insert the Spike's contents, without emptying the Spike, point to **AutoText** on the **Insert** menu, and then click **AutoText**. In the **Enter AutoText** entries here box, click **Spike**, and then click **Insert**. To learn more about using Spike, press function key **F1** and type **Spike** in the **Search** box.

To highlight or select a single word, left double-click on the word. To highlight a sentence or group of words, place your cursor at the beginning of the chosen text and drag the mouse across the text to include the sentence or group of words then release the mouse button. To select an entire paragraph, left triple-click on any word inside the paragraph. To select only one line of text at a time (whether in a paragraph or not), place the cursor outside the left margin where it appears as a arrow and left-click once.

After you have completed building your Web site

- Spell check everything one more time.
- Test the appearance of your Web pages from different types of computers (PCs, Macs, and so on) and test the appearance using different monitor resolutions (800 x 600 or 640 x 480, and so on). Web page layouts and graphics look visually different on dissimilar screen sizes.
- Test that your pages will work on a variety of browser types (at least IE, Netscape, and AOL).
- Develop a detailed online Web site promotional plan that will include keyword search engine placement, online and offline press releases, notification to your existing customer base, announce your new Web site in "announcement newsgroups," and so on. Additional suggestions are found in the chapters "Internet Marketing" and "The Key to Success."

[1] Excerpted from an interview with Tom Heatherington in the Business Strategies Quarterly, Volume VII, Fall Edition - 1996

Microsoft FrontPage 98

He, whose first emotion on the view of an excellent production is to undervalue it, will never have one of his own to show.

- John Aiken

FrontPage 98 introduction

Microsoft FrontPage 98 is a Web site creation and management tool that requires no programming knowledge. FrontPage 98 includes the FrontPage <u>Explorer</u>, where you create, design, and manage your *entire* Web site, and the FrontPage <u>Editor</u>, where you create and edit *individual* Web pages without needing to know HTML.

Also included are the FrontPage <u>Server Extensions</u>, which run on your PC's Personal Web Server and the Netcom Web server. These are behind-the-scenes software applications that permit you to perform complicated tasks with no programming expertise. <u>Image Composer</u> is a graphics creation and management program and Internet Explorer 4.0 is your Internet browser.

FrontPage is a member of the Microsoft Office family of products, and shares many of the features of Microsoft Word and Excel, such as the clip art gallery, global spell checking and thesaurus, and easy table editing. FrontPage 98 also manages hyperlinks created in Microsoft Office 97 documents.

FrontPage Explorer

You will use the FrontPage Explorer to create the structure or layout of your Web site, apply graphical themes to its pages, organize its files and folders, import and export files, test and repair hyperlinks, administer access privileges, track tasks, and launch the FrontPage Editor to design and edit the contents of your Web pages.

When your FrontPage Web is completed, you use the FrontPage Explorer to publish it on your organization's intranet or your new domain hosted by Netcom. Following is a Folder View of FrontPage 98 Explorer listing the files in the Drew Bledsoe Foundation Web site.

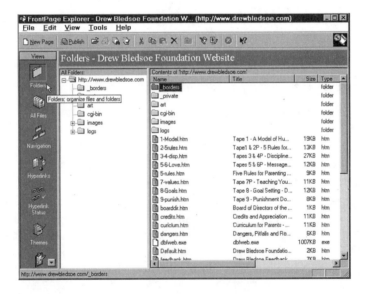

Viewing and working with the FrontPage Explorer

The seven buttons on the FrontPage Explorer's Views bar provide different ways of looking at information in your FrontPage Web. You can choose how you want to view the contents of your Web site throughout the project—from the early steps of creating a new Web site, to the moment it is ready to be published on the World Wide Web. We already examined a **Folder** view in the previous example.

The All Files view

Choosing the **All Files** view is similar to the **Folder** view. FrontPage will create a list of all the files located within your Web in alphabetical order. This is a convenient view when searching for a particular file in multiple folders.

The Navigation view

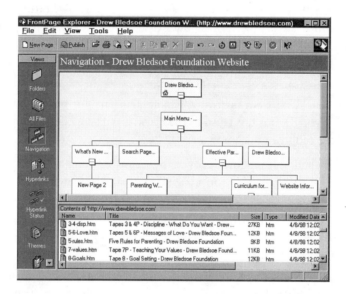

Select the **Navigation** view by clicking the **Navigation** button on the FrontPage Explorer's **Views** bar. The **Navigation** view (as above) consists of a split-screen display that shows the top-level structure of your FrontPage Web in the upper half of the screen (the Navigation pane), and a familiar Windows Explorer-like file and folder list in the lower half of the screen (the Files pane).

The **Navigation** view is the most useful view for constructing a new Web site, because it provides a useful outline of your site structure and it can automatically create navigation bars on all pages in your FrontPage Web. A navigation bar is a page region that provides access to other pages in your FrontPage Web, using textual or graphical hyperlinks. In larger Web sites, linking all of the pages together in a consistent and accurate manner could take hours of work. If you create your site structure in the **Navigation** view, FrontPage can do this work for you.

The Hyperlink view(s)

Hyperlinks and **Hyperlink Status** are the two hyperlink views. The **Hyperlinks** view provides a graphical representation of what pages are linked to a selected page. Explorer manages hyperlinks automatically when you move or rename files and folders. It also provides commands for testing and repairing hyperlinks in your Web site.

The **Hyperlink Status** view lists the status of broken internal and all external hyperlinks in the current FrontPage Web. When you choose the **Hyperlink Status** view, the status of internal hyperlinks is available at once, but external hyperlinks are not immediately verified because they point to pages outside of your FrontPage Web and, depending on network traffic, can take a long time to verify.

Broken hyperlinks are shown with a red "Broken" status and unverified hyperlinks are shown with a yellow "Unknown" status. When an unverified or broken hyperlink has been verified or repaired, it is displayed in the list with a green "OK" status (if **Show All Hyperlinks** is selected from the **View** menu).

Save and close all open pages before verifying hyperlinks. FrontPage may not be able to determine the validity of hyperlinks on a page if that page is open in the FrontPage Editor.

The Themes view

You will use the **Themes** view to apply a set of professionally designed graphics to your Web site. A theme consists of design elements for bullets, fonts, images, navigation bars, and other page elements. When applied, a theme gives the pages and navigation bars in a FrontPage Web an attractive and consistent appearance.

Applying a FrontPage theme to your Web site

On the Explorer's **Views** bar, click the **Themes** button. Click on different themes in the scrolling list box. The **Theme Preview** pane lets you preview the graphical elements as they will appear on your Web pages.

Before applying a theme, you can select theme options that affect the appearance of the theme's components. Selecting **Vivid Colors** will apply brighter colors to text and graphics, selecting **Active Graphics** will animate certain theme components, and selecting **Background Image** will apply a background image to the pages in your current FrontPage Web.

The Tasks view

 The **Tasks** view displays the list of all outstanding tasks associated with a FrontPage Web. Tasks are items that need your attention before you publish a FrontPage Web. In the previous exercises, you added tasks to a list when you deferred certain actions. For example, when you checked the spelling of the pages in your FrontPage Web, you chose to add a new task for each page containing misspellings. By adding tasks to the list, you can complete corrections all at once.

Net Tips If you are working in a Web development environment, such as your company intranet, the **Tasks** view makes it easy to track and assign tasks to other contributors or departments.

Creating new pages

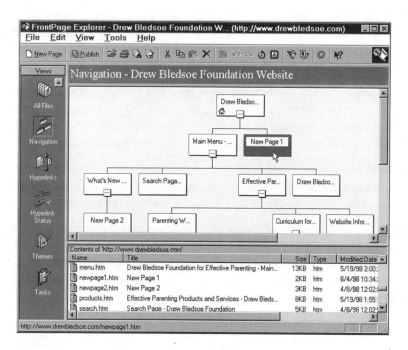

There are a number of ways to add new pages to your Web site. While in the **Navigation** view, select a Web page to which you want to create an additional linked page. On the Explorer's toolbar, click the **New Page** button. FrontPage adds a new page labeled "New Page 1" below the page in the **Navigation** pane.

The **Navigation** view shows the pages connected by lines—much like the relationship of fields in an organizational chart. This is the hyperlink structure that FrontPage will use to generate navigation bars on your pages.

You can also add new pages in the **Navigation** view by *right-clicking* an existing page and choosing the **New Page** command from the shortcut menu. This command will create a new page below the selected page.

Any changes you make to the site structure in the FrontPage Explorer's **Navigation** view are not actually applied until you take one of several actions, including switching views in the FrontPage Explorer, switching to another Windows application, or opening a page in the FrontPage Editor. If you make a mistake or change your mind about a modification you have made, you can use the **Undo** button on the FrontPage Explorer's toolbar to undo the last action.

Before working with the pages you have just created, you should give each page a meaningful title. Page titles not only help you identify and distinguish the pages in your FrontPage Web, they are also displayed in the title bar of the FrontPage Editor, as well as your Web browser. You can change page titles without leaving the **Navigation** view.

With a page selected in the **Navigation** view, press the Tab key on your keyboard. FrontPage highlights the left page below the home page and activates its page title for editing. Pressing the Tab again will select the following page.

Spell checking

While the FrontPage Editor can check the spelling of any *open* page, the FrontPage Explorer can check the spelling of *all* (or selected) pages in the current Web site.

The **Spelling** command works on those page elements that can be edited directly on the page. Other text, such as page titles added in the **Page Properties** dialog box or text contained in FrontPage components, are not included in the **Spelling** command. To check the most current version of pages in your FrontPage Web, you should first save and then close all open pages in the FrontPage Editor.

On the FrontPage Explorer's **Tools** menu, choose **Spelling**. The **Spelling** dialog box is displayed. In this dialog box, you can specify whether FrontPage should check the spelling of all pages or of selected pages only.

In the **Spelling** dialog box, leave **All Pages** selected and click the **Add a Task for Each Page With Misspellings** option. FrontPage will add a task to the **Tasks** view for each page on which misspelled text is found. You will learn about FrontPage Web tasks in the next section.

In the **Spelling** dialog box, click **Start** to begin the spell check. FrontPage displays the progress of the spell check in the **Spelling** dialog box. When the operation has been completed, "Finished checking pages" will appear and the number of tasks that were added to the **Tasks** view will be displayed.

In the **Spelling** dialog box, click **Close**. The spell check is complete.

The FrontPage Editor

The FrontPage Editor is used to create, design, and edit individual World Wide Web pages. As you add text, images, tables, form fields, and other elements to your page, the FrontPage Editor displays your page as it will appear in a Web browser. Although it is a powerful tool, the FrontPage Editor is easy to use because of its familiar, word-processor interface and the WYSIWYG (What You See Is What You Get) results.

You do not need to learn HTML to use the FrontPage Editor because it creates all the HTML code for you as you type. Should you want to edit HTML code for any reason, you can use the FrontPage Editor's HTML view (by selecting the tab at the bottom left of the frame). In this view, you can enter text, edit HTML tags or script code, and use standard word processing commands such as cutting, pasting, finding, and replacing.

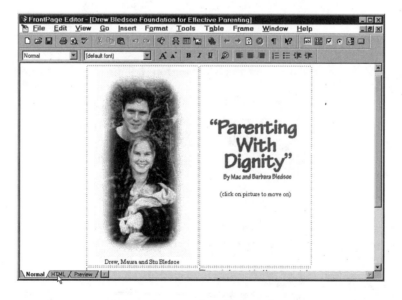

How to use FrontPage 98

Opening existing pages in the FrontPage Editor

Once you have established the layout of your business Web site, you will begin to add content to each of your pages. While page creation and file management tasks are best handled in the FrontPage Explorer, designing and editing pages is done in the FrontPage Editor.

The easiest way to open a page in the FrontPage Editor is to double-click on that page from FrontPage **Explorer**. To open an existing page for editing, from any of the <u>Views</u> options, double-click on a page or select the page and choose (right-click on) **Open** on the Explorer's **Edit** menu. The page will be displayed in the FrontPage Editor.

If you applied a FrontPage <u>theme</u>, all of those page elements will be displayed when your page is opened in the Editor. The page may have a textured background image, a banner with the page's title, and a navigation bar with linked buttons pointing to the other pages in your Web site.

Throughout this book we have used the Drew Bledsoe Foundation as our primary example site when demonstrating various aspects of the Internet. However, the following deals with *your* new page creation and how FrontPage 98 will simplify this process for you.

Let's begin

1. On the Windows taskbar, click the **Start** button, point to **Programs**, and then click **Microsoft FrontPage**.

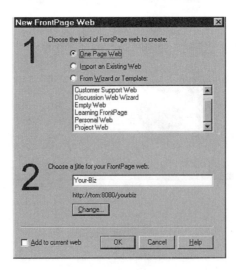

2. The FrontPage Explorer opens and the **Getting Started** dialog box is displayed. The **Getting Started** dialog box is a convenient starting point whenever you begin working in FrontPage. You can open an existing FrontPage Web from a list of recently opened Webs, or you can create a new FrontPage Web.

3. In the Getting Started dialog box, choose **Create a New FrontPage Web** and then click **OK**.

4. The **New FrontPage Web** dialog box is displayed. Here, you tell FrontPage what kind of FrontPage Web you want to create and what will be the title of the new Web site.

5. In the **New FrontPage Web** dialog box, select (for our example) One Page Web next to the large number **1**.

6. Next to the number **2** in the **New FrontPage Web**dialog box, type **Your-Biz** into the title field.

7. "Your-Biz" is the title of your new FrontPage Web. This title helps you distinguish between multiple Web sites you create with FrontPage. As you type the name of your new FrontPage Web, the FrontPage Explorer suggests a location where this FrontPage Web will be stored. For your purposes, accept the suggested location.

8. Click **OK**.

9. FrontPage creates a new FrontPage Web called "Your-Biz."

Building a new page—entering content

To add text on your new page, simply begin typing as you would in any word processing document. The toolbar at the top (middle) of the Editor window will look familiar as it contains many of the same options found in most word processing programs. You can increase/decrease the size of your font, apply **B**old, *I*talic , or <u>U</u>nderlined characteristics, change text color, justify text positioning, and more.

1. Type **Welcome to my Business Web site!**

2. Highlight the sentence and press the **Increase Text Size** button on the toolbar two times.

3. Move the cursor to the end of the line of text you just typed, click the **Center Text** button on the toolbar to center the text and press Enter two times which will create a new paragraph.

4. On the new line, type **Be sure to see our specials of the day**.

5. Press **Enter**. You can later replace this text with your own text, along with a description of what your site has to offer.

6. On the **Insert** menu on the toolbar, choose **Horizontal Line**.

A horizontal line is inserted on the page, just below the text you typed.

In the following steps, you will add a bulleted list to your page. To align your list with left alignment, click the **Align Left** menu button.

Add a bulleted list

On the Editor's toolbar, click the **Bulleted List** button (1,2,3). FrontPage begins a bulleted list and displays the first bullet. If you applied a theme to your Web site, graphical image bullets replace the normally plain list bullets (or numbers). Type:

- About Our Company
- Our Products
- Order Online
- Send us an e-mail

Then press Enter two times. Pressing Enter twice ends the current list. You can copy and paste text in the FrontPage Editor exactly as you do in a Windows word processor. Text from other documents or spreadsheets, graphics, etc. can be selected and saved to memory and pasted into your Web page.

Create a hyperlink

- Click and drag the mouse over the words **About Our Company** to select them.
- On the **Insert** toolbar menu, choose **Hyperlink** (or **Ctrl+K**).

- The **Create Hyperlink** dialog box is displayed. At the bottom of this dialog box, you select the target of your hyperlink. This link can be a page or a file in your current Web directory, on your local (PC) file system, on another Web server, or on the World Wide Web. You can also create an e-mail (*mail to:*) hyperlink in this manner.

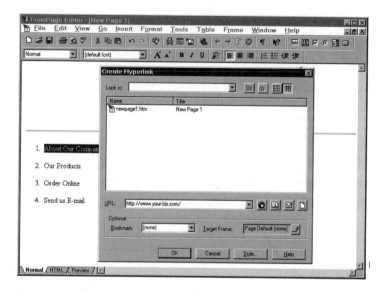

1. Choose a hyperlink from the World Wide Web by visiting that site with your Internet Explorer browser.
2. Select a file on your computer.
3. Create an e-mail (mail to:) hyperlink, or
4. Create a new page in your Web site and link the two pages.

The other option is to enter the Internet address in the **URL** field. Type http://www.your-biz.com and then click **OK**.

On your keyboard, press the down-arrow key to deselect the text.

The words **About Our Company** have changed from black default text to colored text and the words are now <u>underlined</u> to indicate the hyperlink. When this page is displayed in a Web browser, clicking this hyperlink will retrieve and display that linked page.

Net Tips You can also create an automatic hyperlink and bypass the **Create Hyperlink** dialog box by typing the URL directly on the page. Type http://www.your-biz.com/.

As soon as you press the Enter key, the URL you just typed changes from black to colored text and the address is underlined to indicate the hyperlink. Since a URL by itself is not always very descriptive, however, you may want to change it to the name of the site the hyperlink points to. You can overtype the text without erasing the hyperlink

1. Using the mouse, click and drag over the URL you just typed to select it
2. Now type the words **My Business Web site** to replace the selected text.
3. The hyperlink still points to the same URL, but it is now labeled with the site's name instead of an ambiguous address.

Importing an image

Now you will see how easy it is to import an image from another location and insert it on your Web page. Place your cursor under the numbered list you just created.

1. On the **Insert** menu, choose **Image**.
2. The Image dialog box is displayed. In this dialog box, you can select an image to be inserted from the current FrontPage Web, from another Web server, from a scanner, from the Microsoft Clip Gallery, or from a file on your computer.
3. In the Image dialog box, click the **File** button. The File button lets you browse your computer for an image to insert. For this exercise, we chose an image of a pencil included in the FrontPage graphics collection on your CD.
4. In the **Select File** dialog box, navigate to the folder containing your images.
5. Select the file you want to include and click **OK**.

Importing Files

There will be times when it will be easier to transfer content to your Web pages from other documents. With the FrontPage Editor, you can insert the following types of text files directly into your pages.

- ASCII Text (TXT)
- Rich Text Format (RTF)
- Hypertext Markup Language (HTM or HTML)
- Word Processing (including Microsoft Word)
- Spreadsheet (including Microsoft Excel)

Setting the page properties (and other page elements)

Every item on a Web page has *properties* that are embedded in the HTML code. You control these properties and configure them in the FrontPage Editor. These properties affect the page's appearance, give information to Web browsers about how to display the page's hyperlinks, and specify other page settings.

To set the properties of the current page in the FrontPage Editor, choose **Page Properties** on the **File** menu (or "right-click" anywhere on the open page and select **Page Properties** from the menu). Some important page properties include:

- The title, a descriptive word or phrase that is displayed in a browser's title bar when the page is viewed.

- The background image or watermark, an image that is displayed on the page behind the page's contents.

- The background color, the color that is displayed behind the page's contents.

- The text color, the color of the page's text.

- The hyperlink color, the color in which all hyperlinks on the page are displayed before they are visited. (A hyperlink is visited after the user has clicked it.)

- The background sound, a sound file that you associate with the page.

Net Tips

You can specify another page in the Web site to use as the source for the current page's background and colors. Using a single page in your Web as the source of background and color properties gives a consistent, recognizable appearance.

Setting the properties of other page elements

Every item on a Web page has properties that are encoded in the HTML that FrontPage generates to describe the item. Some items' properties are used by Web browsers to determine how to display them. For example, a character has font properties that control its size and font style, and a paragraph has properties that control its alignment on the page.

In the FrontPage Editor, you can edit any item's properties in its properties dialog box. For example, you can edit an image's properties in the **Image Properties** dialog box or a **Radio Button** form field's properties in the **Radio Button Properties** dialog box. To open an item's properties dialog box, select the item and press **ALT+ENTER**. You can also open a selected item's properties dialog box from the shortcut menu. For example, when you select a **Radio Button** field, the Form Field Properties command appears in the **Radio Button**'s shortcut menu.

Because of the way HTML is designed, an item you see on the page is often a part of other larger items. For example, a character in a table is a member of a paragraph, a table cell, a table, and a page. In the FrontPage Editor, you can view a list of all the relevant properties dialog boxes for a selected item by clicking the right mouse button to open its shortcut menu.

Saving the current page

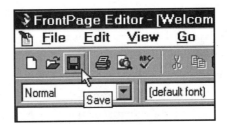

On the FrontPage Editor's toolbar, click the **Save** button. In the **Save Embedded Files** dialog box, click **OK** to save the image(s) you inserted.

All images you placed on your page are added to your FrontPage Web and the current page is saved. As with all computer programs, it is a good idea to *save your work frequently*.

Previewing your new page

Now that you have created a Web page, you can display it in your Web browser to preview your site's layout and appearance. You can also navigate between other pages and test the hyperlinks you created. Previewing a FrontPage Web works just like browsing to a site on the World Wide Web.

In the FrontPage Editor, click **Window** on the menu bar to list all open pages. Choose one.

On the **File** menu, select **Preview in Browser**.

Preview in Browser lets you see exactly how the page will appear in your favorite Web browser before you publish your FrontPage Web. Your new page should look like this.

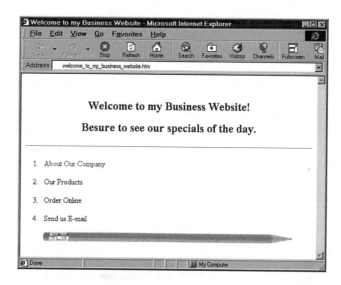

Shared borders and navigation bars

Shared borders are a useful way to present recurring information in a consistent manner. In the FrontPage Explorer, you can specify that one or more shared borders be included on all pages that are part of the FrontPage Web's navigational structure (as displayed in the **Navigation** view).

You can also add or omit shared borders for individual pages, using the Editor. In the following example, the Top Shared Border is selected as indicated by the solid black border. The Left Shared Border is outlined in a dashed line.

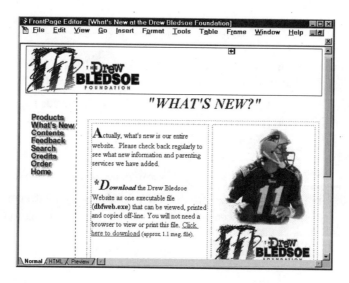

Shared borders are typically used on every page in a FrontPage Web. When you edit the contents of a shared border, the changes apply to *all* pages in the current FrontPage Web that use shared borders.

To add, modify, or delete Shared Borders on a page, do the following.

- On the FrontPage Editor's **Tools** menu, choose **Shared Borders** (or right-click anywhere on the page). The **Page Borders** dialog box is displayed. In this dialog box, you can override the default border settings for the current FrontPage Web. In the **Page Borders** dialog box, choose **Set for this Page Only**.

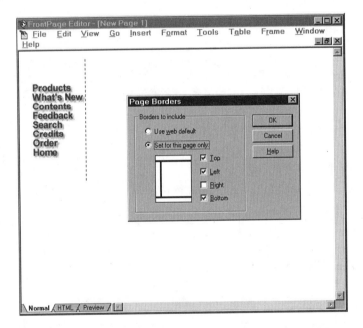

- To remove the Shared Borders for this page deselect the **Top, Bottom,** and **Left** check boxes so that those borders are not selected, then click **OK**.
- The page borders and navigation bars are now invisible on this page and only the background image remains visible.

Navigation bars

To navigate through your Web site, users will follow hyperlinks in a Web browser from one page to another. FrontPage manages these hyperlinks for you with navigation bars—page regions that provide access to other pages in your FrontPage Web, using textual or graphical hyperlinks.

Navigation bars can be added automatically when you create a new FrontPage Web in the FrontPage Explorer's **Navigation** view, or when you create a FrontPage Web from a Web wizard or template. You can also insert navigation bars on individual pages using the FrontPage Editor.

Typically, navigation bars are placed inside a shared border, which displays the navigation bar on every page in the FrontPage Web that includes that shared border. If you change the FrontPage Web's structure in the FrontPage Explorer's **Navigation** view, FrontPage will update the hyperlinks on the navigation bar automatically. Remember that your navigation is one of your strongest influences on the reader's attention.

What are tables? (Pay attention to your table manners)

One of the confusing topics for many new users is the use of tables on a Web page. **Tables**. The name conjures up images of spreadsheets and complex calculations, but nothing is further from the truth. In FrontPage, tables are content organizational tools. Tables are used to position text and graphics on a page and control their appearance and presentation. Tables are how you create newspaper type columns on a page. After you understand some basics, creating and using tables is quite easy.

To create a new table, either select the **Insert Table** button on the toolbar menu (it looks like a small spreadsheet) or click **Table**, then **Insert Table** and fill in the number of **Rows** and **Columns**. The illustration below shows that we have created a table with four individual cells.

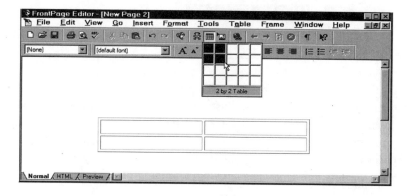

One great aspect about using tables is that you do not need to know how many rows, cells, or columns you will eventually need. You can add or delete them as your imagination, or the volume of information dictates. Also, tables are elastic. When you first create a table, it looks balanced and precisely defined.

Insert a graphic or a block of text inside a cell and that row and/or column will expand to accept the new size. The following illustration demonstrates this elastic cell capability and also shows how each individual cell's properties can have unique alignment characteristics.

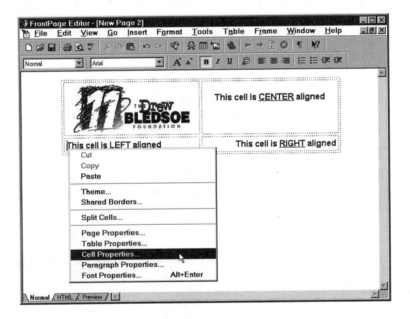

For design and positioning control you can place tables inside of tables and even inside of individual cells. The next diagram illustrates all of these points. The top table is only one row deep, but the right cell has another table of four cells centered inside it with graphics embedded in each of those four cells. The bottom table comprised of one row with two cells is used to center two columns of text newspaper style.

Speaking of table manners, when using "tables" within your pages, take note. Before displaying the contents of a table on the screen, a browser must render the entire table. What this means is that a large table, or one with unsized graphics, will make you wait until the browser assembles everything before it paints the screen. To avoid this, size your graphics and break large tables up into smaller tables.

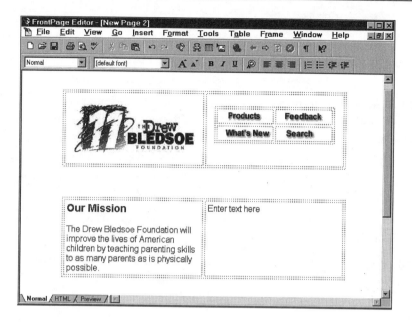

HTML META tags

What are META tags and why must I use them?

META tags permit us to thoroughly utilize little known attributes of HTML. These inconspicuous codes let us take full advantage of the major search engines and the different ways in which they catalog Internet documents. This becomes *vitally important* when we begin to promote our site online and encourage users to locate our domain on the Net.

The META tag is a descriptive set of words that encapsulate the "essence" of your site. You can use the META tags to define your site and what is important to a search engine. Quite simply, proper utilization of <u>META</u> tags will influence the results of your ultimate success or failure when marketing your site on the Internet. Having your domain online without taking the proper steps to promote it correctly is comparable to building a tourist resort in the desert with no roads leading to it and having an unlisted telephone. A great idea poorly executed.

META tags render a number of important administration tasks, which are performed behind the scenes and are not perceptible to the viewer. These tags (instructions) issue commands that generate the appropriate response of the browser program. For our purposes, we will only discuss a few of the key META tags that are important from a marketing perspective.

META tags will instruct some search engine <u>spiders</u> how to list your site based upon your choice of keywords and site description. It is more advantageous that you tell your story to the world than trust some database engine to extract random words from your site.

META tags are placed at the top of the HTML document located between the <HEAD> and </HEAD> tags. You can look at different examples of this with any Web page by selecting **View/Source** on the top menu bar of your browser.

Many search engines rely upon META tags to capture a description of your site and assist with the indexing of the keywords. In addition, various search engines look for different things when they visit your site. Some examples include:

- Search engine spiders like Alta Vista's and Lycos' place greater emphasis on words located nearest the top of a page.
- Infoseek looks at the first 200 characters after the <BODY> tag (except when you apply META tags).
- Yahoo! uses the words in your URL and up to 25 of the words you included when you submitted your URL.
- Webcrawler compares the number of times a word(s) is repeated and awards significance to that, the more repetitions, the more validity to the search.

If you are utilizing <u>Java script</u> (especially near the top of your page), it is extremely important to include a META tag description. Otherwise, the Java script will serve as the text that will be indexed for some search engines. Using <u>frames</u> in your pages can present the same problem unless you counter the effect by proper use of META tags.

If your home page (default.htm or index.htm) consists primarily of a graphic or image map, some search engines may not index your site properly unless you adhere to the suggestions outlined in this book.

FrontPage automatically produces some META tags as you create or edit your Web pages. Other tags must be inserted manually. The following is an example of what correct (multiple) META tag format will look like in HTML.

```
<HEAD>
<META  name="description" content="This is where you insert descriptive text that
will be displayed when a search lists your site.">
<META  name="keywords" content="Insert keywords words here that are related to your
business and separate words by commas">
<TITLE>A Descriptive Title of Each Page Goes Here</TITLE>
</HEAD>
```

Please feel free to use these tags as a guide and add to your Web pages. Also, be sure to change the description, content, and keywords illustrated in black italics to reflect your products and/or services. Now let's look at each META tag individually using the Drew Bledsoe Foundation pages to demonstrate our utilization.

The <Keywords> tag

Keywords are a critical component of your Web marketing strategy. In many cases, the keywords you associate with your domain will determine the success of search results, the confidence factor returned by the search engine and the frequency with which your site appears. Search engines will rate your keywords to determine the relevance of your site to a query.

Understanding this, one would logically conclude that keyword repetition is the secret to success. At one time, this was a universally true statement, but search engines have gotten more intelligent and more sophisticated. Today, this is considered SPAMming the search engine and some engines will actually penalize you by dropping your site from their listing.

 It is permissible to repeat keywords in the META tag a number of times, but our research shows that more than five or six mentions may be considered SPAMming by the search engine. Including singular and plural cases of words, active and passive verbs and capital and lowercase letters can increase the value of your keywords. Do not forget the most important keyword, the name of your company. Also, it a good idea to provide spelling variations as in the example below of *super bowl, superbowl* and Super Bowl.

<META name=" keywords" content= "Drew Bledsoe, Drew Bledsoe Foundation, quarterback, nfl, New England Patriots, NFL Football, Patriots, super bowl, superbowl, Super Bowl, parenting, children, self esteem, love, respect, happiness, honesty, discipline, punishment, teaching, seminar, workshop, videotapes, parents, child, attention deficit, hyperactive, A.D.D., ADD, parenting, family, teen, teens, teenage, self esteem, self-esteem, relationships, adolescent, adolescents, victim, divorce, workbook, tape, tapes, VHS, prevention, substance abuse, drugs, avoiding drugs and gangs, sport, sports, Drew Bledsoe Foundation, Mac Bledsoe, NFL ">

Configuring the *Keyword* tag using FrontPage 98

To embed the *Keyword* META tags using FrontPage 98, follow these simple steps:

1. **Right-click** anywhere on the page that you are editing.
2. Choose **Page Properties** from the menu.

3. Select the **Custom** tab.

4. You will see two windows **System Variables** and **User Variables**.

5. Select **Add** (to the right of the **User Variables** window). A new window appears with two fields.

6. In the **Name** field type **keywords**.

7. In the **Value** field enter the list of important keywords as described above.

8. Click the **OK** button.

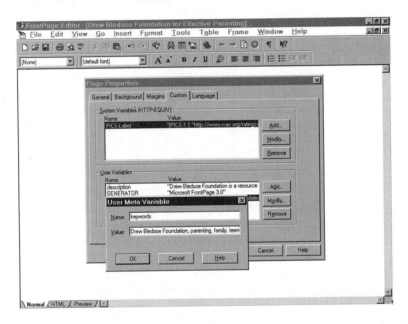

Because each search engine imposes its own rules on how much text it will index, it costs you nothing to make your keyword tags as lengthy as necessary. In this way you can benefit from those engines that will catalog an entire site regardless of size. For those engines that limit their indexing to the first 25 words, strive to place your most effective keywords at the beginning.

The <Description> tag

The description META tag is self-explanatory, in that this is where you will provide a comprehensive description of the content of your Web site. The description META tag is also used to help determine relevancy by search engines in response to a query. This description will be displayed following your URL when the search engine displays the list of results meeting the search criteria.

In the first 25 to 40 words, you should present a concise summation of your site, your mission and/or products. Many search engines will use this wording when displaying the results of a search. Following this 25 to 40 word summary, you should add a substantial amount of supporting relevant text.

<META name=" description" content= ”Drew Bledsoe Foundation is a resource where parents learn new effective parenting skills. This foundation provides a source of information for parents, giving them the tools necessary to create an encouraging, and loving home for their children"**>**

To embed the *Description* META tag using FrontPage 98, follow the same procedures as outlined above for the Keyword tags.

1. Select the **<u>A</u>dd** button again.
2. In the **<u>N</u>ame** field type **description**.
3. In the **<u>V</u>alue** field enter the site description as outlined above.
4. Click the **OK** button.

The <TITLE> tag

In spite of the fact that FrontPage prompts you to add a title for each new page as you create them, the significance of proper titling warrants our covering this topic in greater detail. The title of *every* page should be notably descriptive.

If at all possible, your most significant key words should be in the title of your pages. The importance of the title to the search engines can not be stressed strongly enough. This text will appear in the title bar of a browser, and how your Web page description will be displayed in the list of <u>keyword</u> search results. This will also be beneficial when someone includes that page in his or her bookmark file. See example:

`<TITLE> Drew Bledsoe Foundation for Effective Parenting</TITLE>`

This is much more descriptive than:

"The Drew Bledsoe Foundation Home Page on the Internet."

In our chapter on marketing, we will explain the idiosyncrasies of the major search engines in great detail. You will learn how you can improve your chances of better placement.

Ultimately, it never hurts to over explain and over communicate with your META tag descriptions and title descriptions. It can mean the difference between you and your competition when a customer is looking to buy.

Optimize your page titles wherever possible

After rating keyword relevance, some search engines will display sites in alphabetical sequence applying the order to the first word (or letter) in the title. Identifying the title of your page with a character that appears early in the alphabet hierarchy is a good positioning tip. The hierarchical indexing sequence used by many search engines is as follows:

```
! @ # % ^ & ( ) _ + 1 2 3 4 5 6 7 8 9 0 - = \
A B C D E F G H I J K L M N O P Q R S T U V W X Y Z
a b c d e f g h i j k l m n o p q r s t u v w x y z
```

With the exception of the text that appears in the <TITLE> tag, your META tags will not be visible to the enduser browsing your pages. However, many search engines will index the *description* and *keyword* META tags as searchable words.

Miscellaneous <other> META tags

There are numerous varieties of META tags with more being created every day. META tags can also be used to include a name or a value that describes properties of your document, such as the author, date, disclaimers, copyright announcements, and so on. The NAME attribute specifies the property name while the CONTENT attribute specifies the property value, e.g.

```
<META NAME=" Author" CONTENT="Your Name Here" >
```

Only the 'description' and 'keywords' tags are associated with search engines at this time.

Be careful about updating or deleting pages on your site *after* the search engines have indexed them. Deleting a page (*filename.htm*) or changing the name of a page after the search engines have indexed the content can be a problem. Many of the large search engines are so busy that their agents may not revisit your site again for months. This means that a page you deleted may still be displayed on a keyword search months after you removed it. For this reason, it is imperative that you plan your directory structure and page naming convention as thoroughly as possible before you publish.

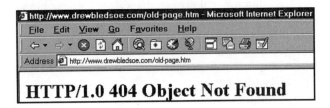

However, at some point even the most well-planned Web site will eventually have pages deleted or information repositioned. You can do a number of things to avoid those dreaded *"File Not Found"* errors. You may want to run a parallel site until your new pages have been indexed or better yet, re-edit the old pages to automatically move (point) a user to the newer page. Here are the **Refresh** META tag instructions you would include in your old HTML page:

```
</HEAD>
<META http-equiv=refresh content=" 2;URL=new_page_here.htm" >
<HEAD >
```

The browser reads this command (**content=2**) as the number of seconds before automatically transferring to the next page. One minute would equal 60. The new_page_here.htm is the name of your new page or hyperlink.

Configuring the Refresh option using FrontPage 98

To embed the *Refresh* META tag using FrontPage 98, follow the procedures outlined below.

1. **Right-click** anywhere on the page that you are editing.
2. Choose **Page Properties** from the menu.
3. Select the **Custom** tab.
4. You will see two windows **System Variables** and **User Variables**.
5. In the top window **System Variables** [HTTP-EQUIV].
6. Select **Add** (to the right of the System Variables window). A new window appears with two fields.
7. In the **Name** field type **refresh**.
8. In the **Value** field type the number of seconds (2) for delay, a semicolon(;), and the URL and name of the new page.

As long as your "target" page and the original (refresh) pages are located within the same directory, the URL does not have to be shown as a fully qualified address, i.e. "new_page_title_here.htm". If the target is in another location use a fully qualified URL address: http://www.your-biz.com/new_page_title_here.htm

You can also use this refresh option to create a slide show within your Web site . A slide show is a series of Web pages that automatically change after a preprogrammed time. This can be used to display products, tell a story, or create effects using different background colors or images.

This would be a good place to remind your visitors to "Update Their Bookmarks" with the new page.

HTML—tips, tricks, and *help*

Although it is called *"code,"* HTML programming is essentially text editing of commands that are read and displayed by a browser. In its most basic form, HTML resembles the onscreen commands that word processors used 15 years ago. As an example, to make a word appear in bold type, the actual HTML code looks like this:

Type:	`Vote early and vote <b>often</b>`
The browser displays:	Vote early and vote **often**

To change the font (Arial) and color (red) of the text you would need to insert the following code:

Type:	`Vote early and vote <font color="#FF0000"`
	`face=" Arial" ><strong>often</strong></font>`
The browser displays:	Vote early and vote **often**

Notepad

WordPad

Fortunately, FrontPage 98, will do 99.9% of the hard work for you and insert the code as you select the commands from the toolbar. FrontPage 98 will automatically perform most of the HTML programming functions discussed in this book. However, at some time it may be necessary for you to edit some of your pages manually. This editing can be done using FrontPage 98, Microsoft Word or any text editor such as Notepad or WordPad (included in Windows 98).

An example of a page that may require manual HTML editing is the default.htm page. As its name implies, this is the default, or main page of any directory or domain on the Web. This is the page that is *"defaulted to"* when you type an address that does *not* specify an exact page name:

`(i.e. http://www.your-biz.com/products.htm)`

Without boring you with the details of how UNIX and NT servers recognize and process Internet addresses, suffice it to say that the server makes certain assumptions when it processes a URL request from a browser.

If you enter the address `http://www.your-biz.com/` and that domain is hosted on a UNIX server, the "index" page will be displayed. This is the same as typing the "index.htm" file name—`http://www.your-biz.com/index.htm`.

With an NT (FrontPage) server, that same address will "default" to `http://www.your-biz.com/default.htm`.

If you have standardized on FrontPage, this is one of those instances where you may never see this again. However, this has been a source of confusion for some new users or those who changed to FrontPage from another HTML authoring program.

HTML reference sites online

A Beginner's Guide to HTML presented by the National Center for Supercomputing Applications (NCSA) located at the University of Illinois at Urbana-Champaign.[1] This is a great starting point to understanding HTML. `http://www.ncsa.uiuc.edu/General/Internet/WWW/HTMLPrimerAll.html`

Interactive Tutorial for Beginners is a "hands-on" tutorial for anyone who is serious about learning HTML. `http://www.davesite.com/Webstation/html/`

Microsoft's **HTML Authoring for Internet Explorer** focuses on working with content and using HTML to present information effectively. `http://www.microsoft.com/workshop/author/default.asp`

Microsoft FrontPage Support site will help you find answers to common questions and locate other resources for helping you learn FrontPage. `http://support.microsoft.com/support/frontpage/fp98.asp`

PMP Computer Solutions provides Web pages that are intended to enhance the support already available for Microsoft FrontPage.[2] `http://www.pmpcs.com/support/frontpage.htm`

W3C, founded in 1994, is the official standards body for determining the evolution of Web protocols. `http://www.w3.org/`

Web Developer's Virtual Library includes demos, tutorials, resources and tools for HTML. `http://wdvl.com/WDVL/`

Project Cool includes demos and tutorials, as well HTML tricks and links to excellent examples of good Web page design. `http://www.projectcool.com/`

Web page design for designers is aimed at people who are already involved with design and want to explore the possibilities of the Web. `http://www.wpdfd.com/wpdhome.htm`

You may also want to pick up a copy of *Sams Teach Yourself Web Publishing with HTML 4 in a Week* by Laura Lemay. Her book is consistently reviewed as *the* book to own to learn HTML.

Advanced features of FrontPage 98

Using the advanced features that are built into FrontPage, you can take advantage of the latest developments in Web browser technology. You can add your own ActiveX controls, Design Time controls, scripts, plug-ins, or Java applets. You can use Microsoft Visual SourceSafe® to control the versions of your pages, and you can protect your content using built-in Secure Sockets Layer support. What follows is an overview of some of the advanced features included in FrontPage 98.

Active Page Elements

You can add Active Page Elements such as hover buttons, marquees, search forms, page counters, and video clips in FrontPage 98. These elements can make your pages come alive and appear more interesting and useful.

All Active Page Elements are inserted on your page in a similar fashion. As an example, we will step through the process of adding a marquee to a page.

1. On a new page, press the Enter key twice to create some space below the top of the page.

2. Type some text such as **Welcome to Your-Biz.Com!**

3. Select this text and click the **Bold** button on the format toolbar. Formatting of marquee text must occur *before* you insert a marquee region. If the current FrontPage Web has a theme applied, text color, size, and font may change dynamically.

4. On the **Insert** menu, point to **Active Elements**, and then click **Marquee.** The **Marquee Properties** dialog box is displayed. In this dialog box, you can adjust several properties, including the speed and direction, as well as marquee size and background color.

5. On the **Background Color** drop-down list, choose a color and click **OK**. FrontPage adds a marquee region to the current page.

Other Active Elements are similarly created by following the simple directions from the menu.

Interactive Web page forms

A form is a collection of form fields on a page along with a form handler, a method of collecting information from the form. Forms are a key to making your FrontPage Web interactive. Users can "talk back" to your FrontPage Web by filling in forms in your FrontPage Web and submitting them. The layout of a form can include form fields, text in all paragraph styles, tables, images, and most other objects that can be inserted on a page. In FrontPage, you create forms using a simple point-and-click interface. Some typical uses of forms are:

- To collect names, addresses, telephone numbers, e-mail addresses, and other information to register users for a service or event.
- Receive feedback about a Web site, product, or service.
- Gather information for the purchase of an item or service.
- Collect payment information, such as credit card type, number, and expiration date.
- Moderate a discussion forum about a topic of your choice. Using the FrontPage **Discussion Web Wizard**, you can create an entire FrontPage discussion Web.

A user fills in a form by typing into text fields, clicking radio buttons and check boxes, and selecting options from drop-down menus. The user then submits the form by clicking a button, usually labeled "Submit." When this happens, FrontPage appends the contents of the form to a file in your FrontPage Web. This is the file you will periodically open to gather the collected information from the form. You can also configure a form to send its data to your e-mail address.

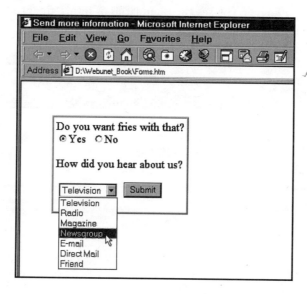

A form's handler is not visible to a user but is associated with a form by FrontPage. It is invoked when a user submits the form. FrontPage automatically assigns a default form handler to each form that you create. You can also select from a set of FrontPage form handlers or add you own custom form handler to any form.

You can place a form field anywhere on the page where you can enter text. On the **Insert** menu select **Form Field** and click the type of form field that you want. You can also create form fields using the **Forms** toolbar. To create a simple form, do the following:

1. Insert the fields.
2. Lay out the form.
3. Set the properties of each field.

Adding a feedback form

One of the best ways of collecting feedback on the Web is to place a comment form on your page. This lets people who visit your site send you feedback without the need to open their e-mail application. In FrontPage, you make a new form by creating a form field anywhere on the page outside of other forms. To Add a Feedback Form to your page:

1. Press the Enter key to create some space below the top of the page. Type **Please send me feedback about my Web site**.
2. On the Insert menu, point to Form Field, then click **Scrolling Text Box.**
3. FrontPage inserts a form containing a **Scrolling Text Box** and **Submit** and **Reset** push buttons. (To help you see the boundaries of forms, the FrontPage Editor can display them as dotted lines.)

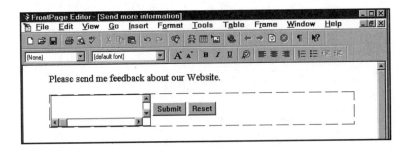

The default properties of a feedback form specify that the (form results) will be saved to a default file in your Web site. You can see the results of your feedback by viewing the saved file.

Viewing the Feedback Results File

The responses from your feedback form are stored in a file that is added to your FrontPage Web. By default, this file is located in a hidden folder that cannot be accessed by a Web browser. No one but the administrator or author (you) of the FrontPage Web site can view this information. To View the Feedback Results File switch back to the FrontPage Explorer.

1. On the FrontPage Explorer's **View** menu, click the **Folders** button on the **Views** bar.

2. In the **All Folders** pane, click the private folder to select it. By default, text submitted through the feedback form that you placed on your page is stored in the private folder in your FrontPage Web.

3. Next, double-click the file form results.txt file shown in the **Contents** pane.

4. The file is opened and displayed in your default text editor (Notepad), where you can see the text you typed into the form from the Web browser.

5. Close the text editor.

Publishing your Web site on the Internet

You will now return to the FrontPage Explorer to prepare your FrontPage Web for publication on the World Wide Web. Before you publish a FrontPage Web, you will want to make sure your pages and files are organized, your hyperlinks are working, and your pages are free of spelling errors. The FrontPage Explorer can help you complete and track these important tasks.

When your FrontPage Web is ready to be published on the World Wide Web—or on your company's intranet—the FrontPage Explorer makes it easy for you to transfer the pages and files to the World Wide Web while automatically verifying the addresses of your pages and the paths to your files.

Normally, moving pages and files from one folder to another would break the hyperlinks between your pages. However, if you move files in the FrontPage Explorer's Folders view, FrontPage updates every page and hyperlink in your FrontPage Web to track the new location of files and folders that have been moved.

1. Close all open pages in the FrontPage Editor.

2. In the FrontPage Explorer, click the **Publish** button on the toolbar.

3. The **Publish FrontPage Web** dialog box is displayed. In this dialog box, specify the location on the World Wide Web or your corporate Intranet to which you want to publish your FrontPage Web.

4. Enter the address of your new domain, for example, www.your-biz.com.

5. In the **Publish FrontPage Web** dialog box, click **OK**. The FrontPage Explorer publishes the FrontPage Web from your computer to the Intranet Web server or World Wide Web server you specified.

ActiveX controls are software components that provide dynamic features on your pages. For example, a stock ticker control could be used to add a live stock ticker to a page, or an animation control could be used to add animation features. For more detailed information about ActiveX controls, and to see a gallery of free controls visit the Microsoft Web site.

In the FrontPage Editor, you insert an ActiveX control into your page on the **Insert** menu by pointing to **Advanced** and then clicking **ActiveX Control** or **Design Time Control**. To insert a control, you must first have it installed on your machine. If you choose the **ActiveX Control** command and the **Pick a Control** drop-down list in the **ActiveX Control Properties** dialog box is empty, you do not yet have any ActiveX controls installed on your system.

After you pick the control to insert, you can adjust the control's settings in the ActiveX Control Properties dialog box. For example, all standard size and alignment options for objects that can be placed on a page are available. You can also specify an Alternate Representation that users will see if their Web browser does not support ActiveX controls.

Once you've picked an ActiveX control from the **Pick a Control** drop-down list in the **ActiveX Control Properties** dialog box, you can set control-specific options by clicking **Properties** in the ActiveX Control Properties dialog box. This opens a dialog box with options that are specific to the ActiveX control that you want to insert. As you change the control-specific values, you can click **Apply** to immediately see the impact of those changes on the appearance of the ActiveX control. Some ActiveX controls also come with documentation that describes the control's properties.

Java applets are similar to ActiveX controls. They are software components written in a programming language called Java that provides dynamic features on your Web page. A software vendor might choose to create a product as a Java applet because its interpreted nature lets it run on several different hardware platforms. Inserting a Java applet is similar to inserting an ActiveX control. Java doesn't support a customized property-setting interface, so a generic one is provided for you.

In the FrontPage Editor, you insert a Java applet into your page on the **Insert** menu by pointing to **Advanced** and then clicking **Java Applet**. In the **Java Applet Properties** dialog box, type in the name of the applet source file that you want to insert. Java applet source files usually have a .CLASS extension. Enter any general size and alignment options properties, and then use the **Applet Parameters** section to set particular properties for a control.

Because Java does not provide a mechanism for displaying the valid properties and values are for a given control, you'll need to consult the documentation that comes with the Java applet and input the right property names and legal values for each property.

When you're done configuring the Java applet, click **OK**, and FrontPage inserts an actual-size placeholder icon on the page to retain your page layout. You preview a Java applet in the FrontPage Editor's **Preview** tab (if you have Microsoft Internet Explorer, version 3.0 or higher, installed) or by choosing **Preview** in **Browser** on the FrontPage Editor's **File** menu.

Scripting is a type of programming language that you can use to write custom code for your Web page. This is an advanced FrontPage feature that requires knowledge of programming. Scripting is useful for custom Web-based solutions development. It provides a full object model for the Web browser and the objects on the current page. This makes it easy to write code that manipulates elements on the page without knowing the details of the HTML or how the objects are implemented.

FrontPage 98 provides a range of scripting features that are compatible with JavaScript and Visual Basic Script. In the FrontPage Editor, you insert a script into your page on the **Insert** menu by pointing to **Advanced** and then clicking **Script**. The Script command lets you easily insert scripting code inline on your page. You pick the scripting language you want, type in the script code, and click **OK**. The script will appear on your page as a small icon. You can double-click this icon at any time to edit the script.

Secure Sockets Layer (SSL) allows software to communicate with Web servers in a secure, encrypted manner. Many Web sites that conduct electronic commerce use SSL to securely transmit credit card numbers from a customer's Web browser to the Web server.

FrontPage Server Extensions

FrontPage 98 automatically includes a set of programs—the FrontPage Server Extensions—that are installed on the Web server computer on which your FrontPage Webs are stored. If you installed the Microsoft Personal Web Server or Microsoft Peer Web Services, FrontPage Setup installed the FrontPage Server Extensions on your PC.

The Server Extensions support authoring and administering FrontPage Webs, along with browse-time FrontPage Web functionality. For example, when an author is editing a FrontPage Web, the Server Extensions support copying or publishing it to other Web servers, creating a table of contents for the Web, adding themes and navigational structure to it, and updating hyperlinks to any pages that have been moved or renamed. Using the Server Extensions, an administrator can give a user, group of users, or specific computer permissions to edit a FrontPage Web, browse to it, or administer it. When a user browses a FrontPage Web, the Server Extensions support search forms, discussions groups, form processing (including sending form results using e-mail), and other runtime features.

FrontPage database integration

More and more organizations are publishing their databases on corporate intranets and on the World Wide Web to offer convenient access to data for employees and customers alike. The benefits of making existing information widely and easily available quickly become evident. A retail business can create an online product catalog that tells customers which items are currently in stock. A computer software company can give its customers round-the-clock self-help information and troubleshooting tips through an online knowledge base. A human resources department in any organization can post directories of up-to-date employee information right on the company Intranet.

With FrontPage, you can easily create custom database queries on dynamic, richly formatted Web pages, providing visitors to your Internet or Intranet site with information at their fingertips.

FrontPage database integration is based on Active Server Pages (ASP). An Active Server Page is an HTML document that contains embedded server-side scripting. What this means is that a query initiates a process that generates the HTML code "on-the-fly" and returns a standard HTML document viewable on any platform using any Web browser.

Before you can integrate a database into a FrontPage Web, you must follow a series of steps that take place outside of FrontPage. These include configuring your Web server and workstation, and building (and modifying) Structured Query Language (SQL) queries in a database management tool such as Microsoft Access. However, you can use any database with an available Open Data Base Connectivity (ODBC) compliant driver to publish data on a Web site.

Check the Net!

To learn more about this process of integrating a database, visit the Microsoft Web site resources located at:

`http://www.microsoft.com/frontpage/resources/access97.htm`

`http://support.microsoft.com/support/kb/articles/q175/7/70.asp`

---

[1] The National Center for Supercomputing Applications, University of Illinois at Urbana-Champaign. http://www.uiuc.edu/

[2] PMP Computer Solutions specializes in providing technology solutions in the areas of application development, competitive analysis, Internet and Intranet development, networks, and research. http://www.pmpcs.com/index.htm

Graphics and FrontPage 98

A picture may be worth a thousand words, but don't make me wait long enough to count them!

- Tom Heatherington

Working with graphics

How do I ensure that my graphics are not too large? And that my pages will download as quickly as possible?

Unlike conventional printing applications, the foremost challenge in creating images for the Web is to control the physical file size.

Big graphic = slow download = goodbye viewer

A file's size (for example, 11KB) is a combination of the image's physical dimensions, appearance, color palette, and file format. The most obvious method of reducing a file's size is to do just that, reduce the physical dimensions of the graphic. A one-inch by one-inch image can be 1/3 to 1/4 the size of a two-by-two-inch graphic. In most instances, reducing the size will not detract from the look of the image.

Resizing an image can be done either in your graphics program, *or* in the FrontPage Editor. While in the FrontPage Editor, you can resize an image by selecting the image and dragging any of its corners to the desired size. The Editor is capable of displaying an image at any size specified by the <u>HEIGHT</u> and <u>WIDTH</u> tags. However, the actual physical size (KB) of the graphic remains intact. After resizing an image, it is necessary to click the "resample" button on the bottom toolbar to reduce the physical size.

Net Tips

When you save a page on which you have resized an image, you will have an opportunity to overwrite or rename the image. This is a great way to produce "thumbnails" of larger images. By renaming "*myphoto.gif*" to "*myphoto-a.gif*," you create and save another image as opposed to replacing the original.

There are primarily two graphic file formats currently being used on the Web, <u>GIF</u> and <u>JPEG</u>. The rule of thumb when deciding upon which format to use—JPEG is best for photographs and GIF files are excellent for <u>screen captures</u> and images created in painting programs (PhotoShop, CorelDRAW!, and so on). The GIF 89a format also permits <u>interlacing</u> and <u>animation</u>.

FrontPage 98 will permit you to import many different file formats and will automatically convert them to Web ready files. Because of this feature, you will not have to manually convert image files created in other programs. Drag and drop, import, or paste from the clipboard, FrontPage 98 takes the mystery out of this confusing process.

Graphic resolution is measured in <u>DPI</u> (dots per inch), the number of color dots packed into one inch. In photography and high-end graphics creation, the greater the DPI, the higher the quality of the image. Details are sharper; colors are richer and look closer to natural.

Color depth is another aspect of graphic quality. The more colors, the better the gradient, shadows, and overall natural look. Although most monitors are capable of displaying millions of colors, many users only have 8-bit color display cards in their computer.

As a further complication, Windows and Mac computers employ unlike color palettes. This means that colors will not look the same on different computers. Fortunately, the color palettes of these two operating systems overlap and produce 216 colors from which to standardize. To be on the safe side it is recommended that you save your images using a 216-color palette.

Net Tips

Most computer monitors are limited to a display resolution of only 72 DPI. This means that the digital images you will use should have their resolution reduced to 72 DPI (or thereabouts). If you do not do this, the graphics will load much slower because the file is larger, but the screen *will not* display a clearer or better picture.

Speed thrills—think fast! (as in download)

How quickly your pages download can literally mean the difference between a quick visit (and a sale) or a speedy exit (and a lost opportunity). When you have images *or portions of images* that can be reused throughout your site, take advantage of that. Whenever possible, divide your graphics into reusable sections. In this way, the browser need only download those other image sections that are required.

The Drew Bledsoe Foundation offers a description of each of 10 videotapes on individual Web pages. The Web site displays a picture of each tape(s) on the corresponding page. Typically, you would need to use a separate image on each page.

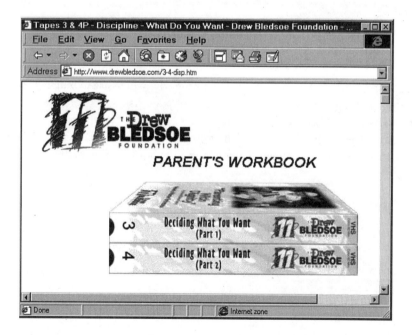

To solve this problem and speed the download of pages, the Drew Bledsoe Foundation sliced up the graphics to reuse the common sections. In this example, the largest graphics were reused (loaded once) and the small tape number and title sections were loaded as necessary. They are assembled in a <u>table</u> to preserve the grouping.

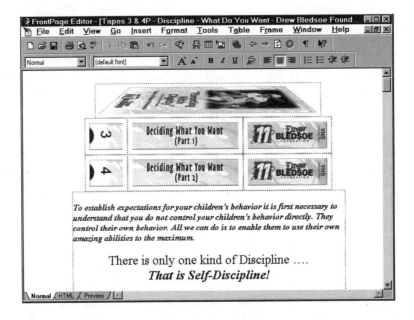

Size is important—think small!

There are numerous other things that if done properly, will assist in making your pages load quicker and enhance the overall experience of your visitors. There are steps you can take to precipitate the process of displaying a page. A big part of this process is to ensure that completing the Image Properties dialog box has optimized all of your images. You invoke this menu by right clicking on any image and choosing the menu selection **Image Properties**.

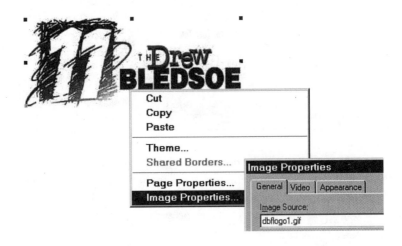

The **Image Properties** menu has three tabs. We will typically be concerned with the choices listed under the **General** and **Appearance** tab only . Most of the fields are self-evident, in that they list the image name, source, the type of graphic, its location, and some other miscellany that will require more in-depth study (the manual or help screens) if you want to learn more.

Under the **General** tab, the **Alternative Representations/Text** field (in the center) is important. This is where you provide a text description of the image. This addresses some significant Web site downloading and marketing issues. While a page is loading in a browser, the text description or message is visible until the image appears, and browsers that view *text only* will receive a detailed description of your image. There are few limitations about the message you can include under this description.

<u>ALT</u> tags should always be included in your page programming because some search engines also read the "ALTernative" description. ALT tags follow an image statement in HTML and generally look like the following:

```
<A HREF=bio.htm><IMG SRC = " dbflogo3.jpg" alt=" Drew Bledsoe Foundation Logo"
width=" 250" height=" 100" border=" 0" align=" left" ></A>
```

Make sure you include alternative text if the graphic has significance. For those users who have graphics turned off (in their browser), or for those who may be sight challenged, having alternative text will keep the context of your images in tact. If they are not important enough to have descriptive text, they should be considered for removal.

If your image is to be a hyperlink, the **Default Hyperlink/ Location** field is where you enter the URL, filename or bookmark location for the target link.

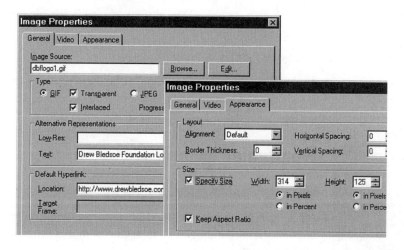

Net Tips

Under the **Appearance** tab, you have two sub-menus, **Layout** and **Size**. The Layout selection deals with the images position on the page (or in a cell) right, left or center. The **Border Thickness** is used when an image is hyperlinked (clickable) to indicate the density of the border around the image. You can select 0 to make the border frame disappear.

You should always check the **Specify Size** box for most images. FrontPage will automatically size your graphic in pixels and gives you the option of including this invisible **Height** and **Width** HTML code.

Providing the **Height** and **Width** attributes for the browser can make a huge difference in how quickly a page loads. With this option selected, the browser reserves the space on the page while continuing to load the text and other images on the screen. Without this option selected, some browsers must wait for the image to load before drawing the remainder of the page. The **Keep Aspect Ratio** box will remain checked by default.

You can further reduce the size of GIF files by reducing the number of colors and saving them as 16 color images. This is a **File/Save As** command for most graphics programs. Also, additional compression of 20–30% in size (in most cases) can be achieved by using an online utility that will help reduce the size of GIF files so that they load more quickly. Visit the GIF Wizard Web site. `http://www.raspberryhill.com/gifwizard.html`

Get the jump on the next page

Whenever you have pages that are light on graphics, but have large graphics further into your Web site, here is a trick to make your pages load more quickly. Without anyone being the wiser, you can *sneak* a graphic into your visitor's cache while they are reading a heavy content text page. By setting a graphics IMG dimensions to 0, the file can be placed into cache and called up later when needed.

```
<IMG SRC=" image01.gif" height=0 width=0>
```

This is not a wise thing to do all the time and should never be done if there are many images (or a large image) on a page. The required graphics for the current page will share the download time with the invisible graphic. Be careful.

Fine-tuning graphics

What are transparent graphics?

All images are rectangular (or four-sided) in shape. The purpose of adding transparency to an image is to improve the appearance of the object and its relationship to the page layout.

By removing the visible background of a graphic, you can create a more aesthetic presentation. This picture of Drew Bledsoe illustrates this point. The background detracts from the scene.

By removing the background color of the image (making it invisible), the three-dimensional image seems to rise out of the page. It appears cleaner, less cluttered, and it calls attention to the image. When exhibiting a picture of a product online this can be very important to the overall presentation.

Most graphics programs today offer this transparency capability. Typically you would select a background color (such as neon green) that is not being used in your image and apply the transparency option as dictated by the program. Also, if you are using a solid background color for your Web pages (such as this white page), you can achieve the same effect by painting your image's background with that fill color.

How to make an image (color) transparent

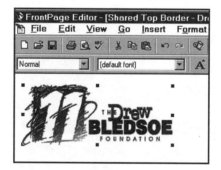

1. In the FrontPage Editor, click the image to select it. When you select an image, the Image toolbar is activated and appears on the screen.

2. Click the **Make Transparent** button on the image toolbar. Move the mouse pointer over the image. The pointer changes to a pencil eraser.

3. Click the left mouse button anywhere on the background behind the subject in the image. The background of the image is now transparent, allowing the color or backdrop of the page to show through.

This technique works only with a background consisting of one color. The backgrounds of most photos, scans, or screen captures will be comprised of many colors. In these instances, you will need to paint out the background with a single color before applying this effect.

The background can be removed either by painting over it with a solid color or "masking" the foreground image. Most graphics programs are capable of masking objects in an illustration. Consult the programs help section for instructions regarding masking.

Creating image maps

You have already learned how easy it is to place images and text on a Web page. Now you will discover how to create an image map—an image that contains one or more (invisible) hyperlinks.

When a graphic is formatted as an image map, a user can click on certain regions of the image and trigger image "hotspots." These hotspots trigger the hyperlinks that have been added to the HTML code by the FrontPage Editor.

The Drew Bledsoe Foundation Web site uses a graphic for one of its menus. Although the menu features text links, it obtained a pleasing drop-shadow effect by using a graphic instead of simple HTML text.

Video Series - Workbook - Website - Order - Home

Send comments to the Drew Bledsoe Foundation
Copyright © 1997, 1998 Drew Bledsoe Foundation
Last Updated: May 19, 1998

How to create image hotspots

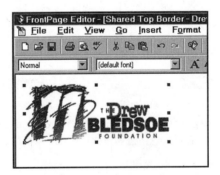

A hotspot is an area on an image that contains a hyperlink. While in the FrontPage Editor, click anywhere on your image to select it. Next, click the **Rectangle** button on the Image toolbar at the bottom left of the Editor window. The Rectangle button will create a rectangular hotspot on an image. The Circle button creates a round or oval hotspot and the Polygon button is used for free style hotspot creation.

1. Move the mouse pointer over your image and the pointer becomes a pencil.

2. Click and hold the left mouse button, then drag the rectangle until it outlines the words "Video Series." When you let go of the mouse button, the **Create Hyperlink** dialog box is displayed. If you let go of the mouse button too soon, you can always adjust (size) the hotspot region after completing the remaining steps.

3. In the **Create Hyperlink** dialog box, choose to link to an existing page in your Web site, create a new page, or choose a URL on the Internet.

4. Click **OK**.

Using our menu example, following these steps will result in an image with the hotspots outlined and displayed by FrontPage as illustrated here. Note the sizing "handles" on the word Web site.

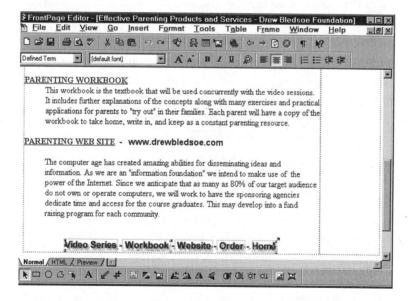

Hotspots can be resized. If you need to adjust the size and position of the hotspot, move the mouse over the hotspot borders until you see the resize pointer (a double-headed arrow). You can then click and drag the hotspot borders into position. The associated hyperlink will be retained.

Placing text over images

In the FrontPage Editor, you can place formatted text on top of any image. This feature is useful for creating graphical banners, labeling image buttons, and creating text on image maps.

To Place Text over an Image:

1. On the FrontPage Editor's **Insert** menu, choose **Image**. The **Image** dialog box is displayed. In the Image dialog box, select the image you wish to use as a backdrop, then click **OK.**

2. Next, click on the image you just inserted which will activate the image toolbar. On the image toolbar, click the **Text** button. A text field with file handles and a flashing cursor appears over the center of the image.

3. Type the text you want to enter (for example, **Click Here**). The text appears centered in the text field. The default text color is black and the default font formatting is 12-point Arial Bold. The next step is to make the text stand out from the image.

4. To format the image text, double-click the text to select it. On the Format toolbar, click the **Text Color** button and the **Color** dialog box appears. Click on a contrasting color for the image text, such as yellow, and then click **OK.**

5. On the **Format** menu, choose **Font**. The **Font** dialog box appears. In the **Font** field, choose **Times New Roma,** in the **Font Style** field, choose **Bold** and in the **Size** field, choose **4** (14 pt.), then click **OK** to apply the formatting changes.

To make the larger size text fit the text box, click and drag a corner size handle until your text is fully displayed. You can move the text box back to the center (or any part) of the image by clicking and dragging the word with the mouse button.

When you place formatted text over an image on the current page, FrontPage does not modify the original image. When you save the page, FrontPage stores a combination of the image and the image text in a separate, new image file.

Provided that you previously allowed FrontPage to save the original image to your FrontPage Web (by clicking **Yes** in the **Save Embedded Files** dialog box), you can revert to it at a later time

Where can I find royalty-free graphics?

The Internet offers hundreds of sites where royalty-free (and also those available for license) graphics, photos, and clip art are available for download. To avoid the possibility of copyright infringement, it is *very* important to make note of the permissions given at these sites. Some artists offer their graphics for free to the Internet community while others require a link back to their site or ask for other special provisions. Companies like Disney will sue like crazy to keep control over their properties.

How can I transfer my company logo and brochures to my Web site?

If you have brochures or copies of advertisements, someone produced those graphics for you and may still have a digital copy you can use. If applicable, contact your ad agency, printer, or your marketing department and ask for the digitized files of those items. If they are not accessible there are a number of other inexpensive options open to you.

- Consider buying an inexpensive scanner ($150–$300) or have your images scanned for you by a third party.
- Use a service such as <u>Seattle Film Works</u> who will convert your undeveloped film to digital images. `http://www.filmworks.com/`
- Contact local printers or graphics houses that can perform scans for you. Many now do this rather quickly and inexpensively.

Check the Net!

Hit the Net. Conduct an Internet search using the keywords scanning + services. A recent search uncovered the following companies offering scanning services starting as low as $.70 per scan.

<u>ActionScan</u> offers scans as inexpensive as $1.50 each for high resolution with a choice of formats—JPG, GIF, TIFF or BMP, size, and delivery options that include e-mail, FTP, or floppy disk. `http://www.actionscan.com/`

<u>Mystic Color Lab</u> will deliver your pictures on a 3-1/2" floppy disk or deliver to you over the Internet. `http://www.mysticcolorlab.com/`

<u>Wink Photo Services</u> started as an image provider to online services such as CompuServe and AOL in 1989. Wink Photo Services can scan your images for you, to any format you want from the basic "Raw Scan" all the way to "Full Image Restoration" quality.[1] `http://www.tiac.net/users/winkfoto/contents.htm`

Graphics resources online

<u>Andy's Art Attack</u> bills itself as a "One Stop Resource for Web Designers." This site contains thousands of original images that include gif89 animations, buttons, bullet points, and backgrounds. `http://www.andyart.com/`

<u>ImageOrama</u> offers over 3,000 freeware images of buttons, bars, and miscellaneous graphics that they have collected and give away freely. `http://members.aol.com/dcreelma/imagesite/image.htm`

<u>Psyched Up Graphics</u> touts itself as "the ultimate clip art collection on the Web!" `http://www.econ.cbs.dk/~gemal/psychedupgraphics/index.html`

<u>Sausage Software</u> permits you to use, alter, or reproduce its graphics. Use on your Web site is actively encouraged.[2] `http://www.sausage.com.au/clipart.htm`

<u>WebExplosion</u> is one of the largest collections of professional-quality Web graphics on a two CD set sold via retail. It includes neon, art deco, Southwest, and retro-style graphics, plus 3D and futuristic shapes. No image editing required. Available as a Windows and Macintosh; two CD-ROM set. `http://www.novadevcorp.com/Webexplosion/index.html`

---

[1] Source: Wink Photo and Scanning Services Web site. http://www.tiac.net/users/winkfoto/contents.htm

[2] eVend, Inc. (http://www.evend.com/evend_info.html) is a wholly owned subsidiary of Sausage Software Ltd. Sausage Software Ltd. is a publicly-traded corporation based in Melbourne, Australia. http://www.sausage.com/

CHAPTER 11

Open for Business

People don't necessarily want more things to buy; they want more convenient ways to buy things.

Before you flip the switch

Intellectual property and Internet law

There are some outstanding legal resources available on the Web. However, acquiring advice from the Internet on matters of law is not much better than getting legal *counsel* exclusively from Court TV. In all matters of law, common sense dictates that we speak to a practicing attorney. Heeding our own advice, we asked attorneys Bret A. Madole and Larry E. Jones to provide some guidance with respect to legal considerations involving the Internet.[1]

The chicken or the egg? The debate rages on.

The Internet or Internet law? An equally difficult issue.

As you take your business online, be aware that legal issues related to cyberspace are still developing. In some instances, the law definitely came first, but it must be stretched, twisted, and applied with a certain degree of legal creativity to this relatively new technology. In other instances, the Internet has created issues that could not have been contemplated until now, and new statutes and regulations have become necessary.

The result of all of this has been a certain amount of uncertainty. Courts and legislatures are beginning to settle many legal issues related to the Internet, but the law is still developing, and in many cases, the winner in a cyberspace legal dispute will be determined by innovative lawyering.

The purpose of this section is to summarize some of the legal concerns you may face doing business online. The list is not exhaustive and the discussion of the issues cannot be comprehensive. Further, this chapter is no substitute for professional legal advice. If you find yourself stuck somewhere between the cyber-chicken and the cyber-egg, consult an attorney.

Building your Web site development team

Make sure all the players are on your side.

Most of you reading this book will design your own Web site, watch it climb the various "Top 100" charts (such as Yahoo!, Infoseek, and so on), and amass thousands of "hits" daily. While others will likely turn to outside consultants to design and implement their Web sites. Whether your development team consists of your internal staff or an outside firm, there are a number of legal issues that could negatively affect your project without proper planning in the beginning.

Some sites will be complex and very intricate and, therefore, relatively expensive. Others will be elegantly simple and less costly. However, in both situations, if you are considering hiring a developer, you should consider several issues and enter into a written agreement to protect your interests. As in any business dealings, contracts are also important in cyberspace. Any Web site development agreement should address the following issues:

> **Scope.** How do you want your site to look? You need to let your developer know what you expect and make sure your agreement sets forth, in detail, the exact scope of work to be performed to meet your expectations. Consider asking that a prototype site be developed first so that you may approve the concept before the developer undertakes the detailed, in other words expensive, work.
>
> It does not matter whether you have retained your developer on a fixed, or flat, fee basis or whether you are paying an hourly fee. A developer working for a fixed fee will not react favorably to spending countless hours in redesigning a site because he did not have an understanding of what you expected. You will not enjoy paying the developer's hourly rate for him to redo something that you thought he understood the first time. Avoid disputes regarding the "look" and cost of developing your site through a concise "statement of work" in your agreement. This statement can be modified as the project develops.

Payment. Fixed fee, hourly, or something in-between, gets it in writing. Be clear on when the developer will be paid, either monthly or through progress payments when certain milestones are accomplished. Allow for the flexibility of increasing the payment to the developer if the statement of work expands.

Delivery and Acceptance. If you order a candy-apple red Buick from a car dealership, and a candy-apple red Buick of the appropriate model is delivered, you can be relatively sure that you got what you ordered. However, Web site design is complicated and technical, and what you see may not fully reflect what you get, or what you do not get. As a result, it is crucial that your agreement set forth a comprehensive testing procedure before the end result is accepted. Depending upon the degree of complexity of your site, it may be advisable to set up the testing and approval process in stages so that each portion of the work is approved before development continues.

Allow yourself enough time to thoroughly test the Web site's performance before you approve and accept the work. You should have ample time to test the Web site from a variety of combinations of software and hardware and determine how the site responds in normal day-to-day usage. Your agreement should set forth specific notice procedures and deadlines to inform the developer if the site does not perform as expected, as well as "cure" procedures and deadlines for the developer to correct the work. And, just in case you cannot agree, a good development agreement will include a process for dispute resolution of material disagreements.

Necessary Web site materials. Who will provide the content for the Web site, such as audio and video materials, or editorial matter? In many instances, it makes sense for the customer to do so. In all instances, it makes sense to spell out these requirements in the contract. Otherwise, deadlines may be missed, and the parties will waste valuable time casting blame on each other. Additionally, who provides project materials will affect the development cost.

Ownership of the Web site. The most important provision of any Web site development agreement relates to who owns the intellectual property created as a result of the relationship. Significant intellectual property is created in the development of a Web site—layout, graphics, custom scripts, and other programming— which you might be surprised to learn may not be yours unless those rights are conveyed to you in the contract.

Absent clear provisions in the agreement setting forth the respective intellectual property rights in a Web site, copyright law will determine the ownership issue. And, generally speaking, if you hire an independent contractor to develop a Web site, the developer owns most of the rights in the site. The customer owns a copy of the graphics and program, but cannot reproduce it, prepare derivative works, or use it to the detriment of the developer's exclusive rights under copyright law. If the customer is to obtain copyright ownership of the site, the developer must assign to the customer the copyright to the entire work, including graphics, programming and data.

You may think initially that you do not care who owns the copyright as long as you own one copy and can use the Web site in your business. However, think ahead. Web sites should be updated periodically to include fresh content or to incorporate new technological innovations. You must own the copyright, or have adequate licensing rights, to modify it. The same goes regarding creating derivative works of the site, such as conforming it to suit the purposes of another business you may own. And, perhaps most importantly, you do not want to see your site cloned for some other business, perhaps a competitor, which the developer may have the right to do in the absence of contractual provisions to the contrary.

The area of ownership is likely to be the prime area of negotiation in a Web site development agreement. Make sure your interests are adequately represented in the negotiation and reflected in the final agreement.

Copyright infringement

If your work is on the Net, it will be copied. Deal with it!

Original works of authorship are protected by law, specifically by the federal copyright act. The protection is in the form of exclusive rights granted to the copyright owner. These exclusive rights include (1) reproduction; (2) preparation of derivative works; (3) public distribution; (4) public performance; (5) public display, and (6) public performance via digital audio transmission.

Perhaps the foremost of these rights is the right of reproduction, that is, copying. As with the other exclusive rights, the right of reproduction belongs to the author or third parties who have taken an assignment of the right or have obtained a license for the work. The Internet has raised some interesting issues as to what constitutes a "copy" within the meaning of the copyright act and what constitutes copyright infringement. For instance:

- The random access memory (RAM) in a computer of an Internet user may copy a portion of copyrighted work. Is this a "copy?"
- An entire Web page could be cached on a mirror site. Is this a "copy?"
- A Web site could be "linked" to another site or "framed" by another Web site. Prohibited by the copyright act?
- And, of course, it is reasonable to anticipate that somebody accessing your Web site might deliberately download or print your copyrighted material. Plus, because the Web is literally worldwide, the copying may take place in China, the Netherlands, anywhere.

We do not want to put you to sleep with a legal analysis of what constitutes a copy within the meaning of the copyright act, as it applies to the Internet, and what legal defenses might exist for someone copying your work. The analysis is technical and, frankly, boring. Simply recognize that if you post material on the Internet, it is available worldwide, it will be copied, and you can easily loses control of it. Recognize these facts and, then, *protect yourself.*

Copyright notices have never been more important. Be specific as to what reproduction of your work you will allow and what is prohibited. Address linking and framing issues. Discuss with your attorney the prospects of infringement occurring in another country and the best way to deal with it. Consider so-called "Web-wrapped" licenses granting controlled use of your work under specific circumstances. Make your notices noticeable.

Trademarks on the Net

Marking your domain.

In the early 1900s, thousands of pioneers gathered their covered wagons in western Arkansas in preparation for the much-anticipated land rush. The most enterprising, and least honest, of these pioneers crossed over to Oklahoma just a little bit early to put their names on a piece of the vast prairie. The Internet experienced similar poaching when domain name registrations were first taken.

Trademark infringement on the Internet occurs in its most traditional sense, but has raised particularly interesting issues in the area of domain names. Many businesses initially did not realize the importance of having a domain name that included its well-known trademark. This oversight led to the "domain name rush" in which household names were snatched up by these cyber-Sooners. "Candyland.com" was not registered by Hasbro, Inc., maker of the popular children's game, but by the operator of a sexually explicit site. A former employee snatched "MTV.com" through registration and "plannedparenthood.com" was registered and operated by the Catholic Church. Hundreds of disputes over domain name selections have been reported.

The registration process has evolved and today provides more protection for trademark owners. Additionally, the federal Trademark Dilution Act now protects the dilution of "famous" trademarks used to describe dissimilar services or products, such as the "Candyland" example. In selecting and registering your domain name, consider the following:

Does the name you have selected infringe upon an existing trademark or dilute a "famous" mark as defined by the federal statute? A trademark search of federal and state registrations, commercial directories, and databases should provide the answer.

If your domain name does not infringe or dilute others, consider federal trademark registration to prevent its infringement or dilution.

Register your proposed domain name with the Internet Network Information Center (InterNIC). This can be accomplished by following the procedures specified in the Netcom Business Center. `http://www.netcomi.com/nbc/domain.html`

Consider trademark and domain name registration in other countries. Most countries do not recognize trademark rights unless the trademark has been registered in that country. Additionally, there are domain name registries outside the United States responsible for administering geographical domains.

As a last resort or worst case scenario, be prepared to defend your rights in court if necessary. New dispute resolution procedures protect trademark owners from "poachers." However, if you do not possess a valid United States or foreign registration, you must litigate your rights to the trademark in court before the registrar will prevent a registrant from registering and/or using a domain name. Additionally, if the proposed registrant owns the trademark in another class, your best result with the registrar may be that the domain name is put on "hold" until rights are determined in court. The formalities for a challenge are relatively complicated and subject to change. Be careful out there.

Monitor the use of your trademark or trade name online. You can check registered domain names by accessing InterNIC's "whosis" service at `http://rs.internic.net/cgi-bin/whosis`. A search will provide the name, address, and other information relating to the owner of a particular domain name.

Jurisdiction over online activities

Upstate New York is a nice place to visit, but would you really like to get sued there? One of the most vexatious areas of law as it relates to the Internet is that of jurisdiction. The key question is does the establishment of a presence on the Internet accessible from another jurisdiction constitute sufficient contacts with that jurisdiction to subject an individual or company to the long-arm jurisdiction of that forum? Translation: If you host your Web site in Texas that can be accessed from New York, can you be sued in New York?

The answer is not clear. The law is developing, primarily in the area of trademark infringement. The standard for the exercise of personal jurisdiction over a defendant in a foreign forum is whether the defendant has sufficient contacts with the forum and/or whether it has "purposefully availed" itself to the forum making the exercise of jurisdiction fair, just, or reasonable. Some courts seem to believe that the establishment of a Web site alone is enough. Decisions to date from these courts seem to follow the rationale that Web site owners realize that their messages will reach all states, and indeed chose to advertise on the Internet for this reason. If the Web site gives rise to a cause of action in another forum, these courts reason, then jurisdiction should be extended.

Other courts argue that a "passive" Web site should not automatically result in the exercise of jurisdiction. They want more. The inclusion on a Web site of 800-numbers or 900-numbers soliciting telephone calls has been found to weigh in favor of exercising jurisdiction, as has evidence that products actually were shipped to or downloaded in a particular forum. If information is exchanged over the Internet, such as via e-mail, the courts lean toward exercising jurisdiction.

Our best advice at this time is to realize the possibility that if you are on the Internet, especially if you conduct commerce online or otherwise "nonpassively" interact with Internet users, you could find yourself in a courtroom thousands of miles away. Stay tuned as this area of the law is defined.

Conducting sweepstakes and contests online

Make sure you aren't the big loser.

With so much competition for attention on the World Wide Web, sweepstakes and contests offer an attractive promotional technique for generating traffic to a site. A month-long contest, for example, can keep visitors coming back day after day for further exposure to your products or those of your advertisers. However, operating a contest or sweepstakes online also can create one of the biggest legal nightmares in cyberspace.

Start with the fact that all cyberlaw is somewhat uncertain, and then add the variable that any contest or sweepstakes could be rendered illegal under the law of the federal government, any of the 50 states, or a foreign government, and you can understand that sweepstakes and contests can be tricky. However, if carefully designed, they are legal and can be a lucrative promotional gimmick.

Generally speaking, a sweepstakes is a game of chance in which the winner of a prize is determined entirely by chance. A contest is a game of skill in which the winner is determined on the basis of that skill, and the outcome is not in any way affected by chance. A sweepstakes is universally deemed illegal if the participant is required to provide consideration (a legal term meaning anything of value) in exchange for playing. A contest is usually deemed illegal if an element of chance controls the outcome. In either of these situations, the sweepstakes or contest could be considered a lottery, something that is illegal in all 50 states unless operated by the state.

If consideration is required by the entrant to enter a sweepstakes, the penalties and fines could be significant. If you charge a fee to enter the sweepstakes, or charge an access fee for the sweepstakes site, you are obviously requiring consideration. However, consideration is defined as "anything of value." Could the fee charged by an Internet Access Provider qualify as consideration? The answer is a murky maybe. As a result, allow alternate entry methods, such as a toll-free telephone number or mail, to avoid this result and make sure that telephone and mail entrants have an equal chance of winning.

What if the sweepstakes requires you to spend significant time navigating a Web site or asks you to complete a lengthy survey in order to enter?

Another murky area, but a high degree of effort in entering could be construed as consideration.

Most states allow an entry fee in contests, although several specifically prohibit it. However, fee or not, in a contest in which a prize is awarded, the outcome must be determined solely on the basis of skill or the contest or it will be considered an illegal lottery. Additionally, the skill must be a bona fide skill, as determined by the regulators, and the contest must be judged using objective standards known by all participants. The definition of "bona fide skill" and the specificity of the standards likely will vary jurisdiction to jurisdiction. After you have addressed the consideration issue for sweepstakes and skill requirement for contests, it is time to formulate the rules. Consider the following issues:

- Involve a "techie" in the development of the rules and the implementation of the contest. Make sure the rules are on a separate Web page which entrants are required to access before reaching the game area. Discuss with the technician how to limit the number of computer entries by an individual to avoid the situation where an Internet user enters hundreds of times at a lower cost than entrants using the mail and thereby creating an unfair and potentially illegal advantage. Have the technician design the contest so those individuals using a faster modem do not have an undue advantage. Make sure the game is secure from would-be hackers.

- Do not forget the basics. The rules should include the popular "no purchase necessary" disclaimer and specifically describe the prizes, the number and value of the prizes, and the odds of winning. Some states require these details. Be clear about the deadline for entries. Disclose alternate methods of entry.

- Remember that a game on the Web can be accessed worldwide. Review your promotion in light of the requirements of all 50 states and if it does not pass muster in a state, or if it is not feasible to offer the contest in a particular state, void it there. Then, consider foreign jurisdictions. If you do not intend to accept entries from outside the United States, disclose this fact.

- Protect yourself from techno-glitches. Disclaim liability for failures in hardware, software, transmission lines, servers, or from corrupted data transmitted by entrants. Reserve the right to cancel the promotion if the game is corrupted by a hacker or infected by a virus.

Framing, linking, and META lines

The dirty tricks of the World Wide Web.

Technology is a wonderful thing. And one of the wonders is that it may be used to create a distinct competitive advantage. These uses may skirt, most say violate, emerging Internet law.

You will find a more comprehensive description in other sections of this book, but we need to start with a few working definitions. "Links," more accurately called hyperlinks, allow browsers to jump from one site to another. Links make the Web "Web-like." "Framing" is sort of a cyber "picture-in-picture." It allows the initial site to remain as a frame of a linked site. The monitor will display the border of the initial site, the URL of the initial site, but the content of the "framed" site. "META lines," or META tags, are embedded in the HTML code used to create Web sites. These are invisible to viewers of the Web page, but contain information such as keywords used by search engines to catalog and retrieve Web pages.

Most Web site owners encourage linking. Links are often reciprocal in nature and can benefit both sites by channeling surfers between Web sites offering services or information complimentary to the linked location. However, disputes involving linking have occurred. In the most famous case to date, heavyweights Microsoft and Ticketmaster have squared off in a California court. The case was still pending at the time this material was written, but could have a significant effect on linking, which is the lifeblood of the Web.

Here's what happened: Microsoft operates a Web site offering information regarding regional entertainment. The site lists a variety of leisure-time events. Ticketmaster operates a site with information on nationwide sporting events and concerts and allows Internet users to purchase tickets on line. Both sites contain advertising. The controversy arose when Microsoft, without Ticketmaster's permission, created a link from its site, called "Seattle Sidewalk," to Ticketmaster's site.

Ticketmaster claims that the link dilutes the commercial value of its own site to advertisers. Ticketmaster also believes that the link increases the advertising opportunities for Microsoft's site without any compensation to Ticketmaster. Perhaps the biggest complaint, however, is that Microsoft's link is deep into Ticketmaster's site, directly to the point-of-purchase page. This bypasses messages from Ticketmaster and its advertisers.

The framing controversy first grabbed attention when a relatively small company called Total News framed the content of several worldwide news organizations on its Web site. When the news sites were framed by Total News, the advertising of the framed site was bypassed or distorted. Web users could not "bookmark" the framed site because Total News' URL was the only one displayed. Through framing, Total News was able to offer a "megasite" with world-class news content without spending a dime to gather it. A number of the framed news organizations sued, stating that Total News "engaged in the Internet equivalent of pirating copyrighted materials from a variety of famous newspapers, magazines, or television news programs; packaging those stories to advertisers as part of a competitive publication or program...; and pocketing the advertising revenue generated by their unauthorized use of that material." The case has been settled. Total News will continue to provide links but will do so without framing the linked sites.

META tags also have been used to appropriate the goodwill created by other—often times larger—competitors. A hypothetical: ABC Tractor Company, a new manufacturer and supplier of tractors in the United States, creates a Web site. Within the META line, which is not displayed on its site, ABC inserts the words—and registered trademark—"John Deere." Someone looking for information about John Deere online would type "John Deere" into one or more search engines commonly available and as the search engine crawls through the META lines, the ABC site would be included in the search results. Courts have found little difficulty in determining this to be trademark infringement even though ABC, in our hypothetical example, never used "John Deere" in the visible contents of its Web page.

Linking, framing, and misuse of META tags are stretching and reshaping the law as it applies to the Internet. A fervent debate abounds as to whether linking and framing violates the Copyright Act. Innovative lawyers are attempting to convince the courts that these cyber-age dirty tricks violate laws prohibiting unfair competition and misappropriation which were written decades before the Internet was contemplated. As with all areas of Internet law, the answers will become clearer in the future.

Related online reference sites

Cornell Law School's Legal Information Institute offers a no-nonsense Web site with a collection of recent and historic Supreme Court decisions. It also has hypertext versions of the full U.S. Code, U.S. Constitution, Federal Rules of Evidence and Civil Procedure, and other important legal materials.[2] http://www.law.cornell.edu

CCC Online Copyright Clearance Center (CCC) is a not-for-profit organization created at the suggestion of Congress to help organizations like yours comply with U.S. copyright law. http://www.copyright.com/

Legal Documents Online USA Law Publications, Inc. offers a Web site that lets you prepare legal documents online and instantly obtain a completed will, estate plan, contract, or other document "on-the-fly." http://legaldocs.com/.[3]

Creating your online store

Why would you want to? Let's explore that first.

The are many software applications that will help you create an online store that incorporates order processing. For the sake of a through overview, online store is also synonymous with storefront, virtual showroom, online catalog, and so on.

Some of the commercial software programs available are quite complex and may require that you hire a technically savvy employee or outside consultant to implement and maintain your site. At the other end of the spectrum are programs that are fairly simple, intuitive, and easy to use. To determine what is most appropriate to satisfy your requirements, you will want to consider the following characteristics of a good program:

- Catalog creation and management tools
- Secure shopping basket
- Real-time credit card authorization
- A site search engine
- Detailed sales and traffic statistics
- Features that make handling larger product databases easier and more efficient
- Scalability

Remember, when planning the look of your online store, consult Chapter 8, "Creating Your Web Site." Keep in mind the general rules for creating professional looking Web pages. When organizing your site's pages, use frames and links. Since fast loading pages are important, keep your <u>animations</u> and <u>applets</u> to a minimum. Also, consider your target market as you design your online store. Know who your customers are, what they demand, and then deliver.

There are companies that provide this service for someone who doesn't want to make this kind of investment.

What is a shopping basket?

Electronically speaking, a shopping basket or cart is a virtual tracking system that emulates a real world shopping experience. Shopping baskets allow customers to select items with the click of the mouse while they maintain an inventory of selected quantity and price. The selected items are virtually stored in the shopping basket until the customer is ready to check out. At checkout time, the quantity and price totals are tallied.

Most shopping baskets have customizable payment, shipping, tax, and handling options. Customers should be able to view their shopping baskets at any time, as well as add and remove items before final checkout. Most catalog/storefront applications have a shopping basket feature built into the software. However, be advised that the amount of difficulty in setting up these options will vary.

Providing Internet business solutions and hosting the domains of small and medium sized companies is Netcom's *primary* business. Their advertising slogan exemplifies their corporate mission…

"Putting the Net to Work for You"

Netcom

The Netcom staff evaluates most of the commercial tools that appear on the market and selects only those that will best support their customers' needs. For a complete store building and transaction processing solution Netcom selected **Open Market, Inc.** Some of the information in the following section is from Open Market's online help and information section at URL: http://www.shopsite.com/help/.

All of the features mentioned above and more are found in **Open Market's ShopSite** product available through the Netcom Business Center. http://www.netcomi.com/

ShopSite Manager is an easy-to-use Internet e-commerce package. Its intuitive design allows a merchant to easily build and maintain an e-commerce Web site. Even Internet users with very little experience will find this program easy to navigate.

ShopSite Manager resides on an Internet server but can be accessed through a standard Web browser from any personal computer. ShopSite calls this browser-based interface the "back office." The back office is the virtual location where merchants build their e-commerce sites, update or make changes, and check on their online orders and Web site statistics.

What do I need to know about taking credit card payments online?

In order to do real-time credit card authorization and delayed settlement processing, there are a couple of things you must first have in place. To process Internet transactions, the following events need to happen in sequence. (If you already have a merchant account you can skip over this information.)

- Obtain an Internet merchant bank account. A merchant bank is a banking company that handles corporate (merchant) transactions. The merchant bank enables a business to receive and clear credit card transactions online. Merchant banks actually transfer money from the buyer's account to the seller's account from an online store.

- Choose an Internet Transaction Gateway Service Company (ITGSC) that will link your Internet store to a respected processing network (*not the credit card company itself*). The ITGSC provides a software interface that will communicate with the credit card clearinghouse (processing network). The processing network is a financial center used for financial transactions between banks or other financial institutions. It compares and clears accounts based on the value of differences between collections of the transactions.

Segue Systems is an ITGSC incorporated into Open Market's ShopSite Manager and ShopSite Pro, who use First Data Corporation's FDC network for processing. They do this through their SocketLink Internet Transaction Gateway. The tricky part is that you actually have to perform these two steps together. Your bank will want to know which Internet clearing service you intend to use and most merchant bank applications require you to indicate which gateway software you will be using. http://www.seguesystems.com/

In short, be prepared to contract with two separate companies, the Merchant Bank Provider and the Internet Transaction Gateway Service Company. Therefore, you will pay two separate set-up charges and two different monthly service fees if you intend to maintain your own merchant bank account and offer real-time credit card authorization over the Net.

How do I obtain a merchant account?

In order to authorize and process credit card transactions over the Internet, most processing services require that you have a merchant account and a merchant account ID number. Be aware that your bank may not yet be capable of supporting Internet businesses. A few Internet-friendly banks include:

BankOne	http://www.bankone.com/
First Bank of Beverly Hills	(800) 515-1616 fbbh@wfsg.com
Wells Fargo	http://wellsfargo.com/home/

All these banks use the First Data Corporation network for credit card transaction processing. The FDC network accounts for 80% of all credit card transactions and is the largest credit card clearing house. The Internet Transaction Service that Open Market has integrated into ShopSite's e-commerce products uses the FDC network as its primary network. http://www.firstdatacorp.com/

By choosing a merchant bank that is not on the FDC network, you may end up paying a higher set-up fee. You may also experience a slower response time because the service may be using a modem connection instead of a leased line connection to the financial network.

If you own or operate a new business and have not applied for a merchant bank account then be advised that the application process can be lengthy while the approval process can be slow. Should you decide to investigate this procedure on your own, the following banks process credit cards through the FDC network:

Bank of Hawaii	Chase Manhattan	PNC Bank
BankBoston	First Bank of Beverly Hills	Wachovia
BankOne	Huntington Bank	Wells Fargo
Barnett Banks	NationsBank	US Bancorp
Boatman's Bancshares		

Segue Systems will help you with the merchant account application process. Usually you will need to send the merchant bank detailed information about your business, how long you have been in operation, the type of business, references, and so on. Your personal credit history is the single most influential element reviewed during the application process for a merchant bank account. Therefore, your personal credit history may determine the initial rates you are offered.

If you cannot or do not want to obtain a merchant bank account of your own, there are many services available that will function in place of a merchant bank account. A few will function as both the online ITGSC and the merchant bank account, such Segue Systems. Whatever route you decide to take, evaluate more than one of these services comparing set-up and transaction fees and the support services you will receive from each.

What if I already have an existing bank relationship?

If you already have a merchant bank account, check with your bank provider to verify that your current account will accept Internet or "non–face-to-face" transactions. Make sure to request the approval details in writing. Some banks may charge a premium charge-back if they discover by accident that you are processing your Internet charges through your "face-to-face" account.

If you already have a typical terminal connection merchant account used to process face-to-face transactions, and decide to have it "Internet-enabled," your ITGSC or merchant bank provider can help you get your account type changed. However, in many cases, once the account type is changed to an Internet-type account, it will no longer support a "terminal" connection.

What should I expect from a merchant bank provider?

Merchant bank providers have different service and fee structures. Check to see if they offer the following and what they charge for these services.

- What type of automatic tracking and reporting system do they offer so you can review a complete daily history of all sales, credits, charge-backs, and discount charges from the previous day's activity? Do they issue daily and monthly reports?
- What are the application fees and when will you be charged? Application fees can range from $100 to several hundred dollars. Some merchant bank providers will not charge the application fee unless you are approved.
- Are there additional hidden fees, such as monthly statement fees, batch header fees, and so on?
- How soon after a credit card is processed will the funds be available to you? Two or three days, or longer?
- What are the bank's competitive and "true" discount rates? The discount rate is the amount of money the bank retains for itself from each order that you submit for processing. For example, if the order total is $20.50, and your discount rate is 2.4%, then the bank retains $.49 of that order and credits the remaining $20.01 to your account.
- What are the bank's competitive reserve rates? Reserve rates range from 5% to 10% of daily sales for merchants processing sales in excess of $25,000 per month.

A reserve is the money set aside by the bank to cover charge-backs or a bankruptcy situation should one occur. Merchants processing sales less than $25,000 per month are covered under the Small Dollar Merchant Program, and are generally not required to maintain a reserve account. The total reserve required for the bank is a function of the merchant's monthly sales volume and the risk analysis process.

- Ask your merchant bank account provider if it charges a premium to process a transaction. Some banks charge a per transaction premium (ranging from 10 cents or more) for certain Internet transaction service companies.

What is a transaction?

The request for credit card authorization is recognized as a transaction by most clearing services. The submission of the order for settlement after you have shipped your goods is recognized as another transaction. Therefore, a typical order will count as two transactions to the processing service. When evaluating credit card clearing services, make sure you ask how the service calculates transactions.

What should I expect from a credit card processing service provider?

Just as merchant bank providers have different services and fee structures, so do Internet Credit Card Processing Services (ITGSC).

- Subscriber Setup Fee for the FDC network can vary with the credit card (CC) processing service, but you can expect to pay around $200.
- Ask if your credit card processing service charges a flat monthly fee, an annual fee, or a per transaction fee. Also ask if it charges excess usage fees or additional per transaction fees if you exceed your standard plan transaction allowance.
- Is there a fee to upgrade your payment plan?
- How long after the transaction has been specified for settlement does it actually occur?
- Does the gateway service allow you to immediately authorize credit card transactions, submit for delayed settlement transaction, or immediately settle transactions?
- How can you view your transaction reports (password protected area)? How often are reports updated and what reports are included? Ask specifically about reports for sales, credits, authorizations, denials, and so on.

Are there other online payment options that I should consider?

Yes, there are alternative methods of receiving online payments and new ideas continue to be introduced. Secure payment can be offered using resources that are already available. A few alternative options are outlined below, but remember that things change quickly on the Internet. Investigate your options thoroughly before you decide.

Online checking account drafts

It is estimated that more than 60 million Americans have checking accounts but do not have or use credit cards. Considering that millions more people have little or no credit available, offering check drafts seems like a winning idea. Similar to how credit cards are handled online, checking account drafts can be instituted over the Net almost as easily as a merchant accepts a check in the real world. There are a number of third-party companies providing this type of service and their terms and operating procedures are competitive with each other.

How it works. The companies provide you with basic HTML code that you insert into your Web pages. The code (usually) produces a **Click here** button. When clicked, an online check appears on the screen. The customer then completes the check using his checking account information. Because authorization for the draft is obtained from the customer, a signature is not required.

The information is then transmitted to the processing company who collects the checking account information and prints a special check draft offline. These check drafts are sent to you via an overnight delivery service or regular U.S. mail. Once received, the check can be treated like any other check. There is a per check processing fee that ranges from $1.00 to $2.00 depending upon the selected level of service, shipping method, and so on. Typically, there should be no other hidden costs.

The following links provide additional information about online checking account drafts:

CheckPro	http://checkpro.com/
Draft Creator	http://www.redbay.com/org/draft/
Redi-Check	http://www.redi-check.com/
TurboCheck	http://www.turbocheck.com/

Virtual cash

No, "virtual cash" is not money that *used* to reside in your wallet. This is a catch-all phrase for third-party payment organizations that act as both the ITGSC and the Merchant Bank on your behalf. These organizations function as agents between you and your customer. Like other ITGSCs, the method they use for transmitting a customer's sensitive financial data is typically based on the encrypted RSA security system. Some have procedures for approving credit card purchases without sending any of the customer's information over the Internet.

The Drew Bledsoe Foundation utilizes this type of fulfillment service to receive orders, verify credit card information, and ship its series, "Parenting With Dignity." http://www.drewbledsoe.com/

A third-party fulfillment service is an ideal solution for businesses that are selling a limited quantity of items such as books, videos, reports, and other items that can be easily inventoried. Typically, orders are received, payments are processed, and products are shipped immediately. This process does not require a merchant account or any involvement from the selling party (you). In this case, the fulfillment house sends the business a statement of activity and a check for proceeds collected on a regular basis.

CyberCash, which requires a Merchant ID, is a digital cash vendor where customers may store their credit card information in a "digital wallet" on their individual computer system. When the customer wishes to make a purchase, the system sends packets of information in encrypted form to the clearinghouse. The order information is "stripped" off as it passes through the merchant's site. Open Market's ShopSite software can help you take advantage of CyberCash with no extra programming. We recommend that you visit the CyberCash Web site and study the benefits of incorporating their functionality in your Web site. http://www.cybercash.com

Digital money has some advantages over online credit card transactions. The digital money method is easy to use, provides service quickly and securely, and (compared to a pure credit card system) is relatively inexpensive to implement. In addition, there is a perception that by using a third party, security concerns are minimized. Although the speed and convenience of this method may favor your customers, it may take up to 90 days before you receive payment from some of these services. If that is going to be the case, you may as well have your customers fax or mail in their orders.

First Virtual—http://www.firstvirtual.com/

The First Virtual solution enables merchants that do not wish to apply for a merchant bank account (or cannot qualify) to offer a credit card based payment option to shoppers that have purchased an First Virtual **PIN**. The First Virtual system is integrated into both **ShopSite Manager** and **ShopSite Pro** and is also a component of the commerce hosting packages available through the Netcom Business Center.

What is a PIN-based online credit card clearing?

A Personal Identification Number (PIN)–based payment system is a secure and easy-to-use payment method that facilitates commercial transactions over the Internet between merchants and consumers. First Virtual Holdings developed and operates the First Virtual Internet Payment System ("FVIPS"). This system seamlessly integrates existing e-mail technologies and a Personal Identification Number with established financial networks by using well-accepted transaction processing practices.

To buy online, the shopper *must* purchase a VirtualPIN from First Virtual, which can then be used on any First Virtual–enabled merchant Web site. The shopper's credit card number is stored offline on secure computers not connected to the Internet. When the shopper makes a purchase on the Internet using the VirtualPIN, the shopper is sent an e-mail message from First Virtual asking for purchase confirmation. The shopper's credit card will not be charged until the shopper responds "yes" to the e-mail.

To get a VirtualPIN from First Virtual, the shopper must have a valid VISA or Master-Card, an e-mail account, and complete an application at the First Virtual Web site. A shopper's PIN currently costs $5 per year, but is expected to increase to $10 per year.

To become a qualified First Virtual merchant, you must register your shopping site with First Virtual at `http://www.fv.com/developer/become_a_VIP`. It will take about 15 days after qualification before you can begin using First Virtual as a payment system. FV offers two different classes of service to merchants:

The Pioneer Seller Program

- Does not require a merchant to get a merchant bank account
- Costs $10 per year (expected to increase to $50 per year)
- Transaction fees of $.29 per transaction, plus 2% of each transaction total
- Money held by First Virtual for 91 days, to cover the charge-back period

Express Seller Program

- Merchants must have an active merchant bank account
- $350 for the first year; $250 per year thereafter
- Transaction fees of $.29 per transaction, plus 2% of each transaction total, plus $1.00 fee for each deposit made into the merchant bank account
- Money transferred to your account within 3 to 5 working days after closing

Summary for taking credit cards over the Internet

In order to take credit card payments online, you need to have a merchant ID, a bank account, and be established with a credit card processing network. In order to process credit cards over the Internet, you also need to have software that can communicate the information to the credit card processing network.

Steps:

- Establish a company bank account
- Obtain a Merchant Account and obtain an ID number
- Select software transaction tool, register, and pay license (if required)
- Install and configure transaction software for your store

For merchants who desire a one-stop-shop approach, The Netcom Business Center provides a turn-key commerce solution for hosting on a secure server. Included with a variety of NBC offerings and features is Open Market's storefront/shopping cart software applications and transaction processing capabilities.

Open Market and **Netcom** offer three ways to link to a credit card clearing service with your domain. *(The following is included in the Commerce level hosting packages available through the NBC.)*

1. First Virtual is offered in ShopSite Manager and ShopSite Pro. Since First Virtual does not require a merchant to have a merchant bank account to accept credit card payments, the set-up fee for FV's entry level plan is nominal.

2. Online Analysis is offered with both ShopSite Manager and ShopSite Pro. To use ONA, the merchant must have a merchant bank account.

For those who want to link to a credit card clearing service of their choice, Open Market offers a real-time CGI interface to the orders database in ShopSite Pro. This choice will require that a programmer write a custom CGI that grabs the order information from the ShopSite CGI in real-time. The information is then delivered to the selected online credit card processing service.

One final thought

If the prospect of developing and managing an online store seems a bit overwhelming to you explore other options. Consider developing a "referral program" whereby you could derive income from traffic your Web site generates to another retailer (on- or offline).

---

[1] Bret A. Madole and Larry E. Jones. Mr. Madole is a shareholder and Mr. Jones is an associate with David, Goodman & Madole, P.C., a Dallas, Texas, law firm with a significant intellectual property and cyberspace practice. Contact David, Goodman & Madole at http://www.david-goodman.com.

[2] The Legal Information Institute, a research activity of the Cornell Law School (taken from their Web site http://www.law.cornell.edu/admit/admit.htm)

[3] Descriptive text obtained from Web page (3/12/97). Legaldocs, Legaldocs.com, and USA Law are trademarks of USA Law Publications, Inc. http://www.legaldocs.com/

12

The Key to Success

Publishing your company on the Web is the easy part. Getting discovered on the Web requires serious effort!

- Lori Heatherington

Positioning your domain on the Web

How will customers find my Web site?

Technology, expanding economics around the world, and the globalization of direct marketing techniques are revolutionizing your market potential. Direct marketing takes many forms—among them direct mail, telemarketing, infomercials, catalogs, home shopping TV channels, and Internet promotions.[1]

Do you remember the movie, "The Jerk," starring Steve Martin?[2] In one scene, Steve got excited because the "phone book" finally listed his name and he began shouting, *"I am somebody . . . I'm in the phonebook!"*

Now that you are somebody and have your own domain it is time to tell *everybody* about it. Like Steve, just because you're "in the book" (on the Internet) means nothing unless the world knows you're there.

If a domain marketing campaign is implemented properly, the Internet becomes a somewhat level battleground for businesses regardless of their size. Potential customers can locate your Web site as easily as Netcom's or Microsoft's *if they can find you*. Therein lies the challenge; how will they find you? The dilemma many businesses face today is that all of the obvious or descriptive domain names are mostly taken.

Let's assume that you own a business called McDonald's Welding Supply. Unfortunately, those people with the "Golden Arches" already registered **mcdonalds.com** and for the purpose of our example, we will assume that **mcdonalds-welding.com** is also taken. You decide to register your company initials, **mws-welding.com**[3] as your domain. Now, how will you get people to visit your site and inquire about brazing rods?

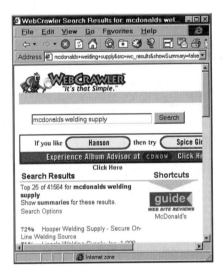

An actual WebCrawler query resulted in locating the Kingsville Chamber of Commerce Buyers Guide listing a McDonald's Restaurant and a local welding supply company, but McDonald's Welding Supply was not to be found.

To be successful on the Internet, you must use a combination of conventional and guerrilla marketing and advertising techniques. Designing your Web site properly and making use of all that you learned about using titles, <u>META tags</u>, and other programming tips and tricks is a critical step in marketing your domain effectively. Your <u>URL</u> and e-mail address should be prominently displayed on every piece of promotional material your business distributes. Your brochures, letterhead, flyers, business cards, billboards, advertisements, radio and TV commercials, and company vehicles should all promote your Web site.

Your Web site speaks volumes for your company. It implies that your company is a progressive firm in sync with new technology. It also says that your company is a leader in your field. Publish your URL everywhere you would include your company phone and fax numbers. It also lifts the veil off your company, so you can truly speak one-on-one with a customer.

Registering your domain with search engines and directories

Proper promotion of your Web site on the Internet is a whole new ballgame and is the single greatest factor determining a Web site's success on the Web. There are a number of things that must be done to ensure that a potential customer can locate your Web site. The first action should be to submit your URL to as many search engines and directory listings as possible. Search engines are the Internet's answer to the "Yellow Pages." There are a number of ways to do this, but nothing beats pure old hard work and perseverance.

One of your first stops on your self-promotion tour of the Internet should be to Submit It, a service that will submit your URL and a brief description of your business to 20 search engines and directories on the Net.[4] This will ensure that the major search engines will visit your site, index your pages and log them in their databases for future queries. It can take weeks for a search engine's spider to visit your site so don't expect to be receiving inquiries immediately. The remaining steps you should take are not necessarily prioritized. `http://www.submit-it.com/default.shtml`

Another good submission site is `did-it.com`, which will submit your site to the top 10 Search Engines and Directories and check the status of your listing every month with their "Detective" service. According to their Web page, if your site comes back not listed, did-it.com will automatically resubmit your site and e-mail you with the latest results of the search along with the previous month's search.

The automatic submission process won't do it all. We would highly recommend that you also register your site manually in specific areas of interest that are directly related to your site or products. As an example, if you sell telescopes, a quick run through sites that offer astronomy information might prove beneficial.

Strategic search engine positioning

What's the difference between a search engine and a directory listing?

The primary difference is that a directory will not list your URL if you do not register it with them. They do not employ indexing software (robots and spiders) and have no way of knowing that your site exists. Directories are usually subdivided into categories, and you must submit your Web site under the appropriate category.

How can I improve the standing of my Web site with all search engines?

It is virtually impossible to have one particular URL score high with *all* of the search engines. The way in which these engines collect, catalog and disseminate information is different from one another and plays a part in relevance rankings. What may increase your position in engine "A" will get you banned from engine "B."

Search engines also change their algorithms frequently, which has a bearing on how relevancy is assessed as a result of a query. In addition, thousands of new Web sites are being added daily which can influence your position and force your site further down the list. You may enjoy a good position today and a less than favorable position when a new rating system goes into effect tomorrow.

The only practical way to address this problem is to continue to query search engines using your keywords and see which sites list most favorably. Then visit those sites, view their source code, and try to determine what they are doing different from you. Imitation is the sincerest form of flattery, but getting convicted for expropriation can ruin your whole day.

If you really want to be seen, get to know the major search engines, what makes them tick, and try several listings until you find the best result.

How long before my site begins to show up in search engines?

Due to the sheer volume of new site submissions, it can take as long as six to eight weeks before your site appears. In most cases, when the search engine determines that it is your turn to be reviewed, a spider is sent to visit your site to ensure that it is a valid submission.

The spider will check your META tags, description, and title for keywords and review the text on your pages and also the other sites to which your pages are linked. This is one way in which the search engine determines your Web site's relevance for future keyword searches.

Will I be notified when my site has been listed with a search engine?

Search engines handle their listing confirmations differently. Some will send you a notification via an "autoresponder" following the tender of your application. Some provide no notice whatsoever while others will post your listing instantaneously. It can take days or you may have to wait for weeks before your site is actually listed. This is one of those instances where good old-fashioned hard work and perseverance will eventually pay off if you exercise a little patience.

What assurances do I have that my site will be accepted by major search engines? Can they refuse to list my site?

No one can *guarantee* that every search engine will list your site. This decision ultimately falls to the discretion of the search engine. The key is to ensure that your Web site has been submitted properly by following the recommendations outlined in this book.

Keep in mind that search engines and directory listing services are in business to catalog sites such as yours. They want to list your site. With the possible exception of illegal or pornographic content, rejections are usually a result of errors when submitting a site.

What is a META (search) engine?

META search engines are searching programs that comb the databases of other engines to generate search results. Confidence ratings are based on details collected from the other engines in the way they list a Web site's "relevancy." One example of a META search engine is `metacrawler.com`.

What about search engines that do *not* utilize META tags?

To improve your odds with search engines that do not use META tags, other than the title tag, requires that you incorporate your keywords and phrases in the text on your page. This is the primary reason you do not want to let a graphic image alone do the talking for you. A picture may be worth a thousand words, but without text, your page may be overlooked.

Hide your text to get discovered!

Okay, you must use text keywords so that your pages turn up as a result of a search. However, if displaying the text is detrimental to your page's appearance, you can hide the text and still satisfy these finicky search engines. As a bonus, you can increase your keyword repetition and not to be accused of SPAMming the engine and face possible elimination.

You can satisfy these provisions by employing a work-around strategy that will permit you to have more repetitions of your key words than would typically be aesthetically desirable on a page. There are some considerations in using this approach.

You must use a solid color (not a graphic) for your page background and your page will appear to have empty space at the bottom. There is still a risk that some search engine may remove you from its list, but if you follow our recommendation of keeping your keyword repetition to a minimum this should not happen.

To insert unseen text at the bottom of your page, change your text color to match your background color (for example, white on white). Next, change your font size to the smallest setting and insert your keywords above the ending </BODY> tag.

191

Hide your hyperlinks and get discovered!

Although there are *rumored* exceptions to this axiom, the more links you have on your page to other topic related pages, the better your chances of returning a favorable search score. Spiders will visit pages to which you are linked and factor the overall relevancy of your page to a particular keyword(s) or phrase.

The greater the number of links to other pages utilizing your keyword(s) or phrase(s), the more relevancy you will receive for a particular search. This is one explanation why some pages score higher on words or phrases that are not found in their page code and why you may wish to incorporate phantom pages in your marketing strategy.

What are phantom Web pages?

Phantom pages are designed entirely to receive higher scores in search engine results and will not usually be seen by a casual Web visitor. In the event a visitor does stumble upon a phantom page, the only visible object ideally will be a link to your primary page. The intent is to have other keyword specific pages linking back to your primary page. Theoretically, the more phantom pages to which you have links, the better your chances will be of receiving high relevancy scores from some search engines.

Producing a phantom page is easy. Create a new page and add hyperlinks that point back to your primary page or other pages in your site that have been seeded with your keywords. You can disguise your links by embedding them as graphics links or hide them at the bottom of your newly created page.

All of your phantom pages and your primary page should be linked to each other using these unobtrusive links. Your keyword text should be hidden on each page as explained above. If you create *five* phantom pages, each page should contain *four* links as it is needless to link a page to itself.

Hiding links is part of a strategy; omitting links can be disastrous.

In many instances, Web pages with the most relevant information are those inside pages buried within the site, as opposed to the default home page. If your default page does not link to any inside pages, some search engines may not fully catalog a site. If, because of design reasons or site layout, your default page (default.htm or index.htm) does not link to the interior of your site, you may want to try directing search engines to the lower levels via numerous manual submissions. If nothing else, consider hiding links as explained above.

Ready, set, submit!

Now that you have created a Web site, tweaked your pages with descriptive text, optimized your titles, keywords, and META tags, it is time to submit your site to search engines. As we mentioned, this can be done manually or you can use one of the automated submission services.

Be mindful that the greatest activity for searching takes place with the top five or six search engines, so make special effort to get your site placed properly. If you choose to do it yourself, we have included some guidelines and helpful tips.

Things *not* to do when submitting your site to a search engine

- Do *not* submit your Web site to search engines before it is ready as this could cause your listing to be rejected.

- Do *not* attempt to list your site in inappropriate categories.

- Do *not* use common words such as "site" or "Web site," "Web" or "Internet" in your listing description. These words will figure toward your maximum word count and some search engines automatically filter out these words.

- Avoid "clever," little-known, or fabricated words or phrases as no one will search for them. For example, a prospect will conduct a search for "hard drives," not your proprietary *"SuperSpin-Swiftly"* model designation.

While some search engines require that you submit only a URL, others will require that you submit specific information, such as keywords, a description of your site, your name, and e-mail address. Rather than typing this data repetitively, it is a good idea to have Notepad (or Microsoft Word) open and have this information typed in a file so that you can <u>cut and paste</u> the appropriate data when required.

Once again, be advised that for your site to be discovered by your target audience via a keyword search, you *must* choose those keywords very carefully. If an automotive speed shop advertised its site as having "Horses to Burn," the only traffic they would receive would be from confused animal rights sympathizers.

Compose your text submission statement *thoughtfully*.

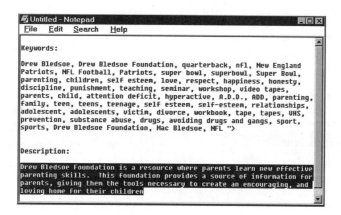

Listing your site with the major search engines

The major Internet search engines and links to their URL submission pages are listed here *in no particular order of importance*. This will be a handy reference when you begin to submit your Web site.

AltaVista

URL: http://www.altavista.digital.com/

Submission Page: http://www.altavista.digital.com/av/content/addurl.htm

Submission Requirements:

AltaVista requires only your URL.

Submission Highlights:

- Submit only one URL per Web site since the AltaVista spider will follow all links found on your Web site.
- URLs are case-sensitive so make sure to check your spelling as you submit your site.

Submission Tips:

- AltaVista limits the index of your description and keyword META tags to 1,024 characters.
- Do not use excessive word repetition, excessive keywords, or keywords that do not relate to your Web site document's content, otherwise you jeopardize your inclusion in the index.
- AltaVista's main page provides a "Add a Page" hyperlink for easy reference.

Tips to Improve Relevance Ranking:

- Make sure that your Web site text accurately describes your site.
- Use META tags to better control how AltaVista will index your site.
- Use synonyms within the document's META tags.

Excite

URL: http://www.excite.com/

Submission Page: http://www.excite.com/Info/add_url.html

Submission Requirements:

Excite requires your URL and your e-mail address.

Submission Highlights:

The Excite spider is programmed to index the text found on your Web pages and will crawl through the rest of your site and index all links. Therefore, submit only your main URL.

Submission Tips:

- Excite does not honor (index) META tags.
- Excite does not index Web sites that use frames.
- Excite's main page provides an "Add URL" hyperlink for easy reference.

HotBot

URL: http://www.hotbot.com/

Submission Page: http://www.hotbot.com/addurl.html

Submission Requirements:

HotBot requires your URL and your e-mail address.

Submission Highlights:

Factors that affect relevance ranking include the words used in the Web site title, META tag keywords, specific word frequency, and the length of the document.

Submission Tips:

- Web sites that use spoofing techniques such as multiple word repetition, META tags that are unrelated to the content in the Web document, or words that are unreadable due to size or color risk being penalized.
- HotBot's main page provides an "Add URL" hyperlink for easy reference.

Infoseek

URL: http://www.infoseek.com/

Submission Page: http://www.infoseek.com/AddUrl?pg=DCaddurl.html

Submission Requirements:

Infoseek requires only your URL.

Submission Highlights:

- Because META tag descriptions determine your Web site's summary description when retrieved via a search, make sure that your META tag descriptions accurately summarize the content of your site.
- META tag keywords may consist of up to 1,000 characters.
- Factors that affect relevance ranking include a very descriptive Web site title, a META tag description, and a keywords META tag.

- Attempts to spam the index will result in Web site exclusion.

Submission Tips:

- Infoseek will index only the page of the URL that you submit. Additional URL's may be submitted one at a time however, a single URL is allowed to be submitted only once in a 24-hour period.
- Do not use HTML tags within the META tag description.
- Do not use repetitive keywords consistently in your Web document.
- If your Web site contains frames, include a <NOFRAMES> section because Infoseek will not analyze URLs within framesets.
- Infoseek's main page provides a "Add URL" hyperlink for easy reference.

Lycos

URL: http://www.lycos.com/

Submission Page: http://www.lycos.com/addasite.html

Submission Requirements:

Lycos requires your URL and your e-mail address.

Submission Highlights:

- The Lycos spider will determine your Web site's keywords and description based on its programming algorithms.
- The spider is designed to examine components of your title, headings, subheadings, word frequency, the appearance of words and where the words appear in relation to one another.
- Lycos will review the links in your URL submission but you should only depend on the spider to index one level deeper than your main submission page.

Submission Tips:

- You are allowed to submit more than one URL from your site as long as the URL's represent distinctly different Web pages.
- If your Web site contains frames, make sure to include a <NOFRAMES> section because Lycos will not analyze URLs within framesets.
- Lycos does not analyze image content.
- The Lycos spider ignores META tags.
- Web pages that spam or hide text will not be added to the Lycos catalog.
- Lycos' main pages includes a "Add Your Site to Lycos" hyperlink for easy reference.

WebCrawler

URL: http://www.Webcrawler.com/

Submission Page: http://www.Webcrawler.com/Help/Results.html

Submission Requirements:

WebCrawler requires only your URL.

Submission Highlights:

- WebCrawler has begun screening new URL submissions for spam. Web sites that use repetitive word lists, irrelevant information, and so on are being ignored.
- Web sites that are found to contain spam are removed from the WebCrawler index.
- WebCrawler will index up to 1MB of text (words) on your Web page.

Submission Tips:

- Submit your main URL as well as the URLs that are subsidiary pages to your main URL. However, do not submit more than 25 URLs per Web site.
- Make sure your Web site has your title name specified in its HTML source file; otherwise, WebCrawler will display the URL as the title of your Web site in search results.
- WebCrawler avoids CGI directories.
- Use the <NOFRAMES> tag, if applicable, to make sure that such pages are indexed appropriately.
- WebCrawler gives slightly more weight to Web site titles than to the text in the body of the Web site in relation to relevance rankings.
- WebCrawler's main page includes a "Add your URL" hyperlink for easy reference.

Yahoo!

Yahoo! is a unique search service in many respects. Most importantly, submissions to Yahoo! are verified by "people," not automated spiders—the same people who take offense at any attempts to SPAM or "fool" the search directory.

URL: http://www.yahoo.com/

Submission Information Page: http://www.yahoo.com/doc/info/include.html

Submission Requirements:

Yahoo! requires that you provide the title of your Web site, your URL, and a description of your Web site limited to 25 words.

Yahoo!'s directory listing structure is comprised of 14 main subject headings such as Business and Economy—with additional subcategories like Companies, Ethics, Labor, and so on. These subcategories organize information from general terms to specific terms. Here is an example of how subcategories appear in Yahoo!'s hierarchical directory:

Business and Economy
Companies
Apparel
Children's
Specialty
(Your Store here!)

Submission Guidelines:

Before submitting your site to Yahoo!, review its subject categories extensively and locate the most ideal subcategory for your listing. Yahoo! places emphasis on whether your site will have regional or nonregional appeal. After you locate the subcategory most appropriate to your business, click on the "Suggest A Site" hyperlink located on the bottom of each subcategory page. Then complete the necessary submission fields and submit your Web site.

Submission Tip:

Do *not* attempt to fool Yahoo! with multiple Web page submissions and reorganized descriptions because it may exclude your entire Web site from its directory.

We mentioned that nothing beats old-fashioned hard work and perseverance. We recommend that you spend a weekend scouring the Net and establishing links and making submissions to every other search engine and directory listing you can find.

Verify your listing regularly

After you have been listed in a search engine, check back there often to ensure that you remain listed. This is the Internet and anything can happen. Listings and links can and do disappear. If you discover that something is wrong with your listing, resubmit it.

Most search engines are revisiting sites on a regular basis. However, some engines are getting smarter and know that some Web sites change their content infrequently and thus, they don't revisit those sites on a regular basis. Feel free to resubmit your site anytime you make significant changes or add content.

---

[1] Trend Letter, published by The Global Network, Vol. 16, No. 5, March 6, 1997

[2] Universal City Studios, 1979

[3] At this writing, mws-welding.com is a fictitious domain name. No resemblance to any business or individual is intended by use of this example.

[4] Service as outlined on the Submit It home page http://www.submit-it.com/

13

Web Site Toolbox

How do I work? I grope.

- Albert Einstein

Netcom Business Center—client resources

The **Netcom Business Center's Client Resource** Web site is a value-added service available exclusively to Netcom hosting customers. "Members Only" will benefit from these tools and you must be a Netcom hosting customer with a valid username and password. *If you haven't done so already, now might be the right time to install the software from the accompanying CD and begin your free trial service.*

The **Client Resources** area of the Netcom Business Center (NBC) is accessible from the main <u>Hosting</u> menu. This is where you will have access to other software programs that you can use to enhance, maintain, and promote your domain. Click on the Client Resources menu option to enter. You will be prompted for your User Name and Password. http://www.netcomi.com/nbc/mainmenu.html

 Among other services, the NBC **Client Resources** site provides access to your domain e-mail maintenance, FrontPage 98 server extensions, interactive SQL, your Netcom Internet access account information and offers a convenient place to change or update your InterNIC information.

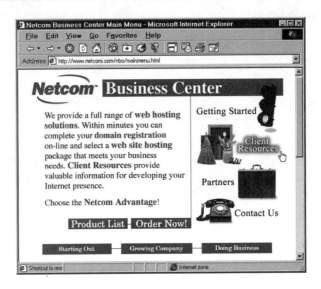

Here you can Password Protect sensitive areas on your Web site, promote your domain via search engine registration tools, and access ICentral's Shop Site software and Netcom's Web Site Builder. http://www.netcomi.com/nbc/resources.html

Additionally, this is where you can obtain extra disk space or purchase more e-mail accounts to your domain. There is an extensive list of other options you can add to your current hosting package. Best of all, you can do all these things (and more) online, instantly, 24 hours per day—any time it is convenient for you.

Toolbox

Need software? The NBC Toolbox provides a convenient place where you can download your choice of browsers, e-mail programs, FTP applications, plug-ins, HTML editors, and more. It would be impractical to mention all the programs offered on the NBC Web site as the list of Netcom partners continues to grow.

Downloading some of these third-party programs will be in the form of self-extracting files, and decompressing a program will occur automatically as you execute (double-click) the file name. However, other programs may require that you "decompress" (unzip) the file manually.

WinZip is a file compression program and a standard for Windows and Windows 98. Its purpose is to *squeeze* files to make them smaller, thus easier to fit on a disk or transfer over the Internet. If you download a program that is "zipped" you may need this shareware program. Installation is easy.

1. Download the zip utility by clicking on the appropriate link at `http://www.winzip.com/` and save it to your Download or Temp directory.

2. Right-click on the **Start** button on your toolbar and select **Explorer**. Locate the file you just downloaded (winzip95.exe). Install the program by double-clicking on the self-extracting file.

3. WinZip will unzip automatically and install files as required.

WinZip is continually improving its software and offering upgrades to registered users. The latest version permits you to download and open archives from the Internet with one click via Microsoft's Internet Explorer and Netscape Navigator. There is no need to "Save to disk" and then switch to WinZip or to the Windows Explorer or File Manager to open the downloaded file.[1]

 TIP Remember that many of these programs are "shareware," *not* freeware. If you like a program and decide to continue using it, be sure to register with the author. It's the right thing to do.

Support

 Customer service and technical support is available exclusively to Netcom customers in a number of convenient ways. Online or off, you can get the help or information you need by contacting Netcom using any of the following options.

contact **US**

Hosting Support	Contact
Online Help and FAQs	`http://www.netcomi.com/help/`
Acceptable Use Guidelines	`http://www.netcomi.com/nbc_usage.html`
Terms and Conditions	`http://www.netcomi.com/nbc/terms.html`
E-mail	
Technical Support	`support@netcomi.com`
General Information	`info@netcomi.com`
Sales	`sales@netcomi.com`
Webmaster	`webmaster@netcomi.com`
Accounting	`accounting@netcom.com`
VAR Partnerships	`varinfo@netcom.com`
Telephone	
Hosting Support	1.888.638.2669
Hosting Sales	1.888.638.2664

dial-up
support support

Dial-Up Support	Contact
Online Customer Service	http://www.netcom.com/netcom/contact.html
Online Dial-Up Support	http://www.netcom.com/support/index.html
Dial-Up Support FAQs	http://www.netcom.com/support/faq.html
Support Knowledge Base	http://www1.netcom.com/bin/webtech
General Support Tools	http://www.netcom.com/support/club.html
Local Access Numbers	http://www1.netcom.com/bin/popinfo
E-mail	
General Information	info@netcom.com
Netcomplete Support	support@ix.netcom.com
Telephone	
Customer Service	1.888.316.1122
Technical Support	1.408.881.1810

Internet Explorer quick tips and tricks

Microsoft® Internet Explorer *e*

Net Tips

- **Save time** when entering a URL in the Address window of Internet Explorer 4.0 by ignoring the "http://www" characters. To visit http://www.netcom.com you can type "netcom.com" and Internet Explorer 4.0 will automatically fill in the rest. (Some domains may require the "www" part of the address, but you can always skip the http://.)

- **To launch a new browser window** before displaying a hyperlinked site, click on the hyperlink while pressing the **Shift** key.

- **To scroll immediately** to the bottom of a Web page, press the **End** key. Press **Home** if you want to zoom back to the top of a page.

- **Printing with Explorer**. To print a Web page, press **Ctrl+P** to open the Print dialog box and press **Enter**.

- **To print a Web page that includes a list of all the URLs** on that page, select **File/Print** and in the Print dialog box, select **Print table of links**. Your Web page will print, and, at the end of the printed page, you'll get a table listing all of the URLs embedded in the Web page.

- **To print a page with frames,** you must click on the frame you want to print and then click **File/Print**.

- **Locate the name of a page using frames**. When you are visiting a Web site that contains frames, click on the framed section for which you want the correct URL and select "open in new window." Otherwise, you will have to view source and look for the URL in simple text and then go back to the browser and input the URL.

- **To empty your cache**, empty your cache, empty your cache! Most problems on the Internet are temporary. Your browser can sometimes display old information, because it was temporarily cached on your hard drive. To empty your cache: Select **View**, and then **Internet Options**. Under the General tab in **Internet Options**, look in the block entitled **Temporary Internet Files** and select **Delete Files**.

- **Get control of your keyboard**. Sometimes it is faster to use the keyboard than the mouse. A few commands that will help speed your surfing include:

Ctrl+A	Selects *all* the text on the current page
Ctrl+Esc	Opens the Windows 98 **Start** menu
Ctrl+F	Opens the **Find** dialog box
Ctrl+N	Opens a **new** browser window
Ctrl+O	Displays the **Open** dialog box

Check the Net!

To learn more about *getting* more from the Internet, refer to the following links for additional Internet Explorer 4.0 tips and tricks:

http://www.microsoft.com/magazine/internet/ie/ie.htm

http://www.microsoft.com/ie/homeuser/tips/?/ie/homeuser/tips/tipsp4.htm

PC World Online will help you get the most from your browser and have fun in the process. http://www.pcworld.com/software/internet_www/articles/sep97/ 1509ietipsa.html

Windows 98 tips

Books explaining the new features of Windows 98 in great detail are plentiful. These few comments of ours are no substitute for a reliable reference book. However, we felt it was important to mention a couple of things about Windows 98 that would provide immediate benefit and help you appreciate some of the new features of Windows 98. These suggestions may help to reduce your learning curve, and we also wanted to point you in the direction of some other resources. First, the *big* question:

Should I upgrade to Windows 98?

Designed for

Microsoft® Windows 98

If you are a Windows 3.1 user (and have a 100 MHz or faster[1] computer), run—don't walk—to your nearest retailer and purchase a copy of Windows 98. The advantages of changing what's under your hood are far too extensive to enumerate here.

If you currently use Windows 95, life as you know it will go on if you choose not to upgrade to Windows 98. *Most* of the changes in Windows 98 are at the OS level and are not readily apparent after installation. If you're a current Windows 95 user, your desktop will look pretty much the same as it does now. This is *not* the major upgrade that Windows 95 was to Windows 3.1.

However, for roughly the cost of an evening out *(the street price of Windows 98 is less than $90)*, you will have little trouble justifying the price of this upgrade. What you stand to gain in speed, system stability, recaptured hard disk space, better Internet integration, and new useful utilities is more than worth the price. A few Windows 98 tips that are worth mentioning are covered here.

Use that "new" button

For years, nearly everyone believed that the right (and middle) buttons of their mouse was another one of life's unsolved mysteries. Every PC mouse had one (or more), but their purpose for being there was not perceptible and most software programs did not utilize them.

Without a doubt, the single most important tip that you should apply to Windows 98 (and most other current version Microsoft products) is *right-click on everything*. A whole new world of file shortcuts, information, and convenience will be opened to you.

A familiar example of this functionality is to right-click on the **Start** button and select **Explore** (File Manager)—you will launch that program.

- While the Exploring window is active, right-clicking on a folder (directory) and selecting **Properties** from the menu will display the size of all the files in that folder. *(This is a very useful feature when you are copying files to a floppy disk.)*
- Right-clicking on a file will produce a new menu with additional shortcut commands such as **Open**, **Copy**, **Delete** and other handy actions.

Update Windows 98 painlessly in the future

By now, no one has to convince you that everything related to the Internet and your computer is changing daily. One outstanding feature of Windows 98 is its ability to update your system software automatically and recommend to you when you should install other updates specific to your computer.

Windows Update is an online extension of Windows 98 that will scan your system to see what is installed and then offer a list of suggested additional components for you to download. It will show a list of fixes, updates, and enhancements to Windows (Critical Updates will fix known issues, such as security patches and so on). Any of the components you select will be downloaded and installed *automatically*.

If you are a little paranoid about sharing your system information with another Web site, your information will not be sent to Microsoft or to anyone else.

- Click on the **Start** button and select **Windows Update** from the main menu.
- Select any components you wish to install and click **Download**.

Need to know your IP address? Most Internet Service Providers automatically assign IP addresses dynamically to users when they log on. What this means is that you are assigned a different random IP number every time you initiate an Internet session. Some Internet programs require that you identify your IP address to make their programs operate properly.

- Click **Start**, and then select **Run** and type **winipcfg**. Press **OK**. This will display the IP address for your current connection to the Internet.

Make your programs open and run faster

Your hard disk is much like your closet at home. Without periodic maintenance (cleaning it out), it gets harder and takes longer to find anything. Periodically, we must do the same thing with our hard drives. This rearranging of old files is called defragging. You perform this process on your hard drive using Disk Defragmenter.

- Click **Start**, select **Programs**, then **Accessories** and **System Tools**, and click **Disk Defragmenter**.
- Select the drive you want to optimize.
- Depending on the size of your hard disk, it can take a while to complete the process. It is worth the wait.

This maintenance procedure can be scheduled to be done after hours and on a regular interval via the Scheduled Tasks folder found under the **System Tools** menu.

Squeeze more space from your hard drive

The Disk Cleanup utility will free up space on your hard disk by searching your drive for files that you can delete safely. Here's how:

- Click **Start**, select **Programs**, then **Accessories**, point to **System Tools**, and click **Disk Cleanup**.

- Select the drive you want to clean up.
- On the **Disk Cleanup** tab, select the files you want to delete.
- To free up more space, click the **More Options** tab. Here you can remove Windows components or other programs or files that you don't use.

Bypass the Recycle Bin when deleting files by holding down the **Shift** key and pressing **Delete**. This will permanently delete the files.

Programs that become unstable can be shut down by selecting **Ctrl+Alt+Delete** (pressing keys simultaneously). This will terminate *only* the program that is slowing or has stopped your system.

If you need to restart Windows 98, if you select **Start, Shutdown, Restart Computer**, and hold down the left Shift key while pressing **OK**, you will restart Windows 98 only and not reboot the computer itself.

Finally, always remember that there are usually at least three ways to accomplish the same thing. If you get confused and can't figure it out? *Right-click on it.*

Check the Net!

The **Microsoft Windows 98 Web site** is the *first* place you should visit to learn more about Microsoft products, get support, and receive valuable user tips at no cost. `http://www.microsoft.com/windows98/basics/tipstricks/default.asp`

Customize Windows 98 desktop - Start menu - Shortcuts and toolbars with ZD Net's 16 tips. `http://www.zdnet.com/wsources/content/0598/feat_tips_desktop.html`

CMP Megasite provides over 50 tips from CMP Media. `http://www.cmpnet.com/win98/displayTipsInSubcat?cat_id=47&mjCatDesc=Win98`

PC Computing Windows 98 Web site offers tips, secrets, and a survival guide. `http://www.zdnet.com/pccomp/features/windows98/welcome.html`

Windows Sources magazine's Web site shows you 40 ways to make Windows 98 fly. `http://www.zdnet.com/wsources/content/0598/feat_tips_splash.html`

PC WORLD online offers "The Hardware Book" for free and is available for download. This book offers nuts-and-bolts technical information about computers in general and is a great reference source to keep handy. `http://www.pcworld.com/cgi-bin/shareware?ID=2705`

---

[1] WinZip is a registered trademark of Nico Mak Computing, Inc.

[2] Although Microsoft says that Windows 98 can operate on a 66MHz machine, it is impractical to overburden such a machine with this 200MB operating system. It will devour your system resources.

CHAPTER 14

What's Next?

If you think that establishing your business online may be too expensive or too time-consuming, wait until you see what it will cost if you don't.

- Tom Heatherington

Your business must continue to grow, or it may eventually go away

In business as in nature, only the fittest or the smartest will survive. One thing will forever remain constant. That is, the pace of change in many areas that affect your business will most assuredly continue to increase.

- Customers will always demand better service.
- Competitors will charge lower prices.
- Vendors will want to impose higher prices.
- Employees will demand larger salaries.
- Talented and experienced employees will be harder to find.
- Marketing effectively will be more difficult.
- Computers will get faster.
- Software will always need to be upgraded.

- Internet bandwidth will continue to expand.
- Your time will continue to be your most valuable and most expensive commodity.

Embracing new technology for technology's sake is an indisputable recipe for disaster. However, selectively choosing technologies that will help you manage the challenges of your changing market is what this book has been about.

What is the migration path of products and services for my business?

Understanding and applying new technology is critical to most businesses long-term survival. Unfortunately, technology always seems to be one step ahead of our understanding of its application or benefits received. As we mentioned previously, most people are far too busy running their business to keep up with every new technological advancement.

Where do I go from here?

The next logical step for many small businesses will be to integrate Internet (TCP/IP and HTML) technology more fully throughout their organization. This will initially be accomplished by incorporating an internal Intranet. An <u>Intranet</u> is fundamentally an internal Internet, a private Web that functions much like a <u>LAN</u> (Local Area Network).

Intranets—interlinking the virtual office

> **intra** -\'in-trä\ prefix adj., inward – more at INTERIOR   **1 a:** within **b:** during **c:** between layers of **2** : INTRO- <an *intra*muscular injection>

As an internal information system, an Intranet uses existing Internet technology such as <u>TCP/IP</u> as its communications <u>protocol</u>, and a Web browser (primarily) as the client side (user) interface. Because the browser performs navigation and interactive functions, the (user) client side of the Intranet equation can be put in place at no additional cost to your company.

Prior to the arrival of Intranet technology, proprietary operating systems (DOS, MAC, UNIX, and so on) made shared communications extremely challenging and often very expensive. By its very nature, an Intranet solves the LAN/<u>WAN</u>, <u>client/server</u> issues with improved efficiency. This independent platform solution allows users of different operating systems to communicate seamlessly. That is, regardless of the different hardware or software used by authorized members, everyone has access to the same information that is associated with a Web page via your Intranet.

Who can use an Intranet?

Using Windows 98 (or Windows 95) permits a small cluster of machines to be connected by <u>ethernet</u> cable and an inexpensive network card to form a "peer to peer" network. No other software or hardware is required. Windows **Help** screens or any

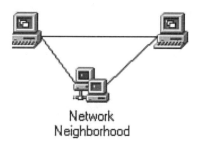

Network
Neighborhood

Windows manual can provide basic information relative to setting-up your own private network. Every company, large or small, can maximize internal communications using an Intranet.

An Intranet is your own *intimate* Internet. You alone decide who will have access to information. When you extend permission to others outside your network to access your intranet, it becomes an Extranet.

What are the benefits of using an Intranet?

An Intranet is an ideal medium for storing and exchanging intracompany communications such as corporate mission statements, goals, forms, policies and procedures, directives, memorandums, schedules, organizational charts, updates, activity reports, and so on. Because most needed components already exist in your organization, Intranets do not always require new technology and software. Also, an Intranet can provide two-way communication with offsite employees, customers, vendors, and associates.

The benefits of utilizing an Intranet include:

- Greater accessibility
- Increased productivity
- Improved efficiency at minimal cost to your company

The Intranet becomes your company's internal communications system and an external communication channel. While the Internet is part of your outside marketing and customer support program, an Intranet functions as an internal communication and support mechanism. Your standalone operation, Intranet, does not have to be connected to the Internet to operate properly.

Check
the
Net!

The Microsoft Web site offers extensive information to help you build an Intranet with their 60 Minute Intranet Kit. Also available are predesigned Intranet templates that follow step-by-step instructions to build a custom Intranet for your company. `http://www.microsoft.com/office/intranet/`

Use the Tour Guide of the Microsoft® Office Demo Intranet Home Page to learn how the Microsoft Office family of products gives you the tools you need to gain the business advantages and value that an Intranet can provide your company. `http://www.microsoft.com/msoffice/intranet/volcano/tourg001.htm`

The Intranet Journal calls itself the "Web's #1 Intranet and Extranet Resource." Here you will find an overview of Intranets, the latest Intranet news, resources, Intranet-related software, and much more. `http://www.intranetjournal.com/`

To get a good overview of what benefits can be achieved utilizing an Intranet, see the White Paper: Intranets: Internet Technologies Deployed Behind the Firewall for Corporate Productivity prepared for the Internet Society by Process Software. http://www.process.com/

For more information, we suggest *Intranets Unleashed*, a massive tome on the subject of the Intranet as a business tool, available at your local bookstore from Sams Publishing.

When will my business need dedicated Internet access?

The SIC code for your business may help the government categorize your type of firm, but in reality, every company is unique in its individual requirements. Your need for dedicated access and the kind of service you will require depend on a number of factors. Considerations such as your company size, Internet usage, applications being used, the number of users, and so on will help answer that question. Netcom can help you determine which service will be best suited for your particular situation.

Netcom offers a variety of dedicated Internet services with the reliability and functionality crucial to meeting your business needs today and into the next millennium. Netcom's DirectConnect solutions will enhance your company's efficiency and effectiveness. They are designed to give you a dedicated port on the Netcom network, a port which only you can use. You get the scalability, flexibility, and security critical to success.

Which dedicated access service is right for my business?

Netcom offers a variety of services from a low-cost, dedicated dial-up connection to high-speed T1 access. All DirectConnect products include determining correct bandwidth requirements, configuring and testing the necessary hardware, setting up lines with the telephone company, round-the-clock monitoring, and support. DirectConnect products also include options for increased performance, including High Performance Routing and AutoReconnect ISDN.

There are six Netcom DirectConnect solutions to choose from. All include 24x7 toll-free technical support, and allow you to use critical business applications such as e-mail, file transfer, Web site hosting, multimedia presentation, and video conferencing. Plus, they'll do all the work coordinating your line installation and maintenance with the local telephone company or carrier, registering domain names and IP addresses, providing domain name services (DNS), and configuring and testing any equipment you might purchase from Netcom.

99.5% As your business grows increasingly reliant on the Internet, you need guaranteed availability for your mission-critical applications. DirectConnect 56K, Frame Relay, Flex T1, and Full T1 services are backed by Netcom's industry-leading Service Level Agreement (SLA) which provides a *99.5% uptime guarantee!*

This industry-leading Service Level Agreement guarantees your entire Netcom Internet connection, including the local-loop (telephone circuit), Netcom POP, and network backbone up to the Network Access Point (NAP). Administration of your router and DSU/CSU is also covered under the SLA if they are purchased from and are managed by Netcom.

To contact Netcom for more information:

On the Web	http://www.netcom.com/offer/connectivity/index.html
E-mail	businessinfo@netcom.com
Telephone	1-800-NETCOM1

Small business networking—the next step

Microsoft BackOffice Small Business Server — As your company grows, the sharing of information and resources between people or departments becomes more critical. In the past, installing a network to link all of this together could be a costly proposition. Today there are intermediate steps you can take which will provide total functionality with minimum investment. One such product is Microsoft's Small Business Server.

The Microsoft Small Business Server features award-winning products that give you everything you need to run a growing business. Designed for companies with 25 or fewer PCs, it's an ideal, integrated solution for sharing files, databases, printers, electronic mail, fax services, applications, and other resources with anyone, anywhere, at any time—all from one integrated server. One integrated installation program that installs and configures all of the major components of the BackOffice Small Business Server. Helpful wizards walk the small-business administrator through the steps of connecting printers and workstations, creating user accounts, and connecting them to the Internet, ensuring that the small business has a complete network.

Everything you need to run your business. File print and application services, essential communication services and a safe, secure Internet connection have all been combined, tested, and optimized to work together.

Communicate in new and more efficient ways. The Internet Connection Wizard automates location, selection and connection to an Internet service provider, automatically configures Microsoft Exchange to send and receive e-mail across the Internet.

Easy to set up, manage, and grow. Installing Microsoft BackOffice® Small Business Server is made easy through a fully integrated setup that silently installs all server applications.

**Check
the
Net!**

When you are ready to upgrade your business to a network, you will need to learn more about this small business networking solution, visit:

http://www.microsoft.com/backofficesmallbiz/default.asp

Y2K —the year 2000 controversy

It has been called by many names, Y2K, the millennium bug, the Cinderella syndrome, the year 2000 problem, and "TEOTWAWKI."[1] Regardless of its label, it is potentially a *real* problem. The question that no one seems able to answer today is, will 2000 be the "year the earth stands still" or just another year with some isolated computer problems?

The Y2K problem will affect almost every computing environment from the mini- and mainframe to UNIX and PCs. Rectifying this problem means that billions upon billions of lines of computer code must be reviewed and fixed. Will we be able to accomplish this in time and if not, what does it really mean? No one has a good answer for these questions.

How did all this happen?

Computer memory today is a dirt-cheap commodity. However, back in the early days of mainframes, computer programmers were forced to conserve what was then, very expensive and very limited memory. One way in which they accomplished this was to use two digits instead of four to identify a year (99 vs. 1999). No one ever dreamed that this code would still be in use 30–40 years later. One minute past 11:59 PM on December 31, 1999, many computers will not be able to discriminate between the years 1900 and 2000.

Our world operates on computers, but it's not *just* computers that may be influenced by this problem. There are *billions* of chips out there that operate everything from bulldozers to bank vaults, our financial system, utility companies and our government. No one knows how many of these chips are noncompliant or will experience *confusion* when the clock strikes twelve. Theoretically, if a computer can't figure out what day it is, it won't be able to balance your checkbook or send electricity to your home.

Due to the *potentially* serious consequences of these and other Y2K issues, it is difficult to talk about it without sounding apocalyptic. There *is* a problem. How serious a problem and whether it will be fixed in time, or have any effect on life as we know it remains a raging debate.

On the extreme negative end of the scale, Dr. Gary North maintains that *"the y2k problem is systemic and that it cannot be fixed."* http://www.garynorth.com/

Opposing this viewpoint is the understanding that some of the best minds in the world are working on this problem. Many large companies are already issuing Y2K compliance guarantees. Most large companies and government organizations have made this a top priority and are allocating resources to it.

What can I do to prepare?

First, get informed—use the Web. One of the best overall sites is <u>The Year 2000 Information Center</u>™. This is a wholly owned subsidiary of **The Tenagra Corporation**—`http://www.tenagra.com/`—and provides a forum for disseminating information about the year 2000 problem and for the discussion of possible solutions. Just about any subject related to Y2K is presented in-depth with links to hundreds of other resources. A must visit: `http://www.year2000.com/`

Microsoft has a very comprehensive site called the <u>Year 2000 Resource Center</u>. It includes detailed FAQs, a Product Guide providing information concerning Microsoft products and a directory of third-party Year 2000 Services and Tools focused on Microsoft products and the PC. `http://www.microsoft.com/y2k/`

Next, look internally. What will your business need to do to become Y2K compliant? Software is now available (and more programs are being developed) that can scan your PC or network, identify programs with Y2K issues, repair some problems and recommend fixes to you. Make it a priority try to find out how Y2K may affect your business.

Broaden your discovery process to include any custom machinery, alarm systems, metering equipment, and so on that you rely on for your business. Begin asking your suppliers and others with whom you do business if they have a Y2K plan in place or are addressing the problem. Develop a probable case scenario of what impact all of this could have on your business and tailor a plan to manage those issues.

Forewarned is forearmed. If you do these things you will be better prepared to assess your individual situation and take steps to correct potential risks to your business. Also, being able to issue a Y2K compliant statement may prove to be a huge competitive advantage in the months to come.

You will hear more and more about this as the year 2000 draws nearer. Our reason for including this was to provide a brief explanation of what are the issues and suggest other resources where you can find help and get detailed answers to your questions.

Check the Net!

Y2K resources on the Web

U. S. Federal Government **Gateway for Year 2000** Information Directories. `http://www.itpolicy.gsa.gov/mks/yr2000/y2khome.htm`

Computer Associates says that it offers more kinds of software solutions for more kinds of computers than any other software company in the world. To receive more information about how CA Discovery 2000 can meet your needs, visit them at: `http://www.cai.com/products/ca2000/disc2000.htm#success`

www.y2k.com explores the multitude of legal issues related to identifying, controlling, and remediating the problem, in addition to the litigation that will arise if/when the malfunctions begin. `http://www.y2k.com/`

ANKH Software Pty Ltd is a software development company specializing in Year 2000 (Y2K) PC compliance tools. According toits Web page, Survive 2000 Professional Version 2.1.1 is the most comprehensive Y2K testing, diagnostic, and remediation tool available in the world today for IBM compatible PCs. `http://www.survive-2000.com/`

Check 2000 PC, a software program by Greenwich Mean Time-UTA, L.C., can be run on most PCs. According to its Web site, it will flag and fix Year 2000 PC Problems. `http://www.gmt-uta.com/default.cfm`

Lessons learned

Embrace the chaos!

After five hectic years of bleeding-edge Internet involvement, we have learned that it is imprudent to "predict" most anything remotely associated with the Internet. Certainly, it is easy to identify trends and draw conclusions based on logic and historical lessons, but this is the Internet. *This is chaos!*

The Internet has been compared to everything from the early days of television to the hype of the CB radio craze, but nothing like this has ever existed before. Our world has been changed forever and the most radical changes may yet be ahead of us. In what specific ways all of this will affect us tomorrow is anybody's guess, but we choose to abstain from such prophesying. No one can accurately predict what impact the Internet will ultimately have on our society, how we will communicate, entertain ourselves, or do business.

Some analysts believe that they can make intelligent guesses, but often their assumptions are based on models that are no longer valid, or are being redefined or invented by "kids" with no preconceptions of how things are supposed to be or have been in the past. *This is chaos! Embrace it.*

The one prediction we feel comfortable in making is that the Internet will radically transform how most businesses do business in the months and years to come. To compete and to survive, you *must* involve yourself and your business with the Internet. You *must* be willing to learn, experiment, make mistakes, reinvent how you do business, and acclimate your organization to this new and constantly changing "standard."

Tom Heatherington	`tom@webunet.com`
Lori Heatherington	`lori@webunet.com`

---

[1] Still yet another new acronym meaning The End Of The World As We Know It.

15

Glossary of Geek Speak

Strange new terms and acronyms related to Internet technology are being created almost daily. It is impossible to keep up with this onslaught, yet these words and definitions are being absorbed into our vocabulary. In the very near future, you will need to understand the meanings of many of these words just to conduct your business.

In an effort to explain some of the more common terms, we have created this glossary of terms. This is not meant to be all encompassing, but the most used words and acronyms are included. If you would like an Internet term defined that is not part of this list, send an e-mail to support@ix.netcom.com.[1]

A

Acrobat Reader™ by Adobe, lets you view and print **PDF** files in your browser window. Adobe Acrobat 3.0 permits anyone to share business documents across platforms. Click here to download the latest version of Acrobat or go to http://www.adobe.com.

ActiveX Microsoft's OLE (Object Linking and Embedding), permits Windows programs to communicate with each other. For example, changing the numbers in a spreadsheet will update a chart in a different program. ActiveX is the Internet-workable version of OLE.

Address There are two types of addresses in common use within the Internet. They are *e-mail* and *IP* or Internet addresses.

ADSL (Asymmetric Digital Subscriber Line)   A term that refers to modems (not wires) that convert an ordinary twisted-pair copper telephone line into high-speed digital access. Like many data transfer methods, it takes two to tango. ADSL requires a pair of modems on both ends of the line. To learn more about this new technology, visit the ADSL Forum.

Agent   A software program (or command) that performs preprogrammed functions such as keyword searches, monitoring incoming data, and so on. An intelligent agent can make decisions about information it discovers and take action such as alerting a user or starting a program.

AI (Artificial Intelligence)   Software that tries to emulate human thinking, emotions, and learning techniques, such as a chess program that memorizes your moves, employs a strategy, and makes comments about your tactics. Software programs, browsers, search engines, and so on will soon be "learning" about your preferences and methods of utilization thus simplifying many repetitive processes.

Alert or Alert Box   An audible and/or onscreen signal from the computer that demands a user's attention. An alert box usually accompanies most alerts requiring a response or acknowledgement.

Alias   An e-mail address that is forwarded to another address, or a group of addresses stored under one name, for example, `all_staff@your-biz.com` . A name, usually short and easy to remember, that is translated into another name, usually long and difficult to remember. Commonly used in the UNIX realm to "abbreviate" verbose commands.

Aliasing   The jagged and stair-stepped appearance of curved and diagonal lines of a graphic image.

ALT Tags (Alternate Tags)   A text description of a photo, graphic, or image map that is read by a browser. This permits users who surf the Web with text-only browsers to "see" an image.

AND   Used when querying many search engines, a Boolean operation which is "true" if both inputs are true.

Anonymous FTP   Allows any user to retrieve files from selected directories. Most anonymous FTP servers implement security measures to prevent users from accessing anything but the designated public information areas. By using the special userID of "anonymous" the network user will bypass local security checks and will have access to publicly accessible files on the remote system.

ANSI (American National Standards Institute)   Defines the U.S. standards for the information processing industry and represents the U.S. on other international standards-setting bodies such as the ISO. ANSI was responsible for developing **ASCII** (The American Standard Code for Information Interchange) that encodes characters in seven-bit units.

Applet   A Java program that is embedded in an HTML page.

Application   A program that performs a function directly for a user. FTP, mail, and Telnet clients are examples of network applications.

Archie   A system to automatically gather, index, and serve information on the Internet. The initial implementation provides an indexed directory of filenames from more than 800 anonymous FTP archives on the Internet—some 100 gigabytes worth of information. This information is accessible through Archie client programs, through servers reachable using the telnet command, through e-mail servers and through forms on the World Wide Web. Later versions provide indexing services for many different resources. *See Gopher.*

Archive   Moving a file, or compressing a file for long-term storage or to save space.

ARP (Address Resolution Protocol)   A means of determining a host's address from its Internet address.

ARPANET   This was the precursor of today's Internet and was transferred by DARPA in July of 1975 as an operational network. Today's Internet became reality when the ARPANET was divided into Military and Civilian sections in 1983. TCP and IP protocols were established by 1980, and adopted throughout ARPANET by 1983. ARPANET was dissolved in 1989 and the National Science Foundation began to manage the network.

ASCII (American Standard Code for Information Interchange)   A code used by most computers and printers in which letters and numbers are represented as a number from 0 to 127 and translated into a 7-bit binary code.

ASP (Active Server Page)   An HTML document that is generated as a result of a request for information as opposed to a static, preformatted HTML document.

ATM (Asynchronous Transfer Mode)   An advanced standard for packet switching which uses packets of a fixed length. These packets are how information (data) is packaged and transferred along a network such as the Internet.

Attachment   Refers to a file that is linked or attached to an e-mail message

Audio Streaming   The capability to play audio as it is being received as opposed to downloading an entire audio file and launching an audio player.

Authentication   Verification of a person's identity or a processes validity.

Authoring   Used in the context as creating World Wide Web documents.

Autoresponder (Infobots)   An automatic response to an e-mail inquiry generated by the mail server that is programmed to acknowledge receipt of an e-mail request. This can be used to send additional information about a specific product or service. *See also* *Infobot*. E.g. *For current pricing, send e-mail to* `prices@your-domain.com`.

Avatar   A graphic or pictorial representation of a user in a 3-D chat area. Usually chosen by each user, the avatar can be an animal or caricature.

AVI (Audio Video Interleaved)   A Microsoft multimedia file format.

AVR   Automatic Voice Recognition.

B

Backbone   A high-capacity network that links together other networks of lower capacity.

Backdoor   Refers to the "private entrance" around the security in a program or network used by programmers or technicians to perform maintenance or gain entry.

Bandwidth   The range of frequencies (data) a transmission line can carry and defined in bit/s (BPS). The larger the bandwidth, the greater the information capacity of a channel. In geekspeak, the term is used to describe one's available time, for example, "I just don't have the bandwidth to accept another project."

Banner   An online advertising graphic.

Baud   A unit of transmission/receiving speed, expressed in terms of the number of different signal events per second. It is the same as bit/s, when it is used to transmit a single bit of data.

BCNU   Be Seeing You.

Binary File   Any file that is not plain ASCII text. For example: executable files, graphics files, and compressed (ZIP) files.

Bit (contraction of binary digit)   A single unit of information that has two values, 0 or 1.

BITNet   Because It's Time Network. An academic computer network that provides interactive electronic mail and file transfer services, using a store-and-forward protocol. BITNet hosts are not on the Internet *per se*, but are reachable by e-mail through BITNet to Internet gateways.

Bounce   The return of a piece of mail because of an error in the delivery process. Mail can be bounced for various reasons. "Bounce" can also refer to the message indicating the error (informal usage).

Bookmark   Saving the location of an Internet address for future reference creates a bookmark with the browser.

Bps (Bits per second)   A measurement of digital transmission speeds.

Broadband   Any network (or frequency) that multiplexes different independent network carriers into a single cable or channel.

Broadcast   The simultaneous transmission of like data from one to many destinations, one to all.

Brochureware   A slang term for Web sites where companies have done little more than scan their companies brochures and mounted them on their Web pages. This is the first step many businesses take while learning to market on the Internet.

Browser   Software program used to display information on the World Wide Web. The two most popular browsers are Netscape's Navigator (http://www.netscape.com/) and Microsoft's Explorer (http://www.microsoft.com/ie/default.asp).

BTW   An abbreviation for "By The Way."

Bulletin Board System (BBS)   A computer, and associated hardware, which typically provides electronic messaging services, archives of files and any other services or activities of interest to the bulletin board system's operator. Many BBSs are currently operated by government, educational and research institutions. Although BBSs have traditionally been the domain of hobbyists, an increasing number of BBS's are connected to the Internet. The majority, however, are still reachable only via a direct modem-to-modem connection over a phone line.

Bulk E-mail   E-mail sent to multiple addresses in one huge mailing. Usually referring to a UCE bombing or SPAM.

Byte   Eight bits forming a unit of data. Typically, each byte stores one character (letter or number).

C

C (and/or C+, C++)   The name of a programming language so called because many features derived from an earlier compiler named "B" in commemoration of its parent, BCPL. Before Bjarne Stroustrup settled the question by designing C++, there was a humorous debate over whether C's successor should be named "D" or "P." C is now the dominant language in systems and microcomputer applications programming.

Careware   Shareware for which either the author suggests that some payment be made to a nominated charity or a levy directed to charity is included on top of the distribution charge. Synonyms include Charityware or Crippleware.

Cache   A temporary storage bin in memory and on your hard drive. Browsers stash the contents from pages that have been downloaded in the event they are called upon to be displayed again.

CGI (Common Gateway Interface)   An accepted standard by which programs interface with Web servers.

CGI-BIN   (bin, short for *binary*) The name of a directory on a Web server in which CGI programs are usually stored.

Channel   The basic unit of discussion on IRC. Once you join a channel, others read everything you type on that channel. Channels can either be named with numbers or with strings that begin with a # sign and can have topic descriptions (which are generally irrelevant to the actual subject of discussion).

Client   A user's software program that interacts with a server and displays information based on the query from the user (client). A browser is a desktop client that requests information from servers located on the Internet.

Client/server   A front-end client and a back-end server allows multiple workstations (client) to access the same server at the same time over the LAN. The Internet is a global client/server network. The goal of such a design is to offload as much processing as possible to the desktop leaving the shared information at the server.

Clipboard   A temporary staging area for copied information stored in memory. The clipboard stores information until you copy more or you exit Windows.

Confidence Factor   The factor by which a search engine rates the relevance or results of a keyword query. *See Weight or Weighted Results.*

Connectivity   The access method through which one is connected to the Internet. Connectivity choices are increasing rapidly. *See Modems.*

Ctrl+C   The keyboard command to copy text or graphics selected (highlighted) by the cursor to the computers temporary RAM memory.

Ctrl+V   The keyboard command to paste an object stored in RAM memory into an open application such as a paint program or word processor.

Cookie   A handle or transaction identifier, or other token of agreement between cooperating programs. Cookies were introduced by Netscape to preserve state information on the browser. This permits a site to recognize you on subsequent visits. Shopping cart programs can record each item you have collected as you navigate through a site. When done shopping, the Web page can use all of your accumulated cookies to calculate the charge. Some people believe that any site you connect to can read all the cookies on your disk. However, only the site that issued the cookie can read it.

CorelDRAW!   A very popular suite of graphics programs.[2] (http://www.corel.com/)

CPM   Advertising term meaning cost per one thousand sightings or impressions.

Cracker   A cracker is an individual who attempts to access computer systems without authorization. These people are often malicious, as opposed to hackers, and have many means at their disposal for breaking into a system. *See also Trojan Horse, Virus, and Worm.*

CSS (Cascading Style Sheets)   A World Wide Web Consortium specification for designing layout and style elements of a Web page. It permits you to control the appearance of fonts, colors, sizes, and so on throughout the entire site by referencing one master page. FrontPage 98 does this by assisting you with the Themes option.

CTR (Click Through Rate)   Advertising term indicating the percentage of viewers who click on a banner advertisement and follow the link.

Cybercitizens   Citizens of the Internet, Net heads, Netizens.

Cybermall   An online shopping mall such as IBM's World Avenue.

Cybersex   As in sex in cyberspace, having never attempted this personally, the authors must ask you to use your own imagination for a description.

Cyberspace   A term coined by William Gibson in his science fiction novel *Neuromancer* (1984) to describe the interconnected "world" of computers and the society that gathers around them. Today, cyberspace is the Internet and the tens of thousands of computers and networks that make up the Net.

D

Daemon   From the mythological meaning, later rationalized as the acronym Disk And Execution MONitor. A program that is not invoked explicitly, but lies dormant waiting for some condition(s) to occur. The idea is that the perpetrator of the condition need not be aware that a daemon is lurking (though often a program will commit an action only because it knows that it will implicitly invoke a daemon).

DARPA   The Defense Advanced Research Projects Agency (now the Defense Information Systems Agency) initiated the DARPA Internet program in 1969. This network, which was called a "CATENET," was the precursor to the modern Internet.

Dialer   A program that establishes and maintains your connection to the Internet, as well as provides Winsock support. NETCOMplete contains a built-in dialer (NETCOMplete for Windows 98 uses the dialer included with Windows 98). Other popular dialers include Trumpet Winsock and the Windows 95 Dial up Networking.

Dialup   A temporary connection between machines established with modems over a standard phone line.

Digital Cash   Electronic cash or bank account. Automatic payroll deposits in your bank are examples of digital cash.

DNS (Domain Name Service)   The Internet's distributed database system used to map names with the appropriate IP address. The DNS is a general-purpose distributed, replicated, data query service. The principal use is the lookup of host IP addresses based on host names. The style of host names now used in the Internet is called "domain name," because they are the style of names used to look up anything in the DNS. Some important domains are .COM (commercial), .NET (network), .EDU (educational), .GOV (government), and .MIL (military). Most countries also have a domain. For example, .US (United States), .UK (United Kingdom), and .AU (Australia).

Domain   The name associated with the numeric Internet Protocol (IP) address of a site on the Internet. Most of the domains that we will frequent are .com, .org, .edu, and .gov.

Download   Transferring or copying files from one computer to your computer over the Internet or any other communications link.

DPI (Dots Per Inch)   The spatial resolution of a graphics image, the number of dots per inch in a graphics image determine the quality of output. A high-end printer can produce 600–1200+ DPI while a computer monitor is only 72 DPI.

E

EDI (Electronic Data Interchange)   The exchange of information through the use of an electronic (and usually secure) messaging system.

EFF (Electronic Frontier Foundation)   (http://www.eff.org/) A non-profit civil liberties organization working in the public interest to protect privacy, free expression, and access to public resources and information online, as well as to promote responsibility in new media. Founded in July 1990, the Electronic Frontier Foundation (EFF) is dedicated to finding ways to resolve these and other conflicts while ensuring that essential civil liberties are protected.[3]

E-mail   An acronym for Electronic Mail. A system whereby a computer user can exchange messages with other computer users (or groups of users) via a communications network. Electronic mail is one of the most popular uses of the Internet. *See Snail Mail.*

E-mail Address   The domain-based or UUCP address that is used to send electronic mail to a specified destination. For example, support@ix.netcom.com is the e-mail address for the user support on the machine **ix** that is part of the **netcom.com** domain.

E-mall   An electronic shopping mall. The cyber version of the Galleria.

Emoticon   E-mail emotions, or faces that you insert to express moods. Examples: Smiley face **:-)** or unhappy face **:-(**.

Ethernet   The most common LAN transmission network.

Eudora™   One of the most popular Windows e-mail programs available. You can download the freeware version, Eudora Light™ or you can purchase the feature rich Eudora™ Pro from here: `http://www.eudora.com/`.

Explorer (Internet Explorer)   Microsoft's Web browser.

Exposures   The number of times a viewer sees an advertising banner.

Extranet   A close relative of an Intranet with the difference being that remote company offices not confined to the corporate location can utilize the Intranet via the Internet.

F

FAQ   An acronym for Frequently Asked Questions.

FDDI (Fiber Distributed Data Interface)   A fiber-based token-passing LAN technology standardized by ANSI, with dual counter-rotating rings. Each ring carries information at the rate of 100 Mbits.

Filtering   An automatic method of screening e-mail messages as they are downloaded from the Internet. An e-mail client can be instructed to deposit (file or trash) qualifying e-mail messages in various folders as they are received. A filter can look at keywords, addresses, domains, subject matter, size, and so on.

Finger   An Internet tool used to locate people on other Internet sites.

Firewall   A hardware and/or software gateway that buffers and shields data passing between two networks.

Flame   **1. vt.** To post an e-mail message intended to insult and provoke. **2. vi.** To speak incessantly and/or rabidly on some relatively uninteresting subject or with a patently ridiculous attitude. **3. vt.** Either of senses 1 or 2, directed with hostility at a particular person or people. **4. n.** An instance of flaming. When a discussion degenerates into useless controversy, one might tell the participants "Now you're just flaming" or "Stop all that flamage!" to try to get them to cool down (so to speak).

Flame Bait   A posting intended to trigger a flame war, or one that invites flames in reply.

Frames   An HTML programming option that permits a Web page to be subdivided into smaller sections of varying size. The "windows" can have no relevance to each other or they can be hyperlinked to each other.

Frame Relay   A communications interface that provides high-speed packet transmission with minimum delay and efficient use of bandwidth. It assumes that all connections are reliable and does not have error detection or control which helps to speed up the protocol.

Freeware   Software that is free for anyone's use (public domain), but can be copyright protected and/or have restrictions concerning duplication or resale

FTP (File Transfer Protocol)   A method of transferring files that permits a user to access a remote network on which he has permission (user name and password) to upload and/or download files in particular directories. FTP is one of oldest Internet conventions still being used today. Click here to download the current version of WS-FTP. (`http://www.ipswitch.com/pd_wsftp.html`)

G

GIF (Graphics Interchange Format)   Developed by CompuServe. A common graphics format for Web images. GIF and JPG are the most common Web graphics formats in use today. **Animated GIFs** are a group of images stored in one GIF file with programmed delays and transitions that create the illusion of animation.

Gigabyte   1,000 megabytes of data. *See also Megabyte.*

Gopher   A predecessor to the World Wide Web, was a means of navigating a sequence of menus on different servers. Gopher created links from one Gopher site to another. With the arrival of the Web and its hypertext navigation ability, Gopher's usefulness has largely disappeared.

GUI (Graphics User Interface)   Pronounced "gooey," a navigational command or menu interface designed to be self-explanatory and easy to use by pointing and clicking on text selections and icons. The Windows GUI interface, although originally pioneered in the 1970s by Xerox, is now the de facto standard for American business.

H

Hacker   A person who delights in having an intimate understanding of the internal workings of a system, computers, and computer networks in particular. The term is often misused in a pejorative context, where "cracker" would be the correct term.

HDML (Handheld Device Markup Language)   A developing programming language for a new class of cellular (wireless) communications.

Header   Information that appears at the top of e-mail messages and newsgroup articles that contains data about the sender and the message. The date and time the message was created, the computer path through which the message traveled and other information is included in the header.

Hex Code   The binary code name for a color used in HTML.

Hit   A request from a browser for a single item from a Web server. An overused term when discussing traffic on a Web site, for example, *"We get 500,000 hits per month."*

Calling one page from a server could result in dozens of "hits" because each graphic is interpreted as a hit. In reality, counting only the "index.htm" page or "default.htm" page would be a more accurate gauge of traffic.

Home Page   A place on the Web where any person, company, or organization can display information.

Host   A computer that allows users to communicate with other host computers on a network. Individual users communicate by using client programs, such as electronic mail, Telnet, and FTP. Every computer on the Internet with its own IP address is designated as a host.

Hotspot   Areas in a Web document or graphic that are hyperlinks to other pages or URLs.

HTML (Hyper Text Markup Language)   The prevailing presentation level standard for authoring World Wide Web documents. In its most basic form, it resembles the early word processing codes of the early 1980s.

HTTP (Hyper Text Transfer Protocol)   The language convention of the Web, used to deliver HTML documents.

Hype   Anything related to the Internet as described by a Wall Street investment banker or Vice President Al Gore.

Hyperlink   A means of "jumping" from one information site to another on the same or a different network server.

Hypertext   A link between one document and other, related documents elsewhere in a collection. By clicking on a word or phrase that has been highlighted on a computer screen, a user can skip directly to files related to that subject.

I

IETF (Internet Engineering Task Force)   (http://www.ietf.org/overview.html) A large open international community of network designers, operators, vendors, and researchers concerned with the evolution of the Internet architecture and the smooth operation of the Internet. It is open to any interested individual. To learn more about this group, what they do and how you may want to become involved, read "A Guide for New Attendees of the Internet Engineering Task Force" at http://www.ietf.org/tao.html.[4]

Image Map   A graphics image (picture, map, and so on) in HTML that maps the pixels or an area of an image to a Web resource via a hyperlink. Clicking on a section of the image is the same as selecting a hyperlinked word or phrase.

IMHO   In my humble opinion.

Infobot   An automatic response to an e-mail or Web inquiry used to provide additional information about a product or service. *See Autoresponder and Mailbot.*

Interlaced Graphics   GIF files that are interlaced permit the graphic to load gradually in the browser window, progressively increasing the clarity.

Internet   A collection of cooperative networks and gateways that functions as a single, virtual network using the TCP/IP protocol.

Internet Address   An IP address that uniquely identifies a node on the Internet.

Internet Protocol (IP)   The network layer for the TCP/IP Protocol Suite. It is a connectionless, best-effort packet switching protocol.

Internet Society, The   A nongovernmental international organization for global cooperation and coordination for the Internet and its internetworking technologies and applications. The Society's individual and organizational members are bound by a common stake in maintaining the viability and global scaling of the Internet. It comprises the companies, government agencies, and foundations that have created the Internet and its technologies as well as innovative new entrepreneurial organizations contributing to maintain that dynamic. Visit its home pages at http://info.isoc.org/ to see how Internet innovators are creatively using the network.[5]

InterNIC   A cooperative activity between the National Science Foundation, Network Solutions, Inc. and AT&T. Network Solutions sponsors Registration Services, Support Services, and Net Scout Services. Click here to visit the InterNIC on the Web. (http://www.internic.net/)

Interpreneurs   A new breed of entrepreneur who develops Internet/Intranet businesses or applications.

Intranet   A private, internal network that operates within the walls of a company (similar to a LAN) and is usually insulated from the outside world via an electronic or hardware impedance called a firewall.

IP Address   The 32-bit address is the basic unit of information assigned to all participants in a TCP/IP network. The four-part number uniquely identifies a client, network, or domain.

IP*ng*   Internet Protocol *Next Generation* is a working group of the Internet Engineering Task Force (IETF) that is responsible for solving the IP address shortage due to occur after the millenium.

IRC (Internet Relay Chat)   A worldwide "party line" network that allows one to converse with others in real-time. IRC is structured as a network of Internet servers, each of which accepts connections from client programs, one per user.

ISDN (Integrated Services Digital Network)   Switched digital networking that handles a range of digital voice and digital image transmission. It provides end-to-end, simultaneous handling of voice and data on the same digital links via integrated switches. For more information about Netcom ISDN services, go to our ISDN Information page (http://www.netcom.com/isdn).

ISP (Internet Service Provider)   A commercial provider of Internet access to the public.

J

Java   A new object-oriented programming language for creating distributed executable applications. Hot Java is a browser capable of carrying out applet commands written in the Java programming language.

Java Script   A noncompiled command language used in HTML applications, in which the instructions are managed by the browser.

JDK   (Java Development Kit) The development kit from Sun Microsystems that provides the basic tools needed to write, test, and debug Java.

JEPI   (Joint Electronic Payment Initiative) developed by the World Wide Web Consortium (W3C) to help facilitate electronic commerce.

J-mail   Electronic junk mail.

JPEG (Joint Photographic Expert Group)   A graphic compression and decompression standard.

K

Kbps (Kilobits per second)   A measurement of digital transmission speeds (1 kilobit = 1,000 bits).

Kermit   A popular file transfer protocol developed by Columbia University. Because Kermit runs in most operating environments, it provides an easy method of file transfer. Kermit is not the same as FTP. Kermit is available for use by Netcom shell account customers. Issuing the command *kermit* by itself starts Kermit in interactive mode.

Keyword(s)   The descriptive text included in HTML programming which is indexed by search engines. For example, keywords such as motor, engine, tires, and so on would be included in a site geared to automobiles.

L

LAN   Local Area Networks are a cabling system (Ethernet, Token Ring, FDDI Leased lines, and so on) which connect users together and permit file sharing and file transfer as in the case with e-mail.

Lexis-Nexis Although fee-based, this database consisting of extensive news and general interest subjects is one of the most powerful research sites in the world. (`http://www.lexis-nexis.com/`)

Link   *See Hyperlink.*

Listservers   (Listserv) A software program used to manage e-mail discussion groups.

Lurk   To hang around a newsgroup without participating. A person who is lurking is just listening to the discussion. Lurking is encouraged for beginning users who wish to become acquainted with a particular discussion before joining in.

M

Magic (or FM)   As yet unexplained or too complicated to explain. (Arthur C.) Clarke's Third Law: "Any sufficiently advanced technology is indistinguishable from magic."

Mailbot   A program that automatically responds to incoming e-mail requests. *See Infobot or Autoresponder.*

Mail Server   A software program that distributes files or information in response to requests sent via e-mail. Internet examples include Almanac and netlib. Mail servers have also been used in BITNet to provide FTP-like services.

Mailing List   An e-mail address that expands to multiple e-mail addresses. Usually they are confined to specific topics of information.

Majordomo   A mailing list processor which runs under UNIX *See also Listserv.*

MAPI (Messaging Application Programming Interface)   Microsoft's standard for the interface to e-mail.

Marketroid   One who works in the marketing department of any software company. More specifically, the person who dreams-up all the "Twonkies" to add to their programs is termed a Marketroid.

Mbps (Megabits per second)   A measurement of digital transmission speeds (1 megabit = 1,000 kilobits).

Megabit   Approximately one million bits of data.

Megabyte   Approximately one million bytes of data.

Merchant Bank   A banking company that handles corporate transactions. A merchant bank enables a business to receive and clear credit card transactions on line. A merchant bank is the one who actually transfers money from a buyer's account to a seller's account as a result of goods or services being sold.

META Tags   Commands in HTML that instruct the browser or search engines to perform specific tasks, identify keywords, site definitions, page authors, plug-in requirements, and so on that are invisible to the user.

MIDI (Musical Instrument Digital Interface)   A protocol that permits sounds from musical instruments to be converted to a program and read by a computer.

MIME (Multipurpose Internet Mail Extension)   A specification in multimedia documents.

Modem   A hardware device that connects to the phone lines that permits computers to exchange information. Modems convert binary data into analog for the purpose of passing that data over copper phone lines.

Moderator   A person, or small group of people, who manage moderated mailing lists and Usenet newsgroups. Moderators are responsible for determining which e-mail submissions are passed onto a list.

Moore's Law   Gordon Moore, a founder of the giant semiconductor maker Intel, proclaimed in 1968 that the number of transistors or switches on a chip would double every eighteen months or two years, making the chip faster, more powerful, and less expensive.

MUD (Multi-User Dungeon)   Adventures, role-playing games, or simulations played on the Internet. Devotees call them "text-based virtual reality adventures." Players interact in real-time and can modify the "world" in which the game is played. Most MUDs are based on the Telnet protocol.

Multitasking   The simultaneous execution of two or more assignments by one program or the coordinated use of one program that performs many functions at the same time.

N

Narrowcasting   A term that describes the distribution of information (or TV programs) designed for minority interests rather than the mass appeal targeted by broadcasting.

NCSA (National Center for Supercomputing Applications)   At the University of Illinois at Urbana-Champaign.

Net Abuse   Net abuse can be either abuse of Netcom's network services or violations of netiquette. Types of net abuse that violate Netcom's Terms and Conditions include:

- Using too many of the system resources.
- Attempting to "hack," or break into accounts.
- Using an account for any illegal activity.
- Evading the 10-minute idle timeout.
- Running background processes or "bots."
- Sending unsolicited e-mail.
- Sending chain letters via e-mail.
- Advertising in inappropriate newsgroups.
- Off-topic posts to newsgroups.
- SPAMming or inappropriate postings to many newsgroups.
- Disruption of newsgroups or IRC channels.
- "Flooding" someone with talk requests.
- Direct threats in newsgroup posts or e-mail.
- Sharing an account (in certain circumstances).

Netcom Account   The standard PPP dial-up account at Netcom. You have such an account if your e-mail address is of the format **you@ix.netcom.com**. The majority of accounts offered by Netcom, including accounts in the NETCOMplete family of service plans and ISDN, are considered Netcom Accounts.

Netcom Account Holder   The person who owns the credit card that the Netcom Account is billed to.

Netcom Services Authentication

Services password
Use this password to access a Netcom service, such as a mailbox or CruzInfo. Your services plan may include a services password.

NETCOMplete Advantage customers use two different passwords: a "login password" and a "separate services password." Each mailbox in a Netcom account has a separate services password. Netcom account holders need to make sure that their own services password and the Netcom login password that they choose are different.

NETCOMplete and shell customers use the same password for both the "login password" and the "services password".

Netcom Shell Account   A special dial-up account that allows access to Netcom UNIX Shell machines. You have such an account if your e-mail address is of the format **username@netcom.com** (without the "ix").

NETCOMplete   A Netcom brand often used to refer to a bundle of software and services. Versions of Netcom client software 2.5 and above are also referred to as NETCOMplete.

Netscape   A Web browser (Navigator) and by default, the name of the authoring company. The Netscape™ browser was based on the Mosaic program developed at NCSA.

Netiquette (network etiquette)   The conventions of politeness (Miss Manners etiquette of the Internet) recognized on Usenet, such as avoidance of cross-posting to inappropriate groups and refraining from "commercial pluggery" outside the biz (business) newsgroups.

Newbie   A new Internet user.

Newsgroup   A series of articles (postings) concerning specific themes. Usenet groups can be unmoderated (anyone can post) or moderated (submissions are automatically directed to a moderator, who edits or filters and then posts the results). Some newsgroups have parallel mailing lists for Internet people with no netnews access, with postings to the group automatically propagated to the list, and vice versa. Some moderated are distributed as digests, with groups of postings periodically collected into a single large posting with an index.

NIC (Network Information Center)   A NIC provides information, assistance, and services to network users. The Internet Network Information Center (InterNIC) is a project administered by AT&T and Network Solutions, Inc. (NSI). AT&T provides directory and database services for registered Internet hosts, while NSI administers the registration process.

Nickname   A name that you select when you connect to an IRC server. Many users choose descriptive nicknames that have no relevance to their real identity.

NOC   Network Operations Center.

NOS   Network Operating System.

Node   A device on a network that requests or provides services. A node is also used to describe a network workstation.

NNTP (Network News Transfer Protocol)   A protocol for the distribution, retrieval, and posting of Usenet articles through high-speed links available on the Internet.

NSFNET   The National Science Foundation started the Supercomputer Centers program in 1986. NSF's idea was to construct five supercomputer centers around the country and build a network that would link them with users. This would be the core of the U.S. Internet, until its privatization and retirement in 1995.

NSI   Network Solutions Inc. was awarded the InterNIC contract worth $5.9 million a year by NSF. NSI began registering domains at the rate of approximately 400 per month.

NT (New Technology)   Windows NT is Microsoft's 32-bit version of Windows. It is a standalone operating system (OS) that is also a network-ready system.

O

OCR (Optical Character Recognition)   Software that converts scanned images of text documents into files, which can then be imported into a word processor.

OFX (Open Financial Exchange)   Messaging specifications created by Microsoft, Intuit (http://www.intuit.com/), and CheckFree (http://www.checkfree.com/).

OS (Operating System)   DOS, Windows 3.1, Windows 98, UNIX, OS2, and so on are basic operating systems for computers.

P

Packet   A set of data (a collection of bits, including the address, data, and control elements) that is processed as a unit in data transmission.

Packet Switching   A method of transferring data in a network where individual packets are accepted by the network and delivered to the prescribed destination. Packets can be distributed in any order because the control data sent at the beginning of the transmission ensures they are interpreted in the correct sequence once received. Because each packet carries its own instructions, it can use any route to reach its destination.

Page   A single (page) file of hypertext mark-up language. A Web site is composed of many pages of information.

Perl (Practical Extraction and Reporting Language)   A scripting language used for text manipulation and popular for writing gateway applications (CGI).

PDA (Personal Digital Assistant)   Handheld computing and communication devices.

PDF   A file format exclusive to the Adobe Acrobat Reader that can be downloaded and viewed offline.

PEP (Protocol Extension Protocol)   An extension to HTTP.

PGP (Pretty Good Privacy)   Encrypts and decrypts files and messages using some of the strongest encryption technology available to U.S. civilians.

Ping   The TCP/IP service that lets you check to verify that you can reach another network node from your local host. Ping is usually a quick test to ensure that your connection is valid. The command will return the time in milliseconds that a packet takes to make the round trip from your local host to the remote host.

Plug-ins   A software application that allows you to view different information formats in your browser window.

POP (Point-of-Presence)   A group of modems, routers, and other equipment, located in a metropolitan area, allowing subscribers to access the Internet through a local telephone call. Also, POP is an acronym for Post Office Protocol.

POP 2/3 (Post Office Protocol)   A protocol designed to allow single user hosts to read e-mail from a server. There are three versions: POP, POP2, and POP3. Later versions are **not** compatible with earlier versions.

Portal   Similar to a launch pad or a default home page on the Web, a portal is a starting point for Web users.

Posting   The method of sending e-mail message to a newsgroup or electronic bulletin board.

Postmaster   The e-mail contact and maintenance person at a site connected to the Internet. Often, but not always, the same as the admin.

POTS (Plain Old Telephone Service)   Copper phone wires or twisted pair, the same wiring that connects to your home or office.

PPP (Point to Point Protocol)   A communications protocol that allows dial-up access to Internet over telephone lines.

Primary Mailbox   The primary mailbox is set up automatically when you get your Netcom Account.

Primary Mailbox Password   The primary mailbox uses the Netcom Account holder's services password to log in to the primary mailbox.

Primary Mailbox Username   The primary mailbox uses the Netcom Account holder's username.

Protocol   Message formats (rules) that two or more machines must observe to exchange information. To print a document on a network printer, strict protocols must be adhered to or the operation can not proceed.

PSTN (Public Switched Telephone Network)   The old-fashioned telephone system with which we all grew up. *See POTS*.

PUSH   (As opposed to PULL technology.) Information is delivered to a desktop or other receiving device in real time as new information becomes available. This is as a result of a user defining areas of interest, industries, and keywords via a personal profile with the PUSH service provider.

Q–R

QuickTime (QT)   A format developed by Apple Computer for working with data files, such as sounds and video. A QuickTime file is indicated by a ".mov" (movie) filename. (http://www.apple.com/)

Radio Button   A round selection (check box) field in software programs and Web forms that, when checked, looks like a knob from an old radio.

RAM   Random Access Memory is *temporary* memory that your computer uses to store information. Text copied to the "clipboard" is stored in RAM until it is replaced by new information or the computer is turned off.

Real Audio™   A browser plug-in used to listen to live or on-demand music in real-time across the Internet at 14.4K baud or higher. Click here to download the current version of the Real Audio player.

Remote Login   Operating on a remote computer, using a protocol over a computer network, as though locally attached. Commonly used protocols include **telnet** and **rlogin**. Telnet is a TC—More—P/IP protocol. The rlogin protocol is specific to Unix environments. Netcom UNIX shell customers can use both telnet and rlogin. The NETCOMplete software includes a telnet client.

RNA (Ring No Answer)   This is the symptom used to describe a modem at a local POP that rings, but does not pick up the incoming call.

Robot ("bots" and personal agents)   A term for software programs that automatically explore the Web for a variety of purposes; robots that collect resources for later database queries by users are also called spiders, worms, and knowbots.

Routing   The process used on the Internet to deliver data packets to their intended destination. A router processes the data packet and reads the destination address included in the IP header then determines the next (router) stop that will take the packet closer to its destination. The process is repeated until the packet arrives at its final target.

RTFM   An acronym for "Read The *Freaking* Manual." Advice given to Newbies who ask questions before looking for the answers in the appropriate places.

S

Screen Capture   A method of "capturing" a snapshot of your computer screen. Pressing the "Print Scrn" key on your keyboard will place an image of your computer screen in memory. Pasting (Ctrl+V) that image into any graphics program will permit you to crop and edit that scene.

Search Engines   Resources that are used to locate information on the Internet.

Server   An Internet computer that stores Web pages and files for downloading. A software application that provides data or services requested from client programs.

SET (Secure Electronic Transactions)   A new Internet standard from MasterCard and VISA.

SGML (Standard Generalized Mark-Up Language)   An international standard for defining special document types and controlling presentation of pages. HTML is an instance of SGML. *See also XML.*

Shareware   Software that you are permitted to evaluate for a specified period of time and then pay the author a fee if you wish to continue using it.

Shelfware   Software purchased on a whim (by an individual user) or in accordance with policy (by a corporation or government agency), but not actually required for any particular use. Therefore, it often ends up on some shelf.

Shell   The user interface to an operating environment. UNIX has several, including the Bourne shell (*sh*), the C shell (*csh*), and the Korn shell (*ksh*).

Shockwave™   A plug-in from Macromedia that permits you to view animated multimedia presentations on the Web. Click here to download the current version. (http://www.macromedia.com/shockwave/)

Signature   Text that can usually be automatically inserted at the bottom of e-mail messages or newsgroups articles. Most e-mail clients and browsers perform this as a default feature.

Site   A file section of a computer on which files reside, for example, a Web site, a Gopher site, an FTP site.

SLA (Service Level Agreement)   Netcom's New Service Level Agreement (SLA) for DirectConnect Dedicated Internet Services guarantees 99.5% uptime. Netcom assures the availability of your Internet access with its new Service Level Agreement (SLA), which is now included as a standard feature of DirectConnect 56K, Frame Relay, Flex T1, and Full T1 services when you sign-up for a one-year term or more. The DirectConnect SLA guarantees 99.5% service availability ("uptime") each month and may offer a credit equal to 25% of your monthly service fee if this guaranteed availability is not met.[6]

SLIP (Serial Line Interface Protocol)   A communications protocol that permits dial-up access to the Internet via telephone lines.

SMTP (Simple Mail Transfer Protocol)   The set of rules that the Internet uses for exchanging e-mail messages. SMTP is a server-to-server protocol, so other protocols are used to access the messages. *See Post Office Protocol.*

Snail Mail   The traditional mail service offered by the U.S. Postal Service. (http://www.usps.gov/)

SPAM   Not the canned meat with which you may be familiar. Internet-speak: flooding a newsgroup with irrelevant or inappropriate messages. You can SPAM a newsgroup with as little as one well-(or ill-) planned message, for example, asking "Does anyone want to lose weight and get rich at the same time?" on soc.women). This is often done with cross-posting (any message which is cross-posted to alt.rush-limbaugh and alt.politics.texas will almost inevitably SPAM both groups). SPAMing is considered one of the worst examples of bad netiquette .

Spider   A software program that traverses the Web to collect information about resources for later queries by users seeking to find resources; major species of active spiders include search engines such as Lycos and WebCrawler.

SQL (Structured Query Language)   A standardized query language used for querying databases in client/server applications.

Sturgeon's Law   "Ninety percent of everything is crap." Derived from a quote by science fiction author Theodore Sturgeon, who once said, "Sure, 90 percent of science fiction is crud. That's because 90 percent of everything is crud." Oddly, when Sturgeon's Law is cited, the final word is almost invariably changed to crap.

Subject Line   The line in e-mail messages where you insert the subject being discussed. This is an important place to add "spin" to a marketing message.

Surfing   Informal term for exploring the Internet (surfing the net). Most often used in reference to accessing sites on the World Wide Web.

SysOp   The person responsible for maintenance of a given computer system. Short for "System Operator."

T

T-1   A data communication line capable of transmitting at speeds of 1.54 Mbps. This is a U.S. and Japanese standard for high-speed data transmission.

T-3   A U.S. standard data communication line capable of transmitting at speeds of 45 Mbps. Also referred to as a DS3, a T-3 provides the equivalent bandwidth of 28 T-1 circuits.

Tag   The code used to make up part of an HTML component. *See META Tags.*

TCP/IP (Transmission Control Protocol/Internet Protocol)   The protocol used to connect two or more computers, and it is the foundation of the Internet communication protocol. The Internet is TCP/IP, and usually it is implemented on top of UNIX, except at the final desktop destination, where it might be on a Windows, NT, DOS PC, or Mac. Also, three main protocols sit above TCP/IP: Telnet, FTP, and SMTP.

Telnet   A protocol for sharing information across networks using a technique for terminal emulation. Using Telnet, it appears as if user is "logged in" to the remote computer.

Terabyte   1,000 gigabytes.

Themes   In Microsoft FrontPage 98, Themes provide a consistent look throughout a Web site. More than 50 professionally designed thematic templates include backgrounds, fonts, page headers, and navigation buttons.

Threads   In a discussion group or mailing list, a message thread is a series of e-mail responses to a particular subject strung together as in "following the thread."

TIA (The Internet Adapter)   A product that emulates a SLIP or PPP connection over a serial line, allowing shell users to run a SLIP/PPP session through a UNIX dialup account. "TIA" is also used informally as an abbreviation for "Thanks in advance."

Transaction Processing   Taking orders (usually via a secure procedure) and processing credit card transactions.

Trojan Horse   A computer program that carries within itself a means to allow the program's creator access to the system using it.

Troll   A term used to define a public message (either on a Usenet newsgroup or other public message board on an online service) that is posted for the sole purpose of offending people and/or generating an enormous flood of nontopic replies.

TTFN   Ta-Ta For Now.

Twonkie   The software equivalent of a Twinkie (a variety of sugar-loaded junk food), a useless feature added to look sexy and placate a marketroid.

U

UCE   Unsolicited Commercial E-mail, or another term for SPAM.

Upload   Moving files (FTP) from your computer to another computer over a communications link.

UPP (Universal Payment Preamble)   Internet payment negotiation protocol that is an extension to HTTP.

Urban Legend   A story, which may have started with a grain of truth, that has been embroidered and retold until it has passed into the realm of myth. Is an interesting phenomenon that these stories become spread so far, so fast, and so often. Examples of

Urban Legends relating to the Internet include "The Infamous Modem Tax," "Craig Shergold/Brain Tumor Get Well Cards," and "The Good Times Virus."

URL (Uniform Resource Locator)   The scheme for addressing on the Web. A URL identifies a resource (http://your-biz.com) on the Web.

Usenet   A system for disseminating asynchronous text discussion among cooperating computer hosts; the Usenet discussion space is divided into newsgroups, each on a particular topic or subtopic.

userID   A compression of "user identification"; the userID always proceeds the @ sign in an e-mail address.

Username   A username consists of one to eight characters, and only uses numberszero through nine and the 26 alphabet letters. Usernames do not have spaces. Usernames are the first part of an e-mail address: **username@ix.netcom.com**. You must have a username and a services password to log in to a mailbox.

UUCP (UNIX-to-UNIX Command Protocol)   This was initially a program run under the UNIX operating system that allowed one UNIX system to send files to another UNIX system via dial-up phone lines. Today, the term is more commonly used to describe the large international network, which uses the UUCP protocol to pass news and electronic mail. Netcom's UUCP customers have their own internal networks and purchase e-mail and Usenet news feeds from Netcom.

UUdecoding   The restoration of uuencoded data to its original form.

UUencode   (UNIX-to-UNIX Encoding) A process used to convert binary files (graphics) to ASCII (text) so that they can be transmitted across the Internet via an e-mail attachment. The new WinZip utility features built-in support UUencode.

V

Vaporware   Products, services, and "hype" promised far in advance of any realistic availability. For example, "Soon you will be able to browse the Internet wirelessly at the speed of light." *Not!*

Veronica   A service that maintains an index of titles of items on Gopher servers, and provides keyword searches of those titles.

Virtual Domain (or virtual server)   .A site on the Internet that exists virtually with other domains on the same network server that has its own IP address.

Virtual LAN   A logical versus a physical (wired) LAN made up of workgroups and individuals brought together for a particular project with most members' locations being apart from the others.

Virus   A program that when loaded infects, alters, or destroys other programs. Some virus programs cause major trouble and some are nothing more than annoying pranks.

VR (Virtual Reality)   A place or event that exists only in cyberspace but is programmed to have the appearance of a *real* experience.

VRML (Virtual Reality Modeling Language)   A specification for three-dimensional rendering viewed with Web browsers (and possibly a VRML plug-in). Visit the VRML Repository is an impartial, comprehensive, community resource for the dissemination of information relating to VRML. Maintained by the San Diego Supercomputer Center (SDSC). (http://www.sdsc.edu/vrml/)

W

W3C (World Wide Web Consortium)   An international industry consortium committed to developing public protocols for the World Wide Web. Currently, the W3C is contemplating HTML 4.0 specs including XML and digital signatures. W3C is the developer of the Joint Electronic Payment Initiative (JEPI). (http://www.w3.org/)

WAIS (Wide Area Information Servers)   A distributed information service that offers simple natural language input, indexed searching for fast retrieval, and a "relevance feedback" mechanism which allows the results of initial searches to influence future searches. Public domain implementations are available. *See Archie, Gopher, and Veronica.*

WAN   Wide Area Networks are basically the same as a LAN. Where a LAN usually involves one wired office, floor, or building, a WAN can traverse the globe and connect geographically dispersed users.

wav   Pronounced "wave," an audio file used extensively on the Internet and in computer software programs. For example, filename.wav.

Web   A set of hypertext pages that is considered a single work; typically, a single Web is created by one or more authors and deployed on a network server with links to other servers; a subset of the Web.

WebBots   *See Robot.*

Web site   A collection of Web pages or a domain on the World Wide Web.

Webutize   A new term, putting a business on the Web.

Weight or Weighted Results   In statistics, results (taken from a survey or behavioral pattern) that have been measured against predetermined methodology.

Whois   An Internet program that allows users to query a database of people and other Internet entities, such as domains, networks, and hosts.

WIMPs   Whining Internet/Multimedia Phobes.[7]

Windows CE   A new operating system for PDAs and handheld devices which is basically a scaled down version of Windows 98. Click here to visit the Windows CE home page. (`http://www.microsoft.com/windowsce/default.asp`)

Winsock   Winsock is a TCP/IP stack that allows you to use your modem to send data to/from the Internet. A Winsock interface is required for Windows Internet applications

like Netscape, Eudora, Free Agent, and many others. Winsock allows true Internet networking via modem.

Wizards   Software "question and answer applications" that perform a function after presenting the user with selectable options. A set-up wizard may ask, "Do you want white or black text?" *or* "Do you want fries with your order?"

Worm   A computer program which replicates itself and is self-propagating. Worms, as opposed to viruses, are meant to spawn in network environments. Network worms were first defined by Shoch and Hupp of Xerox in ACM Communications (March 1982). The Internet worm of November 1988 is perhaps the most famous; it successfully propagated itself on over 6,000 systems across the Internet. *See Trojan Horse or Virus.*

WS-FTP   A file transfer program that is used to upload/download files and text to your Web Site. Designed for nonprogrammers but sophisticated enough for power users, WS_FTP Pro is widely recognized as the fastest, most powerful Windows file transfer client application available. Click here to download the current version. (`http://www.ipswitch.com/pd_wsftp.html`)

WWW (World Wide Web)   A hypertext information and communication system popularly used on the Internet computer network with data communications operating according to a client/server model. Web clients (browsers) can access multi-protocol and hypermedia information (in some instances multimedia helper applications or plug-ins are required for the browser) using an addressing scheme. A home page or a Web page is part of this World Wide Web.

WYSIWYG   An acronym for What You See is What You Get. Pronounced "whizzy-wig."

X–Y–Z

x.25   The most common standard for exchanging information through packet networks and the most widely used interface for WANs.

X.500   The name for a family of international standards used for e-mail directories.

Xanadu   Under development since the1960s, Xanadu is the original hypertext and interactive multimedia program.

XML (eXtensible Markup Language)   Like HTML, is an outgrowth of SGML that permits developers to control and display data in the same way they control text and graphics today. XML is not a replacement for HTML.

YAHOO!   An acronym for Yet Another Hierarchical Officious Oracle. Yahoo! (http://www.yahoo.com/) was one of the first and remains as one of the best Internet search engines.

YP (Yellow Pages)   A service used by UNIX administrators to manage databases distributed across a network. Now known as NIS (Network Information Services).

Zine   As in maga*zine*, a (usually) free Internet publication.

Zip (zipped)   A method of compressing files used often on the Internet to speed downloading. A zipped file will have a name that looks like *filename.zip*. The most popular Windows zip program is WinZip. Click here to download the latest version of WinZip (http://www.winzip.com/).[8]

If you didn't find it here

Check
the
Net!

If you discover a term that is not included here, or you need a better explanation, the following reference glossaries should be of help. They are listed in no particular order of importance.

The Center for Electronic Messaging Technologies (CEMT)   Designed for federal, state, and local employees or anyone else that wishes to gain knowledge in the messaging, electronic directory, and applied technologies field. (http://www.fed.gov/ emailenc/glossry.html)

Net Lingo Dictionary of Internet terms   An online dictionary containing definitions of words that are emerging as a new vocabulary surrounding the technology and community of the Internet and the World Wide Web. (http://www.netlingo.com/index.html)

The Jargon File   A collection of slang terms used by various subcultures of computer hackers. Though some technical material is included for background and flavor, it is not a technical dictionary. It contains the language hackers use among themselves for fun, social communication, and technical debate. (http://beast.cc.emory.edu/jargon30/ HOMEPAGE.HTML)

The Third Age Internet Glossary   A glossary of the most commonly used terms related to the Internet and the World Wide Web. (http://www.thirdage.com/features/ tech/glossary/index039.html)

[1] Some definitions have been "borrowed" from The Jargon File, a collection of slang terms used by various subcultures of computer hackers. The Jargon File is public domain.

[2] Copyright © 1997 Corel Corporation. All rights reserved. Company and product names are trademarks or registered trademarks of their respective companies.

[3] Taken from the Web site of the Electronic Frontier Foundation at http://www.eff.org/.

[4] Taken from the Internet Engineering Task Force's Web page at http://www.ietf.org/overview.html.

[5] Taken from the Internet Society's Web site at http://info.isoc.org/.

[6] Quicken Financial Network is committed to providing convenient, high-quality online financial services within a secure and private environment. (Source: QFN Web site.)

[7] Worcester Polytechnic Institute (http://www.wpi.edu//) Offering a Web based, paperless course on Telecommunications Transmission Technologies (http://bugs.wpi.edu:8080/EE535/).

[8] WinZip is a registered trademark of Nico Mak Computing, Inc. http://www.winzip.com/.

Software Installation

Netcomplete 4.0 for Windows—everything you need to get started on the Internet is in Netcomplete. Within minutes, you can begin exploring your favorite topics on the Net, check out web sites, e-mail, newsgroups, chat, FTP, and more. Netcomplete 4.0 for Windows comes with the Internet Explorer 4.0 web browser.

System requirements

Before installing Netcomplete, make sure your computer meets the following requirements:

- IBM-compatible PC with a 486 or higher processor
- Windows 95 or Windows 98
- VGA graphics card
- Color monitor recommended
- Mouse or other pointing device
- 14.4Kbps modem or faster (28.8Kbps recommended)

 IMPORTANT: If you do not have Dial-Up Networking installed, the Netcomplete Setup application prompts for your Windows 95/98 CD so it can install Dial-Up Networking.

System requirements for Netcomplete with Internet Explorer 4.0

- 16MB RAM
- 51MB free disk space (standard install)
- 86MB free disk space (advanced install)

WARNING

If you already *have* a Netcomplete account, select the option "Use an Existing Account." Do not set up a new account. If you do *not* have a Netcom account, select the option "Set Up a New Account."

Installation instructions

1. Insert the CD-ROM into your CD-ROM drive.
2. From the Windows 95 desktop, double-click on the **My Computer** icon.
3. Double-click on the icon representing your CD-ROM drive.
4. Double-click on the icon titled **SETUP.EXE** to run the installation program.
5. After the installation is complete, the Netcomplete installer may need to restart your computer.

NOTE

If Windows 95 is installed on your computer, and you have the AutoPlay feature enabled, the SETUP.EXE program starts automatically whenever you insert the disc into your CD-ROM drive.

Contacting Netcom

Netcom's Technical Support staff is available to answer your technical questions.

- E-mail: support@ix.netcom.com
- Fax-on-Demand: (800) 638–6383
- Phone: 5am–9 pm (PST): (408) 881–1810
  After Hours: (900) 555–1144

Netcom's Customer Service staff is available to answer your general account and billing questions, Monday through Friday, 6 am to 6 pm (PST). Customer Service can be reached at (888) 316–1122.

Hosting offer

Try it before you buy it! Netcom and Microsoft have teamed up to offer you 30 days of free Internet access and hosting, as well as a 45-day trial version of Microsoft FrontPage 98.

If you already have Internet access. go to `http://www.yourbiz.com/offer` to take advantage of your 30-days free hosting package. You will have your choice of three different Web hosting packages. If you need Internet access with a hosting package, follow the CD installation instructions to sign up.

All hosting packages include

- Domain Name Registration & Routing*
- Plenty of MB Disk Storage
- Generous Monthly Data Transfer
- Pop E-mail Account(s)
- FTP (File Transfer Protocol) Access
- Microsoft® FrontPage® 98 Server Extensions
- Open Market's ShopSite™ Manager Lite
- CGI (Common Gateway Interface)
- E-mail Forwarding
- E-mail Autoresponder
- Log Files
- 14-Day Trial of Virtual WebTrends™

*InterNIC fees may be included with some packages.

To set up a new account, you need a major credit card to complete the registration and to open your Netcom account. If you do not want to use a credit card, please call 1–(888) 638–2664 to speak to a Netcom Hosting Sales Representative.

You will need to enter one of the code numbers on the back of this book during the registration process in order to receive this special offer.

Microsoft FrontPage 98 Trial Version Agreement

1. Microsoft product support is not included with the trial version.
2. Netcom does not provide technical support for Microsoft FrontPage software. After you have signed up for Netcom's hosting services, you may access additional on-line support information in the Help section under Client Resources.
3. The trial version of FrontPage 98 does not qualify users for upgrade pricing.

For complete details, please read the readme.txt file provided on the Netcomplete CD.

All offers are subject to change at Netcom's discretion.

FrontPage 98 installation

You are about to install a complete, fully operational version of FrontPage 98. You will be able to experience the total functionality of FrontPage 98 for 45 days, after which time the program will cease to operate.

IMPORTANT!

Because this copy of FrontPage 98 is an evaluation copy and NOT a registered version of software, there is **NO TECHNICAL SUPPORT AVAILABLE** for FrontPage 98.

Please do not contact Microsoft or Netcom for FrontPage 98 technical support. Without a valid product registration code (only available through retail purchase) you will not be eligible for any support.

This is one of the primary reasons why we have made an effort to explain FrontPage 98's features in such detail. Also, we have provided a number of very helpful support links at the end of the FrontPage 98 chapter.

To load FrontPage 98 with its related components, Internet Explorer and Image Composer on your computer, follow these simple instructions.

- Insert the CD-ROM in your CD-ROM drive.

Select FrontPage from the menu. Setup will first search your computer for required networking components and for Web server software. On Windows® 95 and 98, if Setup does not detect required networking components on your computer, you will be prompted to install them. Click "Yes" and follow the Setup instructions on the screen.

If Setup does not detect a Web server on your computer, you will be prompted to install the Microsoft Personal Web Server (on Windows 98) or Microsoft Peer Web Services (on Windows NT® Workstation). Click "Yes" and follow the Setup instructions on the screen.

 You may be prompted to restart your computer. After restarting, Setup will continue, so that you can install other components of Microsoft FrontPage 98.

If the system setting for your language does not match one of the languages in which FrontPage 98 is offered, Setup displays the **Select Language** dialog box. Choose the language in which you want to use FrontPage and click **OK**.

The Setup dialog box has options for installing all the components of Microsoft FrontPage 98. Click **Install FrontPage 98** to start the Microsoft FrontPage installation.

There are two setup options, **Typical** and **Custom**. The Typical option installs all the components you need to get up and running with FrontPage 98. The Custom option lets you select which FrontPage 98 components to install. The Custom option also includes additional components not available in the Typical option, such as additional clip art. Unless you want to install particular FrontPage 98 components, choose **Typical** and click **Next**.

When it has finished installing the FrontPage Server Extensions, Setup may prompt you to restart your computer. After you restart your computer, Setup will continue.

After FrontPage 98 is installed, you will be prompted to start the FrontPage Explorer. If you choose to start the FrontPage Explorer at this time, you can continue Setup any time in the future. *(We recommend that you complete the entire installation process at one time.)*

Internet Explorer 4.0 installation

 Click Install Internet Explorer to install the latest versions of Microsoft Internet Explorer, the recommended Web browser for use with FrontPage.

Image Composer installation

 When creating a Web site it may sometimes be necessary for you to use a full-featured graphics program. You will need a program more powerful than Microsoft Paint which is included with Windows 98. Microsoft's FrontPage 98 includes a powerful imaging program called **Image Composer**.

- Next, click Install Image Composer on the CD main menu to install Microsoft Image Composer.

Because image creation and manipulation are usually best left to those with experience in that area, we have devoted little time to the explanation of that art. Most of the image management we discuss can be done from within the FrontPage Editor. A brief description of this program follows.

Microsoft Image Composer is an easy-to-learn program that will permit you to arrange, customize, and create your onscreen images.

You can create images for your Web site without having to use traditional image editing concepts such as layers, channels, and masks. With Image Composer™, you simply drag and drop images to arrange them together in compositions.

Open Image Composer directly from Microsoft FrontPage by double-clicking on any image or launch from the main toolbar in the Microsoft FrontPage 98 Editor. You can also click the **Show Image Editor** icon on the Microsoft FrontPage 98 Explorer main toolbar.

Image Composer overview

Working with images and arranging them together can be a difficult and frustrating task, one that typically requires you to use layers, channels, and masks to get the look you want. With Image Composer, Microsoft introduces a new and more intuitive way to work with images.

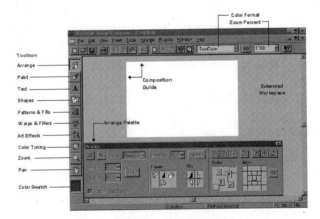

Each image is called a sprite—an independent image with shape. Sprites are easy to move, size, arrange together, and transform with effects. You can get sprites from a variety of sources, including the following:

> ***Import*** sprites from a range of file formats and programs. Image Composer supports the TIFF, GIF, JPEG, Windows BMP, PSD, Targa, and Altamira

Composer formats. Also, you can import and export Adobe Photoshop layers as sprites so you can easily use your existing files.

Scan using Microsoft Image Composer's industry-standard TWAIN interface used by scanners and digital cameras; loading sprites from these devices is easy.

Image Composer includes more than 600 top-quality, professionally prepared sprites on the Microsoft FrontPage 98 CD-ROM. All the sprites have been prepared by digital stock companies, including PhotoDisc, Inc., the industry leader, and all are <u>royalty-free</u> so you can freely use the sprites in projects and on and off the Web.

You can apply a painting effect to the entire sprite by selecting from among the hundreds of art effects in Microsoft Image Composer. In addition to the more than 500 tools and effects within Image Composer, you can install and run hundreds of third-party effects, such as Kai's Power Tools. Because Microsoft Image Composer supports many Adobe Photoshop–compatible filter plug-ins, you can run third-party effects directly from within Microsoft Image Composer.

You don't need to write code to create great animations. GIF Animator creates animations that are based on the GIF89a file format, which stores timing information to create the illusion of animation, much like a cartoon "flipbook."

What is the best way to learn how to use Image Composer?

Although integrally important, image creation and adaptation are not part of the core focus of this book. Detailed instructions on how to use a supplementary program is best done at the source. We highly recommend that you familiarize yourself with Image Composer by taking the time to examine the tutorial. From the Image Composer toolbar **Help** menu, click **Learning Microsoft Image Composer**, then select **Tutorial**.

Image Composer online resources

To learn more about Image Composer, visit the Web site and read the <u>Image Composer FAQ</u> with general and technical answers to common questions. `http://www.microsoft.com/imagecomposer/usingic/icfaq.htm`

Discover Image Composer <u>Tips & Tricks</u> from the experts. `http://www.microsoft.com/imagecomposer/usingic/ictips.htm`

Make your Web site come alive with motion! Microsoft's <u>GIF Animator</u> Web site includes free samples for use on your Web pages. `http://www.microsoft.com/imagecomposer/gifanimator/gifanin.htm`

Microsoft Image Composer and GIF Animator <u>public newsgroups</u>. `http://www.microsoft.com/imagecomposer/usingic/icnewsgrp.htm`

You may also want to check out the <u>Support</u> area. `http://www.microsoft.com/imagecomposer/usingic/support.htm`

- Click Exit to exit the Setup program and begin creating your Web site.

 Please remember that this book is <u>not</u> an all-inclusive software tutorial. We have pointed out a number of times that this book is **not** meant to take the place of other "how-to" FrontPage 98 instruction manuals. You may want to consider *Laura Lemay's Web Workshop: FrontPage 98* available at your local bookseller from Sams Publishing.

The information we have included in this book is intended to get you comfortable enough using FrontPage 98 so that you can immediately begin constructing your business Web site.

Over the years, new users have repeatedly asked us many of the same questions regarding design, layout, execution, and marketing of their Web sites. We have attempted to address most of those topics because they are essential to your understanding of this process and the ensuing success of your Internet business.

---

[1] Microsoft FrontPage 98 is a FREE evaluation program that will expire 45 days after installation.

I N D E X

Symbols

14.4k modems, 78
28.8k modems, 78
33.6k modems, 79
56 kbps modems, 79
60 Minute Intranet Kit, 209
1800 Flowers.com Web site, 53

A

Achoo Healthcare Web site, 47
ActionScan Web site, 165
Active Channels (Internet Explorer), 71
Active Page Elements (FrontPage 98), 146
Active Server Pages, database integration
    (FrontPage 98), 152-153
Activemedia Web site (e-commerce
    statistics), 25
ActiveX controls (FrontPage 98), 73
    Web pages, inserting, 150
adding
    e-mail accounts
        from domains, 103
        Outlook Express, 97-100
    pages to sites (FrontPage Explorer),
        123-124
    user feedback forms (FrontPage 98),
        148-149
ADSL (Asymmetric Digital Subscriber
    Line), 80
Advanced Radio Data Information Systems
    Web site, 81

advertising
    automated mailing lists, 66
    charge fees, 62
    cost measurements, 12
    Link Exchange Web site, 61
    medium potential (Internet), 61
    on Internet newsgroups, 63-64
    online predictions, 62
    positioning
        on local content sites, 62
        online shopping malls, 62-63
    products, 57-60
    Web sites, 12
        local city content, 62
Airborne Express Web site, 48
AltaVista Web site
    free services, 33-34
    language selection, 32-33
    search engine criteria, 32-33
    site submissions, 194
Amazon.com Web site, 44
American Airlines Web site, 51
American Express Travel Web site, 51
American Marketing Association
    Web site, 55
Andy's Art Attack Web site, 165
applying Theme View to Web sites
    (FrontPage Explorer), 122
AT&T Toll-Free Web site, 49
autobots (e-mail)
    configurations, 104-105
    marketing strategies, 65

AutoComplete address feature (Internet Explorer), 71
automated mailing lists, 66
autoresponders
    e-mail marketing strategies, 65
    search engines on new submissions, 190
Award-It! Web site, 52

B

banks (online store services)
    credit card processing, 179-180
    service expectations, 180-181
Banner Ad Manager (FrontPage 98), 73
Barnes and Noble Web site, 44
Bartlett's Quotations Web site, 49
Bell Labs Web site, 8
Benefits Link Web site, 45
Better Business Bureau Web site, 20-21
Bigfoot Web site (locating e-mail addresses), 38-39
Biztravel.com, 51
blocking technologies (pornographic Web sites), 39-40
Bloomberg Web site, 47
broadcast.com, 105-106
broadcasting
    audio/video technologies, 105
    bandwidth intensive, 106
    popularity, 106
    uses, 105-106
browsing Web sites offline, 43
building intranets, 209
bulleted lists (FrontPage Editor), 128
Business Law Site, 46
businesses
    book/magazine sites
        Amazon.com, 44
        Barnes and Noble, 44
        Electronic Newsstand, 44
        Entrepreneur Magazine, 44
        In Touch Networks, 44
        Inc. Online, 44
        Macmillan Computer Publishing, 44
        SmallOffice.Com, 44
    broadcasting uses, 105-106
    communication Web sites
        FaxSav, 44
        Internet News Bureau, 44
    credit cards (processing provider services/ fees), 181
    dedicated Internet access, 210

e-commerce
    elements of, 28
    identifying criteria, 28-29
    planning considerations, 24-25
    statistics, 25
    versus coventional business transactions, 23-27
e-mail
    customer service example, 95
    immediacy of, 96
    SPAM abuses, 96
electronic news Web sites
    CMPnet, 44
    InfoWorld, 45
    Red Herring Direct, 45
    San Jose Mercury News, 45
    Wired News, 45
health Web sites
    Achoo Healthcare, 47
    healthfinder, 47
    MedicineNet, 47
human resource Web sites
    Benefits Link, 45
    Career Mosaic, 45
    Human Resource Store, 45
    Monster Board, 45
    TrainingNet, 45
    U.S. Department of Labor, 45
information
    pull technology, 40-41
    push technology, 40-41
insurance Web sites
    Insurance News Network, 46
    InsWeb, 46
    Quicken InsureMarket, 46
    Quotesmith Insurance, 45
Internet
    broadcasting, 105
    commerce, legal issues, 167-168
    connectivity options, 77
    glossary, 215-242
    help sites, 46
    reasons for connecting, 11
    typical uses, 10-11
intranets, communication directives, 209
legal Web sites, 176
    Business Law Site, 46
    KnowX, 46
    Legaldocs, 46
local content advertising, 62
marketing
    American Marketing Association, 55
    conventional press releases, 60

Four P's, 55-56
  Internet versus conventional, 56
  non-conventional press releases, 60-61
  online advertising, 57-66
Microsoft support links, 53-54
miscellaneous business sites
  1800 Flowers.com, 53
  Kelly's Blue Book, 52
  MapQuest, 52
  Rent.Net, 53
money Web sites
  Bloomberg, 47
  CBS Market Watch, 47
  Motley Fool, 47
  The Final Bell, 47
  TheStreet.com, 47
networking solutions (Microsoft Small
  Business Server), 211-212
office supply Web sites
  Inktec, 48
  Office Depot, 48
  Office Max, 48
  Staples, 48
  Viking Office Products, 48
online commerce Web sites
  Charge.Com, 48
  CyberCash, 48
  First Virtual, 48
online stores
  bank services, 180-181
  credit card authorizations, 178-179
  development issues, 176-177
  merchant accounts, 179-180
  PIN-based payments, 183-184
  question of state jurisdictions, 172-173
  shopping baskets, 177-178
  virtual cash, 182-183
package tracking Web sites
  Airborne Express, 48
  DHL, 48
  Federal Express, 48
  UPS, 49
predictions on future of Internet, 214
printing/faxing Web sites
  Deluxe Printing, 49
  Printovation, 49
  WebRecord, 49
public relations
  elements, 58-60
  tools, 58-60
  uses, 58-60

reference Web sites
  AT&T Toll-Free, 49
  Bartlett's Quotations, 49
  Calendar Land, 49
  OoULook Dictionaries, 49
  U.S. Census Bureau, 49
  U.S. Patent and Trademark Office, 49
  Zip Code Finder, 50
service-based Web site, 27-28
software recommendations
  Internet Explorer, 70-72
  Office 97 Small Business Edition,
    68-75
software Web sites
  CWSApps, 50
  Jumbo Download Network, 50
  Shareware.Com, 50
  Windows Users Group Network, 50
tax Web sites
  Ernst & Young, 50
  H&R Block, 50
  IRS, 50
  Tax Foundation, 50
  Tax Prophet, 50
travel Web sites
  American Airlines, 51
  American Express Travel, 51
  Biztravel.com, 51
  Delta Airlines, 51
  Mapblast, 51
  Microsoft Expedia, 52
  Southwest Airlines, 52
  Travelocity, 52
  VISA Worldwide, 51
  Weather Channel, 51
Web promotion sites
  Award-It!, 52
  Global Information Infrastructure Awards,
    52
  Top 5%, 52
Web sites
  benefits to your business, 11-12
  content decisions, 109-110
  contests/sweepstakes (legal issues), 173-174
  elements to exclude, 115
  evaluating suitability, 13-14
  final tests, 118
  goals, defining, 108
  humor, use of, 114
  layout design, 111
  links to other sites, 113
  maintenance considerations, 113-114

marketing techniques, 187-189
objectives, 108
page size, 112
security, 15-21
strategy development, 108-109
text guidelines, 116
Y2K (Year 2000) problem
  compliance efforts, 212
  personal preparations, 213
  Web resources, 213

C

CA Discovery 2000 software, 213
cable modems
    infrastructure costs, 79
    versus telephone modems, 79
caches (Internet Explorer), 203
Calendar Land Web site, 49
Career Mosaic Web site, 45
CBS Market Watch Web site, 47
CD-ROM contents, 8
Center for Electronic Messaging Technologies (CEMT), 84, 241
channels
    push technology, 41
    subscriptions, 42-43
Charge.Com Web site, 48
Check 2000 PC software, 214
checking account drafts
    CheckPro, 182
    Draft Creator, 182
    online stores, 182
    Redi-Check, 182
    TurboCheck, 182
CheckPro Web site, 182
children (blocking pornographic Web sites), 39-40
CIAC Web site (virus information), 16-17
Client Resource Center (Netcom)
    support services, 199-201
CMP Megasite, 206
CMPnet Web site, 44
commerce (legal issues), 167-168
company logos, transferring to your Web site, 165
Compaq Computer Web site, 76
The Complete Small Business Internet Guide
    CD-ROM contents, 8
    computer fundamentals, 3-4
    focus on Microsoft software, 6
    overall mission, 3-4
    Windows platforms, 6

computers
    connection hardware requirements, 76
    usage statistics (National Federation of Independent Business), 10
    vendors, 76-77
configuring
    e-mail accounts (Outlook Express), 97-100
    keywords in META tags, 139-140
connectivity options
    business uses, 11
    cable modems, 79
    frame relays, 80
    hardware requirements, 76
    ISDN, 79
    modems, troubleshooting, 81-82
    satellites, 80
content (Web sites)
    designing, 114-115
    identifying, 109-110
    text (FrontPage Editor), 127-128
contests/sweepstakes (Web sites)
    legal issues, 173-174
    liability from glitches, 174
    rules development, 174
    security from hackers, 174
    technical design, 174
conventional business transactions
    potential problems
        catalog pricing, 25-27
        mailing lists, 25-27
        out of state checks, 25-27
    versus e-commerce, 23-24
converting graphics (FrontPage 98), 156
copying
    graphics
        from other applications, 116-118
        from other Web sites, 116-118
    text
        from other applications, 116-118
        from other Web sites, 116-118
Copyright Act (debate on linking and framing of Web sites), 176
Copyright Clearance Center (CCC) Web site, 176
copyright laws
    infringement issues, 170-171
    intellectual property, 169-170
Cornell Law School Web site, 176
creating
    graphics, transparent, 160-161
    hotspots for Web sites, 162-163

hyperlinks (FrontPage Editor), 128-130
interactive forms (FrontPage 98),
    147-148
Internet newsgroups, 63-64
online stores (development issues),
    176-177
phantom pages (search engines), 192
tables in Web pages (FrontPage Editor),
    135-136
Web pages (FrontPage Explorer),
    126-127
Web sites (FrontPage 98), 72-75
    elements to exclude, 115
    legal issues, 168-170
    software simplicity, 13
credit cards
    bank processing, 179-180
    merchant bank numbers, 24
    online authorizations
        requirements, 178-179
        vendors, 178-179
    online stores (summary), 184-185
    POS (point-of-sale) terminals, 24
    processing providers
        fees, 181
        monthly reports, 181
        settlements, 181
    Secure Sockets Layer (SSL), 151
    security threats, 19-20
    transaction processing, 181
    versus virtual cash transactions, 183
customer service and e-mail usages, 95-96
CWSApps Web site, 50
CyberCash Web site, 48, 183
CYBERsitter Web site, 40

D

databases, integration with Web sites
    (FrontPage 98), 152-153
Dataquest Web site, 10
dedicated access services (Netcom),
    210-211
dedicated domains versus virtual
    domains, 87
defining goals for Web sites, 108
defragmenting hard disks, 205
deleting e-mail accounts from domains, 103
Dell Computer Web site, 76
Delta Airlines Web site, 51
Deluxe Printing Web site, 49
descriptions, embedding in Web pages
    (META tags), 140-141

designing Web sites
    content, 114-115
    elements to exclude, 115
    graphics versus text, 112
    layout, 111, 114-115
development agreements (Web sites),
    108-109
    content/materials, 169
    delivery and acceptance, 169
    ownership of site, 169
    payment terms, 169
    scope, 168
DHL Web site, 48
dialog boxes, Image Properties (FrontPage
    98), 158-160
Diamond Jim Web site (service-based
    example), 27-28
did-it.com Web site registration, 189
digital IDs (e-mail), 18
    certification, 18-19
    encryption/decryption process, 18
    levels, 18-19
    VeriSign Corporation, 18-19
Direct Mail Manager (Microsoft Office 97
    SBE), 68-69
DirectConnect (Netcom), dedicated access
    services, 210-211
Disk Cleanup utility, launching, 205
Disk Defragmenter, launching, 205
displaying IP addresses, 205
Domain Name Service (DNS), 83
domains, 83
    classifications
        .com (commerical organizations), 84
        .edu (education institutions), 84
        .gov (U.S. government), 84
        .mil (U.S. military), 84
        .net (network providers), 84
        .org (nonprofit organizations), 84
        possible additions, 84-85
    Domain Name Service (DNS), 83
    e-mail accounts, 103
    future implementation, 85
    host selection, 88
    hosting services (Netcom), 88-89
    IP addresses, numeric syntax, 84
    names, 83-84
        22-character limit, 86
        activation fees, 87
        disputes, 86
        Internet statistics, 9-10
        marketing potential, 85-86

monthly charges, 87
obtaining, 86
registering, 85-86
registration fees, 87
reserving, 87
snatching of trademarks, 171
uniqueness, 85-86
owning advantages, 85-86
registration
Center for Electronic Messaging Technologies (CEMT), 84
InterNIC, 84
registration information, 91-92
trademark infringement, 172
virtual versus dedicated, 87
downloading
graphics from Web sites, 157
royalty-free graphics, 164-165
WinZip utility, 200-201
DPI resolution (graphics), 156-157
Draft Creator Web site, 182
Drew Bledsoe Foundation Web site
Front Page Editor, 133-136
META tags, use of, 137-146

E

e-commerce (electronic commerce)
EDI (Electronic Data Interchange), 28
elements of, 28
identifying criteria for businesses, 28-29
ISPs, hosting capabilities, 29-30
planning considerations
design, 24-25
platform selection, 24-25
software, 24-25
predictions, 25
Secure Sockets Layer (SSL), 151
statistics, 25
versus conventional business transactions, 23-27
e-mail
addresses, locating on Internet, 38-39
as business tool, 93
attachments (Outlook Express), 101-103
autobots (Netcom), 104-105
automated mailing lists, 66
customer service example, 95-96
digital encoding development, 17-18
digital IDs, 18
certification, 18-19
providers, 18-19
electronic direct mail (spamming practices), 66
filtering mechanisms (Outlook Express), 100-101
immediacy of, 96
location services
BigFoot Web site, 38-39
Four11 Web site, 38-39
Switchboard Web site, 38-39
Who Where Web site, 38-39
marketing strategies
autobots, 65
autoresponders, 65
electronic signatures, 64-65
newsletters, 65
Netcom
configuration, 103-105
support services, 201
Outlook Express
configurations, 97-100
installation, 97-100
program selection, 96-97
public relations usage, 58-60
SPAM abuses, 96
U.S. Post Office technologies, 17-18
versus telephone usage, 93
E-malls (electronic malls), 62
e-newsletters (marketing strategies), 65
EDI (Electronic Data Interchange), 28
electronic commerce, *see* e-commerce
electronic direct mail (spamming), 66
Electronic Frontier Foundation Web site, 242
electronic malls (E-malls)
Electronic Newsstand Web site, 44
electronic signatures (marketing strategies), 64-65
emoticons, 94
English Server Web site, 4
Entreprenuer Magazine Web site, 44
eRetail.Net Web site, 46
Ernst & Young Web site, 50
evaluating
businesses (Web site suitability), 13-14
Internet connectivity options, 77
Excel 97 (Microsoft Office 97 SBE), 68-69
Excite
search engine criteria, 33-34
site submissions guidelines, 194-195
Expedia Streets 98 (Microsoft Office 97 SBE), 68-69
extranets versus intranets, 208-209

F

FaxSav Incorporated Web site, 44
Federal Express Web site, 48
Federal Trade Commision Web site, 20
file attachments, e-mail (Outlook Express),
101-103
filtering e-mail (Outlook Express), 100-101
Final Bell Web site, 47
Financial Manager (Microsoft Office 97
SBE), 68-69
firewalls, 15
First Virtual Web site, 48, 183
"flame wars"
Internet newsgroups, 64
PIN-based payments, 183-184
Four P's of marketing, 55-56
Four11 Web site (e-mail address location
services), 38-39
frame relays
cost of installation, 80
data transfer rates, 80
LAN applications, 80
framing (legal issues), 175
fraud, 20
freeware, 201
FrontPage 98
Active Page Elements, 146
Active Server Pages, 74
ActiveX controls, 73
Banner Ad Manager, 73
components
Editor, 119-120, 125
Explorer, 119-120
Image Composer, 119-120
Server Extensions, 119-120, 152
databases
capabilities, 73
integration (Active Server Pages),
152-153
Database Region Wizard, 74
graphical bullets, 73
graphics
conversion for Web use, 156
sources, 73
HTML Editor (resizing images), 156-157
HTML programming functions, 144-145
Hyperlink View, 74
Image Properties dialog box, 158-160
Import Wizard, 74
interactive forms, creating, 147-148
Java applets, 73

navigational organization, 74
online reference sites, 145-146
scripting features, 151
Secure Sockets Layer (SSL), 151
templates, 73
text effects, 74
thematic templates, 73
user feedback forms, adding, 148-149
Web sites, creating, 72-75
wizards, 73
WYSIWYG Editor, 73
FrontPage Editor
existing Web pages, opening, 126-127
functional overview, 125
HTML properties, setting, 131-132
hyperlinks, creating, 128-130
images, importing, 130
new Web pages, previewing, 132
shared borders, modifying, 133-134
supported text formats, 130
text, importing, 130
Web pages
adding content, 127-128
bulleted lists, 128
navigation bars, 134-135
properties, setting, 131
tables, creating, 135-136
FrontPage Explorer
functional overview, 120
new Web pages, creating, 126-127
pages, adding to Web site, 123-124
Views Bar, 120
All Files View, 121
Hyperlinks View, 122
Navigation View, 121
Tasks View, 123
Themes View, 122
Web pages
publishing, 149-151
spellchecking features, 124-125

G

Gateway 2000 Inc. Web site, 76
GIF file formats, 156
GIF Wizard Web site, 160
Global Information Infrastructure Awards
Web site, 52
graphic attachments (Outlook Express),
101-103
graphics
colors, number of, 156-157
company logos, transferring, 165

conversion for Web use, 156
copying from other sources, 116-118
download speeds, 157
DPI resolution, 156-157
file size considerations, 155-157
GIF file formats, 156
image maps, 162
Image Properties dialog box (FrontPage
  98), 158-160
JPEG file formats, 156
online resources, 165-166
royalty-free, downloading, 164-165
scanning services, 165
size/complexity, 116-117
transparent, creating, 160-161
versus text on Web sites, 112

H

H&R Block Web site, 50
hackers (damage potential), 16
hard disks
  defragmenting, 205
  Disk Cleanup utility, 205
hardware, connection requirements, 76
healthfinder Web site, 47
hiding
  hyperlinks (search engines), 192
  text keywords (search engines), 191
hiring Web site development teams, 168-170
History Bar (Internet Explorer), 71
hosting services (Netcom)
  comparison to other ISPs, 90-91
  domains
    Submit It! publicity software, 89
    Virtual WebTrends, 89
  e-mail maintenance area, 88-89
  library
    images, 88-89
    programming scripts, 88-89
    tutorials, 88-89
  online FAQ, 88-89
  toolbox, 88-89
  traffic statistics, 88-89
  Web site maintenance, 88-89
HotBot Web site
  pull-down menu options, 34-35
  search engine criteria, 34-35
  site submissions
    guidelines, 195
    rankings, 195
    requirements, 195

hotspots, creating, 162-163
HTML (HyperText Markup Language)
  code visibility on Web pages, 16
  FrontPage 98 programming functions,
    144-145
  META tags, 137-139
  online reference sites, 145-146
  setting properties (FrontPage Editor),
    131-132
  WYSIWYG Editor (FrontPage 98), 73
HTML Editor (resizing images), 156-157
Hughes Network Systems' Direct PC, 80
Human Resource Store Web site, 45
humor (cautionary uses), 114
Hyperlink View (FrontPage 98), 74
hyperlinks
  appearance, 7-8
  creating, 128-130
  hotspots, 162-163
  image maps, 162
  phantom pages, 192
  search engines, 192

I

identifying Web sites
  content, 109-110
  objectives, 108
image maps, 162
Image Properties dialog box (FrontPage 98),
  158-160
ImageOrama (AOL), 165
images
  importing (FrontPage Editor), 130
  text, placing, 164
importing
  images to Web pages, 130
  text into Web pages, 130
In Touch Networks Web site, 44
Inc. Online Web site, 44
information
  content, determining, 109-110
  pull technology, 40-41
  push technology, 40-41
InfoSeek Web site
  personalized news service, 35-36
  search engine criteria, 35-36
  site submissions
    guidelines, 195-196
    rankings, 195-196
    requirements, 195-196
InfoWorld Web site, 45

infringement (copyright issues), 170-171
Inktec Web site, 48
inserting
    ActiveX controls into Web pages, 150
    Java applets into Web pages, 151
Insurance News Network Web site, 46
InsWeb Web site, 46
intellectual property, 169-170
interactive forms (FrontPage 98)
    creating, 147-148
    typical uses, 147-148
Internet
    advertising (medium potential), 61
    broadcasting
        bandwidth intensive, 106
        benefits, 105
        distribution, 105
        uses, 105-106
    businesses
        predictions, 214
        public relations, 58-60
        reasons for connecting, 11
        typical uses, 10-11
    communication technologies, 105
    connection requirements (hardware), 76
    connectivity options, 77
    copyright infringement, 171
    dedicated access, 210
    Domain Name Service (DNS), 83
    domains, 83
        classifications, additions, 84
        future implementation, 85
        names, 83-86
        registering, 91-92
    e-commerce (overview), 23-24
    e-mail
        addresses, locating, 38-39
        SPAM abuses, 96
    glossary, 215-242
    information
        pull technology, 40-41
        push technology, 40-41
    legal issues, 167-168
    marketing
        24-hour audience, 56
        online advertising, 57-60
        versus conventional marketing, 56
    modems, 78
    netiquette
        emoticons, 94
        shorthand abbreviations, 94-95
    newsgroups
        creating, 63-64
        "flame wars," 64
        marketing options, 63
    pornographic (blocking technologies),
      39-40
    press releases, 60
    robots (functions), 30-31
    search engines, 30-31
    security, 15
        credit cards, 19-20
        e-mail, 17-18
        firewalls, 15
        fraud, 20
        hackers, 16
        HTML code visibility, 16
        investment scams, 20-21
        secure versus non-secure trans-
            actions, 21
        viruses, 16-17
    statistics, 9-10
    trademark issues (domain name
      snatching), 171-172
    versus conventional library sources, 31-32
    Web site benefits, 11-13
Internet Credit Card Processing Services
  (ITGSC), 181
Internet Explorer
    Active Channels, 71
    AutoComplete address feature, 71
    browser integration, 70
    Channel Bar, 42
    Favorites list, 70
    History Bar features, 71
    hyperlink selection, 70
    installation, 70
    Links bar, 72
    NetMeeting features, 72
    quick tips
        cache emptying, 203
        keyboard shortcuts, 203
        printing, 202
        URLs, 202
        Web page scrolling, 202
    real-time capabilities, 71
    Search Bar features, 71
    software updates
        Microsoft Web site, 72
    Wallet feature, 71
    Web site content ratings, 71

Internet News Bureau
  as marketing tool, 61
  Web site address, 61
Internet News Bureau Web site, 44
Internet Service Providers, *see* ISPs
Internet Transaction Gateway Service
  Company (ITGSC), 178
InterNIC
  domains
    name disputes, 86
    registering, 84, 91-92
  trademarks
    online searches, 172
    registration protection, 171-172
  Web site, 86
Intranet Journal Web site, 209
Intranets
  building, 209
  company benefits, 209
  overview, 208
  peer-to-peer networks, 208-209
  versus Extranets, 208-209
  versus Internet, 208
investment scams
  Better Business Bureau Web site, 20-21
  Securities and Exchange Commission
    Web site, 20-21
IP addresses
  displaying, 205
  domain names, 83-84
  numeric syntax, 84
IRS Web site, 50
ISDN (Integrated Services Digital
  Network), 79
ISPs (Internet Service Providers)
  as hosts for domains, 88
  comparison to Netcom hosting services,
    90-91
  e-commerce hosting capabilities, 29-30

J - K

Java applets (FrontPage 98), 73
  Web pages, inserting within, 151
JavaScript (FrontPage 98), 151
JPEG file formats, 156
Jumbo Download Network Web site, 50
jurisdiction
  passive Web sites versus active Web
    sites, 172-173
  Web site contests/sweepstakes (legal
    issues), 173-174

Kelly's Blue Book Web site, 52
keyboard shortcuts (Internet Explorer), 203
keywords
  configuring in META tags, 139-140
  search engines (spamming effects), 139
KnowX Web site, 46
Kumite Web site (virus information), 17

L

launching
  Disk Cleanup utility, 205
  Disk Defragmenter, 205
  Outlook Express, 97-100
layout of Web sites (design considerations),
  111, 114-115
Learn the Net Web site, 4
Legal Documents Online, 176
legal issues
  Copyright Act (debate on linking and
    framing of Web sites), 176
  copyright infringements, 169-171
  development teams (Web sites)
    content/materials, 169
    delivery and acceptance, 169
    ownership of site, 169
    payment terms, 169
    scope, 168
  framing, 175
  intellectual property, 169-170
  linking (Ticketmaster v. Microsoft),
    175-176
  META tags, 176
  trademark infringements, 172
  Web site development issues, 168-170
legal resources
  Copyright Clearance Center (CCC), 176
  Cornell Law School Web site, 176
  Legal Documents Online, 176
Legaldocs Web site, 46
LinkExchange Web site, 61
linking Web sites
  copyright infringement, 171
  legal issues, Ticketmaster v. Microsoft,
    175-176
Links bar (Internet Explorer), 72
Liszt Web site, automated mailing lists, 66
local content advertising, 62
Lycos
  site submissions
    guidelines, 196

rankings, 196
requirements, 196
search engine criteria, 36-37
site selections, 36-37

M

Macmillan Computer Publishing
   Web site, 44
Mapblast Web site, 51
MapQuest Web site, 52
marketing
   American Marketing Association, 55
   automated e-mail lists, 66
   conventional press releases, 60
   e-mail strategies
      autobots, 65
      autoresponders, 65
      electronic signatures, 64-65
      newsletters, 65
   electronic direct mail, spamming
      practices, 66
   Four P's
      placement, 55-56
      pricing, 55-56
      products, 55-56
      promotion, 55-56
   Internet newsgroups, 63
   Internet versus conventional, 56
   NewsTarget Direct service, 61
   non-conventional press releases, 60-61
   online advertising, 57-60
   service-oriented businesses, 57-66
   services, 60-61
   Web sites
      business letterhead/advertisements,
         187-189
      META tags, 187-189
      TV commercials, 187-189
      URL displays, 187-189
masking in transparent images, 162
McAfee Web site, 17
   VirusScan software, 17
MedicineNet Web site, 47
memory chips (Y2K problem)
   compliant versus non-compliant, 212
   early programming designs, 212
META search engines, 191
META tags
   descriptions, embedding, 140-141
   Drew Bledsoe Foundation Web site,
      137-146

keywords
   configuring, 139-140
   repetition, 139
legal issues, 176
miscellaneous, 142-143
refresh option, 143
search engines
   hierarchical indexing sequence, 142
   hits, 137-139
   spiders, 137-139
titles, composing, 141
Metacrawler Web site, 191
Metricom Web site, 80
Microsoft Expedia Web site, 52
Microsoft Small Business Server
   award-winning features, 211-212
   Web site information, 211-212
Microsoft Web site, 7
   60 Minute Intranet Kit, 209
   channels listing, 42
   Internet Explorer, software updates, 72
   Office 97 SBE features, 68-69
   support pages, 53-54
millenium bug, *see* Y2K problem
modems (modulator-demodulator)
   connection process, 81-82
   data transfer rates, 78
      14.4k, 78
      28.8k, 78
      33.6k, 79
      56 kbps, 79
      comparisons, 78
      ISDN connections, 79
      T-1, 78
   Internet newsgroups, 82
   signaling process, 78
   troubleshooting, 81-82
   types
      cable, 79
      wireless, 80
monitors, DPI resolution, 156-157
Monster Board Web site, 45
Motley Fool Web site, 47
Mystic Color Lab Web site, 165

N

naming domains, 85-86
   22-character limit, 86
   disputes, 86
   registration fees, 87

National Center for Supercomputing
   Applications (NCSA), 145
National Federation of Independent Business,
   computer usage statistics, 10
navigation bars (FrontPage Editor), 134-135
Net Lingo Web site, 241
Net Nanny Web site, 40
NetBuyer.Com Web site, 77
netcasting, 41
Netcom (On-Line Communication Services,
   Inc.)
      Client Resource Center
         dial-up support, 202
         e-mail support, 201
         services, 199-200
         toolbox, 200-201
      dedicated access services, 210-211
      dedicated Internet access, 210
      domains, hosting services, 87, 88-89
      e-mail configuration, 103-105
      e-mail programs, recommendations,
         96-97
      hosting services, comparison to other
         ISPs, 90-91
      industry awards, 75-76
      Intranet configurations, 210
      modem recommendations, 82
      online store software, 178
      plan options, 75-76
      service summary, 75-76
      signing up, 75-76
      software updates, 75-76
      Web site, 7, 75-76
Netiquette
   e-mail attachments, 101-103
   emoticons, 94
   newsgroups, 63
   shorthand abbreviations, 94-95
NetMeeting
   online conversations, 72
   real-time document collaboration, 72
   whiteboards, 72
new Web pages, previewing (FrontPage
   Editor), 132
newsgroups
   creating, 63-64
   "flame wars," 64
   marketing options, 63
   modems, 82
   Netiquette, 63
NewsTarget Direct service, 61

O

obtaining domain names, 86
Office 97 Small Business Edition
   cursor over function, 69
   document backward compatibility, 70
   features
      Direct Mail Manager, 68-69
      Excel 97, 68-69
      Expedia Streets 98, 68-69
      Financial Manager, 68-69
      Outlook, 68-69
      Publisher 98, 68-69
      Word 97, 68-69
   file conversion, 69
   hyperlinking capabilities, 69
   purchasing criteria, 68-69
   Save as HTML feature, 69
   Service Release (SR-1), 70
Office Depot Web site, 48
Office Max Web site, 48
offline browsing of Web sites, 43
OneLook Dictionaries Web site, 49
online activities, question of state
   jurisdictions, 172-173
online advertising
   financial predictions, 62
   guidelines, 57-60
   service-oriented businesses, 57-66
online checking account drafts, 182
online stores
   advertising positioning, 62-63
   bank services, 180-181
   check drafts, 182
   credit cards
      summary, 184-185
      transaction processing, 178-181
   development issues, 176-177
   merchant accounts, set-up, 179-180
   Netcom software
      Open Market, 178
      ShopSite Manager, 178
   PIN-based payments, 183-184
   shopping baskets, 177-178
   virtual cash, 182-183
   Wallet feature (Internet Explorer), 71
The Open Group Web site, 15
Open Market, online store software, 178
opening existing Web pages (FrontPage
   Editor), 126-127

Outlook Express
  accounts, adding, 97-100
  e-mail
    accounts, adding, 97-100
    attachments, 101-103
    filtering configurations, 100-101
  keyboard shortcuts, 102
  protocols
    IMAP, 100
    POP3, 100
    SMTP, 100

P

packet radio modems, expected costs, 80
PC Computing Windows 98 Web site, 206
PC World Magazine Web site, 203
peer-to-peer networks, 208-209
phantom pages for search engines, creating, 192
PIN-based payments, shopper qualifications, 183-184
placement (Four P's of marketing), 55-56
placing text over images, 164
PointCast, information push technology, 41
pornographic Web sites, avoidance technologies
  CYBERsitter, 39-40
  Net Nanny, 39-40
  SurfWatch, 39-40
PR Newswire Web site, 59-60
press releases
  conventional, 60
  distribution, 60
  non-conventional, 60-61
  question of necessity, 61
  services, 60-61
  templates, 60
PressPromoter, press release tool, 60
previewing new Web pages (FrontPage Editor), 132
pricing (Four P's of marketing), 55-56
printing quick tips (Internet Explorer), 202
Printovation Web site, 49
products (Four P's of marketing), 55-56
  online advertising, 57-60
Project Cool Web site, 145
promotion (Four P's of marketing), 55-56
  offline, 118
  online, 118
Psyched Up Graphics Web site, 166

public relations
  elements, 58-60
  over Internet, 58-60
  tools
    PR Newswire Web site, 59-60
    The Weekley Group PR Notebook
    for Small Businesses, 59-60
Publisher 98, 68-69
publishing Web pages (FrontPage Explorer), 149-151
pull technology, 40-41
purchasing computers, 76-77
push technology
  channels, 41-42
  PointCast, 40-41

Q - R

quick tips (Internet Explorer)
  cache emptying, 203
  keyboard shortcuts, 203
  printing, 202
  scrolling Web pages, 202
  URLs, 202
Quicken InsureMarket Web site, 46
Quotesmith Insurance Web site, 45

RAM Mobile Data Web site, 81
Red Herring Direct Web site, 45
Redi-Check Web site, 182
refreshing Web pages automatically (META tags), 143
registering
  domains, 91-92
  trademarks, Web site protections, 171-172
  Web sites with search engines, 189
Rent.Net Web site, 53
resizing
  graphics for Web site download speeds, 155-157
  hotspots for Web sites, 162-163
Rockwell International Web site, 79
royalty-free graphics, downloading, 164-165

S

San Jose Mercury News Web site, 45
satellites
  Hughes Network Systems' Direct PC, 80
  present and future costs, 80
  Teledesic, connectivity scheme, 80

Sausage Software Web site, 166
scanning services for graphics, 165
Search Bar (Internet Explorer), 71
search engines
    acceptance of your site, 191
    AltaVista, 30-33
    autoresponder notification on new
        submissions, 190
    Excite, 30-31, 33-34
    functions, 30-31
    hierarchical indexing sequence, 142
    Hotbot, 34-35
    hyperlinks, hiding, 192
    Infoseek, 30-31, 35-36
    keywords, configuring in META tags,
        139-140
    Lycos, 30-31, 36-37
    META tags, 137-139
        descriptions, 140-141
        keywords, 139
        miscellaneous, 142-143
        titles, 141
    META type, 191
    new submissions, 190
    phantom pages, 192
    rejection of site submission, 191
    scoring process, 190
    site submission guidelines, 192-193
        resubmission, 198
    text keywords, hiding, 191
    types
        AltaVista, 194
        Excite, 194-195
        HotBot, 195
        InfoSeek, 195-196
        Lycos, 196
        WebCrawler, 197
        Yahoo!, 197-198
    Web pages
        effects of deletion, 142-143
        effects of name change, 142-143
    WebCrawler, 37
    Yahoo!, 38
Seattle Film Works Web site, 165
Secure Sockets Layer (SSL), 151
Securities and Exchange Commission
    Web site, 20-21
security
    credit cards, potential threats, 19-20
    e-mail issues, 17-18
    firewalls, 15
    hackers, 16

HTML code visibility, 16
    viruses, 16-17
selecting
    e-mail programs, 96-97
    hosts for domains, 88
sending e-mail attachments (Outlook
    Express), 101-103
Server Extensions (FrontPage 98), 152
Service Release (SR-1), Office 97 Small
    Business Edition, 70
service-oriented businesses, online
    advertising, 57-66
setting
    HTML properties (FrontPage Editor),
        131-132
    Web page properties (FrontPage Editor),
        131
shared borders, modifying (FrontPage
    Editor), 133-134
shareware, 201
Shareware.Com Web site, 50
shopping baskets, online store software,
    177-178
ShopSite Manager, online store
    software, 178
sites (Web)
    1800 Flowers.com, 53
    Achoo Healthcare, 47
    ActionScan, 165
    Activemedia, e-commerce statistics, 25
    Advanced Radio Data Information
        Systems, 81
    Airborne Express, 48
    AltaVista, search engine criteria, 32-33
    Amazon.com, 44
    American Airlines, 51
    American Express Travel, 51
    American Marketing Association, 55
    Andy's Art Attack, 165
    AT&T Toll-Free, 49
    Award-It!, 52
    Barnes and Noble, 44
    Bartlett's Quotations, 49
    Bell Labs, 8
    Benefits Link, 45
    Better Business Bureau, 20-21
    Biztravel.com, 51
    Bloomberg, 47
    Broadcast.com, 105
    Business Law Site, 46
    Calendar Land, 49
    Career Mosaic, 45

CBS Market Watch, 47
Charge.Com, 48
CheckPro, 182
CIAC (Department of Energy), virus
  information, 16-17
CMP Megasite, 206
CMPnet, 44
Compaq Computer, 76
Copyright Clearance Center (CCC), 176
Cornell Law School, 176
CWSApps, 50
CyberCash, 48, 183
Dataquest, 10
Delta Airlines, 51
Deluxe Printing, 49
DHL, 48
Diamond Jim, service-based Web site,
  27-28
Draft Creator, 182
Drew Bledsoe Foundation, 133-146
Electronic Frontier Foundation, 242
Electronic Newsstand, 44
English Server, 4
Entreprenuer Magazine, 44
eRetail.Net, 46
Ernst & Young, 50
Excite, search engine criteria, 33-34
FaxSav Incorporated, 44
Federal Express, 48
Federal Trade Commission, 20
First Virtual, 48, 183
Gateway 2000 Inc., 76
GIF Wizard, 160
Global Information Infrastructure Awards,
  52
H&R Block, 50
healthfinder, 47
Hotbot, search engine criteria, 34-35
Hughes Network Systems' Direct PC, 80
Human Resource Store, 45
ImageOrama (AOL), 165
In Touch Networks, 44
Inc. Online, 44
Infoseek, search engine criteria, 35-36
InfoWorld, 45
Inktec, 48
Insurance News Network, 46
InsWeb, 46
Internet News Bureau, 44, 61
InterNIC, 86
  trademark searches, 172
Intranet Journal, 209

IRS (Internal Revenue Service), 50
Jumbo Download Network, 50
Kelly's Blue Book, 52
KnowX, 46
Kumite, virus information, 17
Learn the Net, 4
Legal Documents Online, 176
Legaldocs, 46
LinkExchange, 61
Liszt, automated mailing lists, 66
Lycos, search engine criteria, 36-37
Macmillan Computer Publishing, 44
Mapblast, 51
MapQuest, 52
McAfee, 17
MedicineNet, 47
Metacrawler, 191
Metricom, 80
Microsoft, 7
Microsoft Expedia, 52
Microsoft FrontPage 98, 75
Monster Board, 45
Motley Fool, 47
Mystic Color Lab, 165
National Center for Supercomputing
  Applications (NCSA), 145
Net Lingo, 241
NetBuyer.Com, 77
Netcom, 75-76
Netcom Business Center, 7
Netcom Client Resource Center,
  199-200
Office Depot, 48
Office Max, 48
OneLook Dictionaries, 49
The Open Group Web site, 15
PC Computing Windows 98, 206
PC World Magazine, 203
PR Newswire, 59-60
Printovation, 49
Project Cool, 145
Quicken InsureMarket, 46
Quotesmith Insurance, 45
RAM Mobile Data, 81
Red Herring Direct, 45
Redi-Check, 182
Rent.Net, 53
San Jose Mercury News, 45
search engines
  AltaVista, 194
  Excite, 194-195
  HotBot, 195

InfoSeek, 195
Lycos, 196
WebCrawler, 197
Yahoo!, 197-198
Seattle Film Works, 165
Securities and Exchange Commission,
    20-21
Shareware.Com, 50
SmallOffice.Com, 44
Southwest Airlines, 52
Staples, 48
SupportHelp.com, 46
SurfWatch, 40
Tax Foundation, 50
Tax Prophet, 50
TechShopper, 77
The Final Bell, 47
TheStreet.com, 47
Third Age Internet Glossary, 241
Top 5%, 52
TrainingNet, 45
Travelocity, 52
TurboCheck, 182
U.S. Census Bureau, 49
U.S. Department of Labor, 45
U.S. Patent and Trademark Office, 49
UPS, 49
VeriSign, 19
Viking Office Products, 48
VISA Worldwide, 51
W3C, 145
Weather Channel, 51
Web Site Garage, 46
WebCrawler, search engine criteria, 37
WebExplosion, 166
Webhostlist.com, 91
Webmonkey, 46
WebRecord, 49
WebTrends, traffic data software, 12
The Weekley Group PR Notebook Web
    site, 59-60
Windows Users Group Network, 50
Wired News, 45
Worcester Polytechnic Institute, 242
Yahoo!, search engine criteria, 38
Year 2000 Information Center, 213
ZDNet, 46, 206
Zip Code Finder, 50
Sky Station International, 80
SmallOffice.Com Web site, 44

software
    business recommendations
        Internet Explorer, 70-72
        Office 97 Small Business Edition,
            68-75
    freeware, 201
    shareware, 201
Southwest Airlines Web site, 52
SPAM (junk e-mail), 66
    filtering mechanisms, 100-101
spellchecking Web sites (FrontPage
    Explorer), 124-125
spiders, search engines, new submissions, 190
Spike feature (Word) versus copy and paste
    techniques, 117-118
Staples Web site, 48
Submit It! service, Web site registration,
    89, 189
submitting Web sites to search engines,
    192-193
subscriptions to Web channels
    cost, 42
    Web sites, 42-43
SupportHelp.com Web site, 46
SurfWatch Web site, 40
Survive 2000 Professional Version 2.1.1
    software, 214
sweepstakes/contests on Web sites
    legal issues, 173-174
    liability from glitches, 174
    rules development, 174
    security from hackers, 174
    technical design, 174
Switchboard Web site, e-mail address locator,
    38-39

T

T-1 modems, Netcom online quotes, 78
tables in Web pages (FrontPage Editor),
    135-136
Tax Foundation Web site, 50
Tax Prophet Web site, 50
Teach Yourself the Internet in 24 Hours, 4
TechShopper Web site, 77
Teledesic, satellite connectivity options, 80
text
    adding to Web pages (FrontPage Editor),
        127-128
    copying from other Web sites, 116-118
    effects (FrontPage 98), 74
    importing (FrontPage Editor), 130

placing over images, 164
supported formats (FrontPage Editor), 130
versus graphics, 112
Web sites, use guidelines, 116
text keywords in search engines, 191
submission guidelines, 192-193
The Complete Small Business Internet Guide, 7-8
The Final Bell Web site, 47
Theme View (FrontPage Explorer), applying, 122
TheStreet.com Web site, 47
Third Age Internet Glossary, 241
Ticketmaster v. Microsoft, linking dispute, 175-176
titles, composing with META tags, 141
Top 5% Web site, 52
Trademark Dilution Act, 171
trademark infringement
domain name snatching, 171-172
litigation, 172
registration protection, 171-172
Trademark Dilution Act, 171
TrainingNet Web site, 45
transactions
e-commerce versus coventional, 23-24
secure versus non-secure, 21
transferring company logos to your Web site, 165
transparent graphics, creating, 160-161
Travelocity Web site, 52
troubleshooting
graphics, download speeds, 157-160
modems, 81-82
TurboCheck Web site, 182

U

U.S. Census Bureau Web site, 49
U.S. Department of Labor Web site, 45
U.S. Dept. of Defense, implementation of Internet domains, 85
U.S. Patent and Trademark Office Web site, 49
U.S. Post Office, e-mail technology, 17-18
updating Windows 98 future upgrades, 203-205
UPS Web site, 49
URLs (uniform resource locators)
Internet Explorer quick tips, 202
search engines
scoring process, 190
submission guidelines, 192-193

user accounts
adding to domains, 103
deleting from domains, 103
user feedback forms in Web pages (FrontPage 98), 148-149

V

VeriSign Web site, 19
Views Bar (FrontPage Explorer), 120
All Files View, 121
Hyperlinks View, 122
Navigation View, 121
Tasks View, 123
Themes View, 122
Viking Office Products Web site, 48
virtual cash
as business solution, 182-183
CyberCash Web site, 183
First Vitual Web site, 183
versus online credit card transactions, 183
virtual domains versus dedicated domains, 87
viruses
CIAC Web site, 16-17
detection software, 17
Kumite Web site, 17
VISA Worldwide Web site, 51
Visual Basic Script (FrontPage 98), 151

W

W3C Web site, 145
Wallet feature (Internet Explorer), 71
Weather Channel Web site, 51
Web pages
ActiveX controls, inserting, 150
adding content (FrontPage Editor), 127-128
adding to site (FrontPage Explorer), 123-124
bulleted lists (FrontPage Editor), 128
effects of deletion on search engines, 142-143
effects of name change on search engines, 142-143
FrontPage Explorer, creating, 126-127
HTML programming functions (FrontPage 98), 144-145
HTML properties, setting (FrontPage Editor), 131-132
hyperlinks, adding (FrontPage Editor), 128-130

Java applets, inserting, 151
META tags, placement, 137-139
naming conventions, 142-143
navigation bars (FrontPage Editor),
    134-135
opening existing (FrontPage Editor),
    126-127
previewing (FrontPage Editor), 132
properties, setting (FrontPage Editor), 131
publishing (FrontPage Explorer), 149-151
refresh option (META tags), 143
shared borders (FrontPage Editor),
    133-134
tables, creating (FrontPage Editor),
    135-136
titles, composing for search engine
    purposes, 141
user feedback forms (FrontPage 98),
    148-149
Web Site Garage, 46
Web sites
    1800 Flowers.com, 53
    Achoo Healthcare, 47
    ActionScan, 165
    Activemedia, e-commerce statistics, 25
    Advanced Radio Data Information
        Systems, 81
    advertising fees, 62
    advertising positioning
        on local content sites, 62
        online shopping malls, 62-63
    Airborne Express, 48
    AltaVista, search engine criteria, 32-33
    Amazon.com, 44
    American Airlines, 51
    American Express Travel, 51
    American Marketing Association, 55
    Andy's Art Attack, 165
    AT&T Toll-Free, 49
    Award-It!, 52
    Barnes and Noble, 44
    Bartlett's Quotations, 49
    Bell Labs, 8
    Benefits Link, 45
    Better Business Bureau, 20-21
    Bigfoot, e-mail address locator, 38-39
    Biztravel.com, 51
    Bloomberg, 47
    Broadcast.com, 105
    browsing versus searching, 31-32

business benefits, 11-13
    advertising costs, 12
    commerce, 12
    graphic information, 11
    traffic measurements, 12
Business Law Site, 46
Calendar Land, 49
Career Mosaic, 45
CBS Market Watch, 47
Charge.Com, 48
CheckPro, 182
CIAC (Department of Energy), virus
    information, 16-17
CMP Megasite, 206
CMPnet, 44
communication technologies
    audio, 105
    video, 105
Compaq Computer, 76
content
    designing, 114-115
    identifying, 109-110
    ratings (Internet Explorer), 71
Copyright Clearance Center (CCC), 176
copyright notices, use of, 171
Cornell Law School, 176
creating (FrontPage 98), 72-75
CWSApps, 50
CyberCash, 48, 183
CYBERsitter, 40
Dataquest, 10
Dell Computer, 76
Delta Airlines, 51
Deluxe Printing, 49
development team, hiring, 168-170
DHL, 48
Diamond Jim, service-based Web site,
    27-28
download speeds, 157
Draft Creator, 182
Drew Bledsoe Foundation, 133-146
e-commerce
    identifying criteria for businesses,
        28-29
    overview, 23-24
    versus conventional business transactions,
        25-27
e-mail address locators, 38-39
e-mail marketing strategies, 64-65
    autobots, 65
    autoresponders, 65
    newsletters, 65

Electronic Frontier Foundation, 242
Electronic Newsstand, 44
elements to exclude, 115
English Server, 4
Entreprenuer Magazine, 44
eRetail.Net, 46
Ernst & Young, 50
Excite, search engine criteria, 33-34
FaxSav, 44
Federal Express, 48
Federal Trade Commision, 20
final tests, 118
First Virtual, 48
First Vitual, 183
Four11, e-mail address searches, 38-39
framing technology, 175-176
FrontPage Editor, overview, 125
FrontPage Explorer, overview, 120
Gateway 2000 Inc., 76
GIF Wizard, 160
Global Information Infrastructure Awards,
  52
graphics
    bullets, 73
    colors, number of, 156-157
    copying from other sources, 116-118
    file size considerations, 155-157
    GIF file formats, 156
    JPEG file formats, 156
    online resources, 165-166
    transparent, 160-161
    versus text, 112
H&R Block, 50
healthfinder, 47
Hotbot, search engine criteria, 34-35
hotspots, creating, 162-163
HTML online reference sites, 145-146
Hughes Network Systems' Direct PC, 80
Human Resource Store, 45
humor, cautionary use, 114
hyperlinks, hiding, 192
image maps, 162
ImageOrama (AOL), 165
In Touch Networks, 44
Inc. Online, 44
Infoseek, search engine criteria, 35-36
InfoWorld, 45
Inktec, 48
Insurance News Network, 46
InsWeb, 46
Internet News Bureau, 44, 61

InterNIC, 86
    trademark searches, 172
Intranet Journal, 209
IRS, 50
Jumbo Download Network, 50
jurisdictional questions, passive versus
  active, 172-173
Kelly's Blue Book, 52
KnowX, 46
Kumite, virus information, 17
layout, design considerations, 111,
  114-115
Learn the Net, 4
Legal Documents Online, 176
legal issues
    copyright infringement, 169-171
    development agreements, 168-170
    intellectual property, 169-170
Legaldocs, 46
LinkExchange, 61
linking issues, Ticketmaster v. Microsoft,
  175-176
Liszt, automated mailing lists, 66
local city content advertising, 62
Lycos, search engine criteria, 36-37
Macmillan Computer Publishing, 44
maintenance condierations
    monetary, 113-114
    time, 113-114
Mapblast, 51
MapQuest, 52
marketing techniques
    business letterhead/advertisements,
      187-189
    META tags, 187-189
    search engine registration, 189
    TV commercials, 187-189
    URL displays, 187-189
McAfee, 17
MedicineNet, 47
META tags
    placement, 137-138
    search engine success, 137-139
    legal issues, 176
Metacrawler, 191
Metricom, 80
Microsoft, 7
Microsoft Expedia, 52
Microsoft FrontPage 98, 75
Monster Board, 45
Motley Fool, 47

Mystic Color Lab, 165
National Center for Supercomputing
  Applications (NCSA), 145
Net Lingo, 241
Net Nanny, 40
NetBuyer.Com, 77
Netcom, 75-76
Netcom Business Center, 7
Netcom Client Resource Center,
  199-200
Office Depot, 48
Office Max, 48
offline browsing, 43
OneLook Dictionaries, 49
online activities, question of state jurisdic-
  tions, 172-173
online stores
  check drafts, 182
  credit card processing, 178-180
  development issues, 176-177
  shopping baskets, 177-178
  virtual cash, 182-183
The Open Group Web site, 15
page size, 112
PC Computing Windows 98, 206
PC World Magazine, 203
pornographic, avoidance technologies,
  39-40
PR Newswire, 59-60
Printovation, 49
Project Cool, 145
promotion
  offline, 118
  online, 118
Psyched Up Graphics, 166
push technology, 41
Quicken InsureMarket, 46
Quotesmith Insurance, 45
RAM Mobile Data, 81
Red Herring Direct, 45
Redi-Check, 182
Rent.Net, 53
Rockwell International, 79
royalty-free graphics, 164-165
San Jose Mercury News, 45
Sausage Software, 166
search engines
  acceptance of your site, 191
  AltaVista, 32-33,194-195
  autoresponder notification, 190
  Excite, 33-34, 194-195
  hierarchical indexing sequence, 142

  Hotbot, 34-35, 195
  Infoseek, 35-36, 195-196
  Lycos, 36-37, 196
  new submissions, 190
  phantom pages, 192
  registering, 189
  resubmission, 198
  scoring process, 190
  submission guidelines, 192-193
  WebCrawler, 37, 197
  Yahoo!, 38, 197-198
searching versus browsing, 31-32
Seattle Film Works, 165
Securities and Exchange Commission,
  20-21
security, 15
  credit cards, 19-20
  e-mail, 17-18
  firewalls, 15
  fraud, 20
  hackers, 16
  HTML code visibility, 16
  investment scams, 20-21
  secure versus non-secure
    transactions, 21
  viruses, 16-17
Shareware.Com, 50
SmallOffice.Com, 44
Southwest Airlines, 52
spellchecking features (FrontPage
  Explorer), 124-125
spiders, new submissions to search
  engines, 190
Staples, 48
strategies
  business types, 108-109
  developing, 108-109
Submit It! software, 89
subscriptions, 42-43
SupportHelp.com, 46
SurfWatch, 40
sweepstakes/contests, legal issues,
  173-174
Switchboard, e-mail address locator,
  38-39
Tax Foundation, 50
Tax Prophet, 50
TechShopper, 77
templates (FrontPage 98), 73
text
  color, 116
  copying from other sources, 116-118

effects, 74
grammar, 116
keywords, hiding, 191
spellchecking, 116
styles, 116
The Final Bell, 47
thematic templates (FrontPage 98), 73
Theme View (FrontPage Explorer),
   applying, 122
TheStreet.com, 47
Third Age Internet Glossary, 241
Top 5%, 52
trademark issues
   domain name snatching, 171-172
   litigation, 172
TrainingNet, 45
transparent graphics, 160-161
Travelocity, 52
TurboCheck, 182
U.S. Census Bureau, 49
U.S. Department of Labor, 45
U.S. Patent and Trademark Office, 49
UPS, 49
VeriSign, 19
versus conventional library sources, 31-32
Viking Office Products, 48
VISA Worldwide, 51
W3C, 145
Weather Channel, 51
Web Site Garage, 46
WebCrawler, search engine criteria, 37
WebExplosion, 166
Webhostlist.com, 91
Webmonkey, 46
WebRecord, 49
WebTrends, traffic data software, 12
The Weekley Group PR Notebook Web
   site, 59-60
WhoWhere, e-mail address locator, 38-39
Windows 98 resources, 206
Windows Users Group Network, 50
Wink Photo Services, 165
Wired News, 45
Worcester Polytechnic Institute, 242
Y2K resources, 213-214
Yahoo!, search engine criteria, 38
Year 2000 Information Center, 213
ZDNet, 46, 206
Zip Code Finder, 50
Webcasting, 41

WebCrawler
   onsite hyperlinks, 37
   search engine criteria, 37
   site submissions
      guidelines, 197
      rankings, 197
      requirements, 197
WebExplosion Web site, 166
Webhostlist.com, 91
   award to Netcom, 90
Webmonkey Web site, 46
WebRecord Web site, 49
WebTrends Web site, traffic data
   software, 12
Weekley Group PR Notebook Web site, 59-60
WhoWhere Web site, e-mail address locator,
   38-39
Windows 98
   future updates, ease of, 204-205
   Intranets, peer-to-peer networks, 208-209
   upgrade reasons, 203-204
   Web site resources, 206
Windows Users Group Network
   Web site, 50
Wink Photo Services Web site, 165
WinZip utility, downloading, 200-201
Wired News Web site, 45
wireless modems
   connection speeds, 80
   expected costs, 80
Worcester Polytechnic Institute
   Web site, 242
Word 97, 68-69
WYSIWYG Editor (FrontPage 98), 73

X - Y - Z

Y2K (Year 2000) problem
   business/governnmental efforts, 212
   CA Discovery 2000 software, 213
   Check 2000 PC software, 214
   memory chips
      compliant versus non-compliant, 212
      early programming designs, 212
   personal preparations, 213
   pessimism, 212
   Survive 2000 Professional Version 2.1.1
      software, 214
   Web resources, 213

Yahoo!
    site submissions, 38
        guidelines, 197-198
        rankings, 197-198
        requirements, 197-198
    subject categories, 38
Year 2000 Information Center Web site, 213

ZDNet Web site, 46, 206
Zip Code Finder Web site, 50